Called to Serve

Other books published by the Orthodox Research Institute include:

Rev. Dr. Steven Bigham. *Early Christian Attitudes toward Images*

David G. Bissias. *The Mystery of Healing: Oil, Anointing, and the Unity of the Local Church*

Protopresbyter George Dion. Dragas. *The Lord's Prayer according to Saint Makarios of Corinth*

Protopresbyter George Dion. Dragas. *On the Priesthood and the Holy Eucharist: According to St. Symeon of Thessalonica, Patriarch Kallinikos of Constantinople and St. Mark Eugenikos of Ephesus*

Protopresbyter George Dion. Dragas. *St. Cyril of Alexandria's Teaching on the Priesthood*

Alphonse and Rachel Goettmann. *The Spiritual Wisdom and Practices of Early Christianity*

Archimandrite Kyprian Kern. *Orthodox Pastoral Service.* Edited by Fr. William C. Mills

Matthew the Poor. *The Titles of Christ*

William C. Mills. *Baptize All Nations: Reflections on the Gospel of Matthew for the Pentecostal Season*

William C. Mills. *Feasts of Faith: Reflections on the Major Feast Days*

William C. Mills. *From Pascha to Pentecost: Reflections on the Gospel of John*

William C. Mills. *Let Us Atend: Reflections on the Gospel of Mark for the Lenten Season*

William C. Mills. *A Light to the Gentiles: Reflections on the Gospel of Luke*

William C. Mills. *Our Father: A Prayer for Christian Living*

William C. Mills. *The Prayer of St. Ephrem the Syrian: A Biblical Commentary*

William C. Mills. *Prepare O Bethlehem: Reflections on the Scripture Readings for the Christmas-Epiphany Season*

Called to Serve

Readings on Ministry from the Orthodox Church

Edited by
William C. Mills

Rollinsford, New Hampshire

Published by Orthodox Research Institute
20 Silver Lane
Rollinsford, NH 03869
www.orthodoxresearchinstitute.org

Cover art: Washing of the Feet by the artist Zakaré, Armenian Gospel of 1470. Venice, Mekhitarist Brotherhood, no. 1251, fol. 5v. Dickran Kouymjian, *The Arts of Armenia*, Lisbon: Calouste Gulbenkian Foundation, 1992, slide no. 114.

ISBN 978-1-933275-41-3

For

Father Michael Plekon

Friend and Mentor

Table of Contents

Introduction

Within the past several years, there has been a renewed interest in pastoral ministry, especially regarding the relationship between clergy and laity. Ministry was once considered for "clergy only," while the laity remained passive participants. After reflecting on the Scripture, liturgy, and writings of the Church Fathers, we now know that this older ministry paradigm is not accurate.

The Church is not comprised of the clergy alone nor the laity alone but the entire baptized people of God who live a Spirit-filled life seeking God's salvation in this world. The Apostle Paul himself reminds us that while there is one Lord, faith, baptism, and Spirit, there are a variety of gifts; as he says, "some should be apostles, some prophets, some evangelists, some pastors and teachers, to equip the saints for the ministry, for building up the body of Christ" (Eph. 4:11–12). Likewise, in his epistle to the Corinthians, the metaphor of the body is used, just as there is one body there are many members of this body that have different functions, not all parts of the body serve the same function or purpose, so too, in the Church each member serves a different function, "and God has appointed in the Church first apostles, second prophets, third teachers, then workers of miracles, then healers, helpers, administrators, speakers in various kinds of tongues" (1 Cor. 12:27–28).

While, on the one hand, the Church does have a hierarchical structure, including officially sanctioned ministerial offices, including the episcopate, presbyterate, diaconate, and various categories of religious orders, the Church nevertheless is not reduced to these official ecclesiastical offices alone. Through the gift of the Holy Spirit at the feast of Pentecost, the Church has been sanctified and enlivened by the life-giving Spirit to equip the entire people of God for service and love.

Theologians are now taking into consideration the importance and function of all of the members of the Church, both clergy and laity alike, especially in terms of lay ministry, teaching, and pastoral care. Certainly, there is a theological revival that is taking place within the Church, one that broadens and strengthens the entire Body, yet at the same time does not diminish or confuse the various ecclesial offices. Because the Church is always renewed and enlivened, it is always changing and adapting to the growing needs of the local ecclesial communities.

Voices from the Eastern Church. Hopefully, *Called to Serve* will be a contribution to the theological discussion of ministry from a distinctly Eastern vantage point, taking into consideration the numerous discussions, debates, cares, and concerns which are currently at the forefront in the East and West, namely, how both the clergy and laity can work together for the good of the entire Church.

While much of the writing and theological reflection on ministry has predominately come from Western voices, there are indeed theologians in the East who have considered the importance of pastoral ministry; among them are Thomas Hopko, John Zizioulas, John Erickson, Kenneth Paul Wesche, John Chryssavgis, and John Jillions.[1]

[1] See Thomas Hopko, "Ministry and the Unity of the Church: An Eastern Orthodox View," *St. Vladimir's Theological Quarterly* (1990) 34:4, pp. 269–280; Kenneth Paul Wesche, "Pastoral Implications of Orthodox Christology," *St. Vladimir's Theological Quarterly* (1990) 34:4, pp. 281–304; Thomas Hopko (ed.), *Women and the Priesthood*, Rev. ed. (Crestwood, NY: St. Vladimir's Seminary Press, 1999); John Jillions, "Pastoral Theology: Reflections from an Orthodox Perspective," *British Journal of Theological Education* (2003) 13:2, pp. 161–174; John Erickson, "The Priesthood in the Patristic Teaching," in John H. Erickson (ed.), *The Challenge of Our Past* (Crestwood, NY: St. Vladimir's Seminary Press, 1991), pp. 53–64; John Erickson, "Bishops, Presbyters, Deacons: An Orthodox

However, surveying the recent contributions of Orthodox theologians, few have considered important theological questions such as the problem of clericalism, especially the increasing power and authority of bishops, the question of ordaining female deacons, and beginning a discussion of whether or not the Church should consider having a married episcopate. The current practice of bishops coming from the monastic rank is only from the 6th and 7th centuries and was a matter of practice not dogma.

However, underlying these specific theological questions, it was Thomas Hopko, who nearly twenty years ago said that the fundamental question posed to all Christians, especially the Orthodox, is how we should understand the ministry of Jesus Christ, the ministry of the Church and all its members, and the specific ministry of those who are ordained in the Church.[2] Yet, surveying the recent theological literature, one would be hard pressed to find more clarity on this important question.

The essays included in *Called to Serve* are from some of the most noteworthy and ecumenically minded theologians in the Eastern Church. Most lived and ministered on the European Continent, although some eventually immigrated to the United States. Among the authors included in this volume are Metropolitans Kallistos Ware of Diokleia and Maximos Aghiorgoussis of Pittsburgh, Fathers Alexander Schmemann, Nicholas Afanasiev, Kyprian Kern, Sergius Bulgakov, and Georges Florovsky, as well as the lay theologians, such as

Perspective," *Kanon* (1996) 13, pp. 148–64. See also Anton Vrame (ed.), *One Calling in Christ: The Laity in the Church* (Berkeley, CA: InterOrthodox Press, 2005); John D. Zizioulas, *Being as Communion* (Crestwood, NY: St. Vladimir's Seminary Press, 1985), pp. 209–243, and *Eucharist, Bishop, Church: The Unity of the Church in the Divine Eucharist and the Bishop in the First Three Centuries* (Brookline, MA: Holy Cross Press, 2002); Kyriaki Karidoyanes Fitzgerald (ed.), *Orthodox Women Speak: Discerning the "Signs of the Times"* (Geneva and Brookline, MA: WCC and Holy Cross Press, 1999); and Kyriaki Karidoyanes Fitzgerald, *Women Deacons in the Orthodox Church: Called to Holiness and Ministry* (Brookline, MA: Holy Cross Press, 1998).

[2] Hopko, "Ministry and the Unity of the Church," 270.

Anton Kartashev. Also included is an essay by the late Orthodox lay theologian and scholar Elizabeth Behr-Sigel, who well into here nineties, was writing and reflecting on the role of women in ministry and whether or not the Church should rethink the ancient practice of a married episcopate.

These theologians have been influential in a theological and liturgical renewal in the Eastern Church in both Europe and North America and for the most part were very active in ecumenical discussions and debates. They were active in the World Council of Churches as well as many local and international ecumenical organizations. Their writings, essays, sermons, and talks included a wide range of topics and ecumenical interest. Clearly, they envisioned the Church as much broader and wider terms than some of their colleagues.

Likewise, many of these authors have shared rich professional and personal friendships throughout the years; both Fathers Nicholas Afanasiev and Kyprian Kern served together on the faculty at the Saint Sergius Theological Institute in Paris in the early 1940's. Afanasiev was a prolific author whose work on ecclesiology was formative in the pre-conciliar work of Vatican II and the working document *Lumen Gentium* and whose writings are now enjoying a type of renaissance, especially with the new English translation and edition of his work *The Church of the Holy Spirit.*[3] Afanasiev was and still remains to be an important voice within Eastern Christianity, and hopefully, more people will be introduced to his thought through his essays and books. His focus on the Eucharist as the sacrament of sacraments reminds us of our common vocation to offer our common prayer to God. Everything we do in church life, meetings, projects, programs, and projects must flow from the eucharistic table. The Eucharist cannot be reduced to what we do on Sunday morning, but we are called to live the liturgy after the liturgy during the rest of the work week.

[3] Actually, Afanasiev published three works on similar topics, *The Church of the Holy Spirit*, *The Limits of the Church*, and the *Lord's Supper*.

Other Eastern voices, such as Kern, are also important for our understanding of ministry. Kern's work on the theology of the Eucharist was also very influential on many of his students at St. Sergius, especially for the young Alexander Schmemann who was a student under Kern and then later after his ordination to the priesthood was attached to Sts. Constantine and Helen, Kern's parish in nearby Clamart, France, a suburb of Paris. Kern's work on ministry includes important commentary about the problem of clericalism. The abuse of clerical power and authority is one of the greatest temptations and failing of clergy and which is still a timely topic.[4] Kern shows that a proper understanding of the pastoral role is the antidote against clericalism. Of all the authors included in this volume, Kern is probably the least known, yet his essay on ministry and pastoral care will inspire and encourage a new generation of clergy.

Other persons included in the anthology, such as Schmemann and Florovsky, were professors and deans of Saint Vladimir's Orthodox Theological Seminary in New York and were influential in the beginning of the World Council of Churches. Both attended the first Faith and Order meeting in Edinburgh in 1936. Florovsky eventually left St. Sergius and moved on to teach at both Princeton and Harvard University, where he devoted his life to researching early Christian history, producing hundreds of scholarly articles and books. Furthermore, both Metropolitan Kallistos Ware and Elizabeth Behr-Sigel were adult converts to Orthodoxy and were influential in creating a renewed spiritual and theological forum on the European continent. Their writings provide a bridge between East and West as they bring the best of both "Churches" to the table. Until her recent death, Behr-Sigel was personally acquainted with Georges Florovsky, Sergius Bulgakov, Kallistos Ware, and Nicholas Afanasiev.

It is also highly significant that many of these authors were active in a theological renewal and revival in the Church. From the early

[4] Donald Cozzens, *Sacred Silence: Denial and Crisis in the Church* (Collegeville, MN: The Liturgical Press, 2002), especially pp. 112–124.

1920s to the end of the 1950s, the Orthodox community in Paris was reveling in a theological renaissance. For lack of a better term, some scholars, such as Paul Valliere and Michael Plekon, have referred to this major theological movement and body of theological literature as the "Paris School."[5] The Paris School was not a thoroughly organized movement but an informal gathering of like-minded people who were interested in a theological renewal and revival in the Church. Although this was not a single and identifiable school of thought, their mutual reflection on the nature of the Church, the role of the Eucharist, and the liturgical renaissance which was taking place in both the Eastern and Western Church's provided these theologians with fertile soil from which they reflected on theology, ecclesiology, Scripture, liturgy, and the Church Fathers. In many ways, they continued the theological renaissance which was started in theological circles in Russia. In his monumental work on Russian theology, Valliere points out that, dating back to the mid 1800s, one can see traces of a revival of patristic, biblical, and dogmatic theology, first started by Archmandrite Theodore (Alexander) and then later followed by Alexei Khomiakov, Alexander Solovyov, and then brought to the West primarily by Sergius Bulgakov and Nicholas Berdiaev among others.[6] Many of the Paris theologians were theologically trained in Russia and then immigrated West, bringing their thoughts and

[5] Of the Paris School, the Church historian Antoine Arjakovsky has said, "The School of Paris is a reality difficult to identify. It cannot be conceptualized. I would say that it is a movement, a symbolic reality, which the French historian Pierre Nora calls a "place of memory,' that is, a certain relation to the Tradition of the Church ... And then again the collective memory of the Paris school is not very precise. Nobody really knows when it starts and when it finishes!" Antoine Arjakovsky in an unpublished paper delivered at St. Vladimir's Seminary in 2004, "The Paris School and Eucharistic Ecclesiology in the 20th Century." See also Bishop Hilarion Alfeyev, "Theology on the Threshold of the Twentieth Century," paper delivered at the Monastery of Bose (Italy), September 15–17, 1999; Paul Valliere, *Modern Russian Theology: Bukharev, Soloviev, Bulgakov: Orthodox Theology in a New Key* (Grand Rapids, MI: William Eerdmans, 2000).
[6] Alexander Schmemann, *Ultimate Questions An Anthology of Modern Russian Religious Thought (*Crestwood, NY: St. Vladimir's Seminary Press, 1977).

ideas to Paris, inspiring another generation of young people, many of whom are included in this book.

Furthermore, a major theme woven throughout *Called to Serve* is the conciliar or sobornal nature of the Church. The Eastern Church is often described in terms of a "council" or what is often referred to in its Russian term as *sobornost*. The notion of conciliarity or *sobornost* stems from the understanding of the Church as being the living and vibrant body of Christ, each member having its own function yet is under the headship of Christ. It also means that humans have total freedom in Christ, to be active agents in God's saving plan, and fully alive to the world around them. Basically, conciliarity and *sobornost* are reflections of the Trinity. The Trinity is a unity of persons: Father, Son, and Spirit which are intimately connected to one another in a bond of love. While on the one hand they are united in love, they also maintain their individuality. As the Fathers of the Church put it, there is distinction between the members of the Trinity but not confusion. Therefore, the relationship in the Church between the clergy and laity must reflect the Trinity. There is a basic equality among the people of God which begins through the sacrament of baptism; however, there is a distinction when it comes to official ministry such as we see in the three-fold office of the episcopate, presbyterate, and diaconate. The unity is best seen around the Lord's Table. When the whole people of God are united around the Lord's Supper, they offer their common prayer and worship to God through the offering of the Eucharist and then are sent back out into the world to serve others.[7]

Therefore, if both the clergy and laity are truly seeking to live according to the will of God, even among a fallen humanity with hu-

[7] In her thorough history of the Russian Orthodox Church on the Eve of the Russian Revolution, Vera Shevzov states that the term *sobornost* is closely related to the Greek terms *synaxis* and *ekklesia* which means a "to come together" or a "meeting." Likewise the verb *sobriat,* which is related to the term *sobor* means to gather together. Therefore, a sobornal Church is one that gathers together the entire people of God. For more information see Vera Shevzov, *Russian Orthodoxy on the Eve of the Revolution* (New York, Oxford University Press, 2004), p. 30.

man sinfulness, there must be an expression of love based on the example of Christ Himself. Jesus gave us the supreme example of love through his passion and crucifixion on the cross, giving up his life for others. His life was an example of loving and serving others, not using power and authority over his disciples. Clergy are not called to have power and authority over the laity nor area the laity called to increase their power or authority over and against the clergy, but rather work together for the common good of all members of the Church.

However, according to the conciliar model, the Church, which still maintains its hierarchical structure and order, is a community of the baptized saints who work together building up the Body of Christ one person at a time through the exercising of the variety of gifts and charisms that are distributed to each by the outpouring of the Holy Spirit. There is no room for bickering, fighting, power, or authority to be exerted by anyone over someone else or another group of persons. This would preclude any notion of human freedom. The only power and authority in the Church are God working through the Holy Spirit in a life-giving and sustaining way. There are differences in function within the body, yet there cannot be any discrimination or clericalism. So while there is a basic equality among the people of God, there is still order and structure within the Body. The Body only exists because it is Christ's body and is held together by a continual outpouring of love which the evangelist John so beautifully expresses when the post-ressurectional Jesus bestows the Holy Spirit upon His disciples and says, "Peace be with you. As the Father has sent Me, even so I send you" (John 20:21). Michael Plekon comments on the proper understanding of conciliarity in the following manner:

> The church is hierarchical and conciliar, neither a clerocracy not a democracy, but as the Moscow Council of 1917–18 strove to insure, an assembly or communion of all the people of God. The bishops govern only because they have been elected to do so as the presiders at the Eucharist, namely as the servants of the servants of God. There is no division of the church into one part

> that rules and the other which is subject. Every Christian is by baptism prophet, priest and king... There can be as with Christ no separation, division or confusion among those who gather around the Table. The bishops must be present to preside, along with priests and deacon and people. The pastors have no purpose without the flock to shepherd. Bishops lead because the assembly has elected them to preside and serve. All the assembly celebrated the Eucharist, hears the Gospel and seeks to enact the good news in God's world, the place of our everyday lives.[8]

The image of the Church as communion or fellowship or in its Greek form, *koinonia*, is a powerful image, one that is always in front of us. The Church is comprised not just of individuals seeking their own interests but everyone working for the common good of all, which is best seen in the gathering around the eucharistic table. When the entire Church body is present, the full Christ is present. We gather together and are fed with the bread of life in order to go out into the world to provide comfort, forgiveness, mercy, and love to those around us, or as the famous 4th century pastor and preacher John Chrysostom taught, we must live the liturgy after the liturgy. The real liturgy begins when the priest dismisses the people and they are sent back into the world to live a life of faith among others around them, family, coworkers, children, and neighbors. They return the following week to be fed and nourished once again in order to be filled with the Spirit of God. It is this robust and lively image of the Church, centered around the eucharistic table which is seen throughout the pages in this volume.

Not only were these authors active in Orthodox circles, but they were also very active in ecumenical discussions and debates and were open to talking with Roman Catholic theologians such as Louis Bouyer, Dom Gregory Dix, and Dom Botte, as well as Anglicans, Lutherans, and Presbyterians.[9] Alexander Schmemann was often a guest

---

[8] His comments are contained on the Reflections sub-page of www.ocanews.org, which was last accessed on April 25, 2006.

[9] See Brandon Gallaher, "Catholic Action: Ecclesiology, the Eucharist, and the Question of Intercommunion in the Writing of Sergius Bulgakov," M.Div. thesis

speaker at the ecumenical Third Hour meetings in New York City, where such creative people such as Dorothy Day, Helene Iswolsky, and others met for prayer, dialogue, and lectures.[10] Nicolas Berdiaev hosted a regular Sunday salon in his home where Mother Maria Skobtsova, Jacques and Riassa Maritan and others frequented for open dialogue and discussion about religious and philosophical matters.[11] Their sustained dialogue, discussions, and debates were very fruitful, which provided energy and creativity to both parties and which sustained long-standing communication between East and West.

This intense and often strained interrelationship of persons reveals a genuine sense of reflection, investigation, and renewal in the Russian émigré community during this theological flowering in Paris. Not everyone in the Paris School was socially connected to each other, nor were they all friends, but they all were actively seeking the rich theological and liturgical Tradition of the ancient Church which was lost for many centuries. Their attempt was to return back to the sources of the ancient Church, a *ressourcement,* namely re-reading the scriptures, patristics, and the rich diverse liturgical traditions in order to uncover the richness of a theological legacy that was lost in the modern era.

Most, if not all, of the members were active in inter-Orthodox and ecumenical endeavors; Florosvsky, Bulgakov, and Schmemann were active in the World Council of Churches as well as the Fellowship of St. Alban and Sergius which brought together some of the best and brightest theologians from the Eastern Church as well as many Anglicans, Methodists, and Presbyterian clergy and laity in England as well as on the European Continent. Likewise, Sergius Bulgakov, Kyprian Kern, Nicolas Berdiaev, Anton Kartashev were present at the famous Moscow Council of 1917–1918 which brought together bishops, priests, and laity from across the Russian Empire in order to

---

St. Vladimir's Seminary, 2003. See also Donald A. Lowrie, *Saint Sergius in Paris: The Orthodox Theological Institute* (NY: Macmillan, 1954).

[10] Helene Iswolsky, *No Time to Grieve* (NY: Hippodrome Books, 1986).

[11] Donald Lowrie, *Rebellious Prophet* (NY: Harper, 1960).

bring a theological and liturgical renewal to the Church. The Moscow Council was seriously considering restoring the ancient office of the female diaconate, allowing the liturgical services and the scriptures to be translated from ancient Church Slavonic into Russian, allowing parish clergy greater leeway in ministry, and once again empowering the laity as full and active participants in the liturgical services, fostering congregational singing and Church governance. Later these men would emigrate to the West where they continued their vision of theological and liturgical renewal and revitalization.[12]

Of the persons included, only Metropolitan Maximos, a bishop in the Greek Orthodox Archdiocese of America, is the only theologian included from North America. He was born and educated in Greece where he obtained his theological and pastoral training, but lived and ministered most of his life here in the United States, specifically as the Greek Metropolitan of Pittsburgh. In addition to his regular pastoral ministry, Metropolitan Maximos continues to be active in scholarly research and ecumenical activities, most recently participating in the Eastern Orthodox and Roman Catholic bilateral discussions. He also has written numerous reflective pieces and study papers on various ecumenical subjects.

Additionally, these authors also maintained a regular openness to the culture and society around them which is seen in some of the essays included in this book, but throughout their writings as well. They often commented on politics, literature, theology, the arts, and music. One only has to read Sergius Bulgakov or the recent memoirs of Alexander Schmemann and the many essays of Nicholas Berdiaev to see their deep interest in the world around them. They were not afraid or opposed to the Western culture and society, but rather

[12] See Alexander A. Bogolepov, *Church Reforms in Russia 1905–1918: A Commemoration of the All Russian Church Council of 1917–1918* (Bridgeport, CT: Publication Committee of the Metropolitan Council of the Russian Orthodox Church in America, 1966); Nicolas Zernov, *The Russian Religious Renaissance of the Twentieth Century* (NY: Harper and Row, 1963); and Hyacinthe Destivelle, *Le council de Moscou (1917–1918)* (Paris, Cerf, 2006).

were seeking to engage in fruitful dialogue, debate, and discussion. This is seen not only in their writings, but in their personal lives as well. Elizabeth Behr-Sigel was a teacher extraordinaire in both East and West as she not only gave lectures at the University of Paris, but also at St. Sergius, the Ecumenical Institute at Tantur, the Dominican College in Ottawa, and L'Institute catholique in the ecumenical studies department. She was a guest speaker at women's conferences that were hosted by the World Council of Churches. Likewise, Alexander Schmemann was a frequent speaker at ecumenical events, attending conferences and talks at various seminaries, colleges, and graduate schools of theology.[13]

This openness to the West and the need for dialogue, discussion, and debate is something that is much needed today, especially if both the Eastern and Western Church seek to come to terms with the divisions and brokenness of the past. Healing cannot take place if we do not come to the table speaking the truth in love, seeking unity where there is unity and love where there is love. Perhaps these collected essays can assist both East and West in bridging the gap in understanding how we envision ministry in the Church.

[13] His journals reveal his contacts with the Western Church namely that he was an invited preacher and speaker at Schwab Chapel at Pennsylvania State College, Trinity Church on Wall Street, Sage Chapel at Cornell University, as well as at other venues.

CHAPTER ONE

Nicholas Afanasiev (1893–1966)

Nicholas Afanasiev is one of the most important Orthodox theologians of the twentieth century. He was a pioneer in eucharistic ecclesiology and was influential in both the Orthodox as well as Roman Catholic circles, especially in the proceedings of the Second Vatican Council. Afansiev was the only Orthodox theologian who was mentioned in the working session of the Council that eventually culminated in the delivering of The Constitution of the Church, *Lumen Gentium*. His major works, *The Church of the Holy Spirit*, the *Limits of the Church*, and the *The Lord's Supper*, are now appearing for the first time in English translations. Afanasiev was a colleague of other authors in this volume, Anton Kartashev, Sergius Bulgakov, Nicholas Berdiaev, as well as the mentor and teacher of Alexander Schmemann. While many people still might not be familiar with Afanasiev, there has been a renewed interest in his theological writings. In addition to the new English translations of his works, an entire issue of the journal *Sobornost* was devoted to Afanasiev's theological contributions to ecclesiology, which is focused on the Eucharist.

Afanasiev devoted his life and ministry to the proper understanding of the Eucharist. Throughout his writings, especially *The Lord's Supper*, he reminds us that the Eucharist is central to the life and faith of the Church. It is the Eucharist which makes the Church, not the other way around. Since he was first and foremost a student of Church history, he understood that the early vision of the Church, as seen in the writings of Ignatius of Antioch, Irenaeus of Lyons, and Augustine of Hippo, was more than an institution of clergy who performed the sacraments to benefit a passive laity, nor was it the bishops alone, but the entire people of God gathered around the Lord's table.

He also noted the importance and vivifying nature of the work of the Holy Spirit in the Church, the prophetic spirit that enabled the early Christians to spread the Gospel throughout the Roman Empire. The Church was more than an institution, it was the living and organic body of Christ comprised of both the clergy and laity joined around the one altar in order to celebrate the Eucharist. His writings were deeply pastoral in the sense that he encouraged active participation by the entire body of Christ, both clergy and laity alike, and was a proponent of frequent communion during a time when very few people received the Eucharist.

Afanasiev also emphasized the importance of concelebration in the liturgy, that the true concelebration is not only the clergy who concelebrate together in the altar but the real concelebration is the clergy and laity who are gathered together the one altar offering the one prayer and praise to God and who receive the one bread and cup for their salvation of the world. This concelebration of the entire people of God reveals the unity and harmony of the Church. However, Afanasiev, later followed by Schmemann, taught that the Eucharist should not be merely understood in terms of rubrics or ritual, but the worshipping community becoming or being actualized in the Body of Christ.

This essay, "Ministry of the Laity in the Church" was originally published in *The Ecumenical Review*, no. 3 (1958), pp. 255–263.

For Further Reading

Afanasiev, Nicholas. *The Church of the Holy Spirit*, translated by Vitaly Permiakov and edited with introduction by Michael Plekon (South Bend, IN: The University of Notre Dame Press, 2007).

_______. "The Church Which Presides in Love" in *The Primacy of Peter*, edited by John Meyendorff (Crestwood, NY: St. Vladimir's Seminary Press, 1992).

Alexandrov, Victor. "Nicholas Afanasiev's Ecclesiology and Some of Its Orthodox Critics," *Sobornost* 31:2 (2010), pp. 45–70.

Barbu, Stefanita. "Charisma, Law and Spirit in Eucharistic Ecclesiology: New Perspectives on Nikolai Afanasiev's Sources," *Sobornost* 31:2 (2010), pp. 19–45.

Nicholas, Aidan, O.P. *Theology in the Russian Diaspora: Church, Fathers, Eucharist in Nikolai Afanasev 1883–1966* (Cambridge, Cambridge University Press, 1989).

Plekon, Michael. "Nicolas Afanasiev: Explorer of the Eucharist, the Church, and the Life in Them" in *Living Icons: Persons of Faith in the Eastern Church* (South Bend, IN: The University of Notre Dame Press, 2003, pp. 149–176).

______. "Bishop as Servants of the Church," *Sobornost* 31:2 (2009), pp. 70–83.

See also the website maintained by Andrei Platonov: http://www.golubinski.ru/academia/afanasieffnew.htm, last accessed on September 2010.

The Ministry of Laity in the Church

As the title of this article shows, it confines itself to the ministry of the laity within the Church; it does not deal with the very varied forms of lay ministry outside the Church. I recognize the disadvantages involved in restricting my subject in this way, but in my view the ministry of the laity within the Church is much more important than their ministry outside it, because the latter is to a large extent determined by the former. Moreover, the question of the ministry of the laity outside the Church is not a complicated problem for the Orthodox conscience. The Orthodox Church has always accepted and fully approved the principle of the laity undertaking missionary work, education, scientific and social work. For most of the time the Orthodox Church left the laity almost complete freedom in this field of their activity, merely insisting on a minimum of supervision from the ecclesiastical hierarchy.

Today the doctrine of the laity occupies a central position in theology. This may represent an attempt to appreciate the role of the laity after centuries of passivity in the Catholic Church and to a certain extent in the Orthodox Church. The problem of the laity has now been raised, and this fact alone is of value, because it shows a change of mind within ecclesiastical thought; at the same time it may be regarded as "a sign of the times." The laity are regarded as a special state within the Church, differing almost ontologically from the "clergy," and having definite duties and more rarely rights and its own activities, all of which have undergone considerable changes during the course of history. This conception of the laity is a heritage of mediaeval Catholicism, which still carries much weight in contemporary theology. The Catholic theologians always speak of "the Church of the laity" and "the Church of the priests," which shows that there is a split in the theological concept of the Church, the one Body of Christ.[1]

It is hardly surprising that the question of the laity never arose in the Early Church. In accordance with the ecclesiological consciousness of the time, the Church being one body always acted as a whole; any action taken by part of its members involved the action of the whole Church, and, any action undertaken by the Church was undertaken by all its members. To use contemporary terms, which were coined at an early date at any rate they were known to Tertullian, action undertaken by the laity was also action undertaken by the hierarchy of the Church; and action undertaken by the latter was also action undertaken by the laity. They could not act independently, because neither of them constitutes the Church when separated from the other.

In the writings of the Apostles, we only find the word "laos" = the people of God, which included all the members of the Church whatever their position.[2] That does not mean that at the time of the apostles and in the periods which followed all the members of the Church formed a sort of amorphous mass in which there were no distinctions; or that at that time the situation within the Church was as described by Tertullian and opposed by him when he wrote about the Gnostics: "Today they have one bishop, tomorrow a different one; a man who is a deacon today will be a reader tomorrow; a man who is a priest today will be a layman tomorrow."[3] Ever since the time of the Apostles there has been a differentiation between the members of the Church based on the diversity of the ministries accomplished by the members of the Church. In other words, the differentiation was functional, not ontological.

[1] Y. M. J. Congar, *Jalons pour une théologie du laïcat.* Paris, 1954, p. 21.

[2] As far as we know, the word *laikos* was used for the first time by Clement of Rome.

[3] *Praescript.,* c. XLI, 8.

Life in the Church, to which every Christian is called, is a permanent ministry, in which the Christian serves God through the Church, and serves the Church itself. "For the Son of man came not to be ministered unto, but to minister, and to give his life a ransom for many" (Mark 10:45; *cf.* Matt. 20:28.) This was the new principle, hitherto unknown to human society, which was the basis of the Church's life.[4] In the Church, life and ministry are one and the same, because in the Church the Holy Spirit, by which and in which the Church lives, forms the principle of activity. Where the Spirit is, there is life also, and hence action and ministry. The whole of St. Paul's doctrine about "the work of the ministry" is based on the words of Christ quoted above. The work of ministry is incumbent upon all the members of the Church, but they do not all minister in the same way; they render service in accordance with the gifts they have received (I Cor. 12:4–6).

The facts given in the New Testament writings, especially in the Epistles of St. Paul, enable us to distinguish between two kinds of ministry within the Church: one accomplished by the whole people; the other accomplished by certain persons who were specially called. Owing to this, a difference developed between the members who exercised a special ministry and those who exercised the general ministry. During the course of the historical process which I have no time to describe here, this fundamental division between the members of the Church has led to the formation of two groups: the laity and the ecclesiastical hierarchy. This differentiation is based on the diversity between the forms of ministry; it does not mean that some members had ministries and others had not. But during the course of history in the Western Church, and to some extent in the Eastern Church also, the laity were deprived of their ministry; the fact that there can be no inactive members in the Church was forgotten.

The ministry of the laity is the manifestation of the ministry of the whole people of God. The laity serve in the Church when the

[4] Th. W.N.T., B. II., p. 81.

whole of God's people serves. Hence in the Church nothing is done without the people, for the Church *is* the people of God gathered together "in Christ." The laity, as members of God's people, take part in everything that happens in the Church, but they do so in accordance with the ministry to which God's people is called.

After this brief introduction of general premises, I can tackle the question of the ministry of the laity in the Church. At present in accordance with the doctrine of the Orthodox Church and with that of the Catholic Church ministry in the Church is expressed in three domains: the liturgy, church-government and teaching. Catholic theology resolutely excludes the laity from all these activities in the Church, considering that they belong solely to the competence of the clergy. Only recently a few timid attempts have been made to reconsider this question. The Orthodox Church is far less categorical in this domain, and in fact the actual life of the church is to a large extent a contradiction of its "manual theology." According to his theology, the laity "*undergo*" the sacramental acts so to speak, but do not accomplish them; the laity do not participate in the fulfillment of the sacraments. On the other hand the laity have recently been admitted to an important share in the government of the church, and even to some extent in its teaching.

It is one of the paradoxes of our contemporary life that the laity are excluded from the priesthood, although they are called to it as members of God's people in the sacrament of aggregation to the Church.

On entering the Church every member is installed in the Church through the sacrament of aggregation for the ministry of the general priesthood. "But ye are a chosen generation, a royal priesthood, a holy nation, a peculiar people; that ye should show forth the praises of him who hath called you out of darkness into *his* marvelous light" (I Peter 2:9; *cf.* Rev. 1:6; Rev. 5:10). From the time of Tertullian a vast number of misconceptions accumulated around the doctrine of the royal priesthood. On the one hand, there was a tendency to minimize this doctrine to such an extent that it became nothing but a meaningless formula. On the other hand we find erroneous conceptions of this doctrine which consider any member of the Church as a priest entitled to accomplish any of the acts of the liturgy. Under the influence of the individualism, which has penetrated into church life, we are inclined to consider the pronoun "you" in the biblical texts quoted above as being addressed to isolated members of the Church. But in actual fact the pronoun "you" in the New Testament writings does not indicate several persons together, but refers to a whole body—in this case to all the Christians gathered in a church assembly, in other words the Church as God's people. Every member is really installed with a view to the royal priesthood, but he does not fulfill it for himself or for others; he only fulfils it when liturgical acts are fulfilled by the Church as a whole, *i.e.* when God's people is gathered with its head (Greek: *proistamenos)* in the church assembly. Among the many examples of this in the writings of the early fathers, I will merely quote that of Saint John Chrysostom: "It is not the priest alone who renders thanks (he is speaking of the Eucharist); it is the whole people."[5] The Eucharist is celebrated by *the whole people,* but only when its chief is at its head, for without him there is no people; in the same way there is no head unless the people are present also. According to the expression of Theodore of Mopsuestia, the bishop is "the mouthpiece of the Church" for it is through him and in him that the ministry of the priesthood of God's people is manifested. This means that every Christian present, as a member of God's people, is cooperating with the bishop whenever he accomplishes a liturgical act.

This concelebration by the laity is effective and real, not ceremonial. In the liturgy the laity are not passive—for those whom God has appointed to the ministry of the royal priesthood cannot be passive. On the contrary, they participate actively; the liturgical acts are performed by the head of the Church with the con-celebration of the laity. The feeling is deeply rooted in the Orthodox Church though it is not always translated in actual life that the bishop or priest cannot celebrate the Eucharist without the people, and the people cannot

[5] John Chrysostom. In *II Cor. XVIII*, 3.

celebrate the Eucharist without the bishop. The people is appointed for the service of the royal priesthood, and the bishop is appointed to preside over the people. "Thou has made us unto our God kings and priests; and we shall reign on earth" (Rev. 5:10). This refers to all, and not to some. It means that Christ has made all his followers into God's people, so that they may serve their God and their Father (Rev. 1:6) in the Church and through the Church, to serve him when God's people is gathered under the leadership of their head whom God has appointed to *this* ministry.

The priesthood belongs to God's people as a whole, and every member plays an active part in the liturgy as co-minister with his bishop. But in what way do the church-members participate in church-government and in the Church's teaching? Are they the co-ministers of their bishops in these spheres also? As we know, since very early times the people of God was governed and instructed by those who had been set to the ministries of government and teaching. "He gave some (to be) apostles; and some (to be) prophets; and some (to be) evangelists; and some (to be) pastors and teachers" (Eph. 4:11; *cf.* I Cor. 12:28). Like teaching, government is a special ministry in the Church for which special gifts are indispensable. Among God's people there were always some who carried out these ministries. Those who were so destined were called by God not in the sacrament of "baptism by water and the spirit" but by the sacrament of ordination, in which they received special gifts. If church-government and teaching are special gifts of the Spirit which are not given to everyone, but only to those who are called, that means that God's people as a whole do not possess that gift. Church-government and teaching are prerogatives of those who are specially called, and not of the whole of God's people. The people does not govern itself nor instruct itself; it is governed and instructed by its pastors, in accordance with the will of God who gave the work of the ministry. Since they do not possess the gifts of government or of teaching, the faithful cannot be co-ministers of the bishop in the spheres of government and teaching.

Does this mean that in the sphere of government and teaching the faithful are entirely passive? The government and teaching carried out by the bishops does not exclude the participation of the faithful, but their participation is of a different kind from the work of the bishops. The people does not possess the gifts of government and teaching, but it does possess the gifts of "judgment" and of investigation which are a special kind of ministry entrusted to the Church as God's people. "Let the prophets speak, two or three; and let the other judge" (I Cor. 14:29; *cf.* I Thess. 5:21). The task of the people is to "judge" and examine what goes on in the Church; that is the ministry of witness which springs from the ministry of the royal priesthood. The bishop governs God's people not in his own name (*ex sese*) and not as a "right" as if he received the power from the people, but in the name of God, because he is set by God "in Christ" for the ministry of government. Thanks to the fact that it possesses the gifts of investigation and of "judgment," the people testifies that everything which happens in the Church under the leadership of its pastors is done in accordance with God's will according to the revelation of the Spirit. In the early Church, the people participated in all the acts of the church — receiving catechumens and penitents, ordination, and excommunication. For all later times the early Church presented a pattern of church unity, in which the church as a whole, and every individual member, lived and worked in accordance with God's will. The bishop governs God's people not in isolation from it, but from within the midst of his flock (Acts 20:28); and the faithful are governed by their bishop not passively but with their own active participation, thanks to full knowledge of what is happening in the Church and testimony concerning what is God's will.

In the early Church, this testimony was expressed through the consent given by the people to everything that was to be done in the Church, and through the reception of what had happened in it as being in accordance with God's will. However, it would be a mistake to think that the consent of the people had a juridical quality, like that given in representative bodies today. The words "consent" and "reception" do not mean that the people expressed its personal opinion or desire concerning the accomplishment of this or the other church act. The church authorities were not dependent upon the faithful's will, which had not enough authority of its own to take action. The Church does not live and act through the will of men, but through the will of God. Consent and acceptance mean that in accordance with the testimony of the Church the bishops teach and govern according to the will of God. That is the basis on which the faithful participate in church-government, and in teaching. It was observed only during the first centuries. After the time of Constantine the organization of the Church no longer gave any room to the people's ministry of witness and today it has become practically impossible. I cannot trace here the whole history of lay participation in church government. I can only state that little by little the laity had less and less share in it, and sometimes none at all.[6] But the norm remains the same, for it corresponds to the nature of the Church. Even if it cannot be fully applied today, this norm shows us which course we ought to take if we want to revive the work of the laity in the Church. It is thought that we can do so by inviting some representatives elected by the laity to share in the church government, side by side with the bishop.[7] Perhaps this is the easiest way to revive the work of the laity in church-government. But does it correspond to the nature of the Church and to its doctrine of the ministries? How can ordinary elections of lay representatives on the same lines as modern political elections really endow them with the ministry of government and confer upon them the grace required for this ministry? And if the representatives elected by the laity do not possess the gift of government. How can they govern the

[6] The Orthodox Church always retained the idea that it was necessary for the laity to share in the activity of the Church; in proof of this one can quote the epistle of the Eastern Patriarchs, and especially the decisions of the Council of Moscow of 1917–18.

[7] It was in conformity with this way of thinking that the laity were called by the Council of Moscow to participate in the government of the Church. But it's decisions have only been applied by the Russian churches abroad.

Church? It is surprising that this question is not even raised when speaking of the laity. In the Church the different forms of ministry can only be fulfilled through the gift of the Spirit; hence the persons who fulfill those ministries must be appointed by the Church. Orthodox theology, like Catholic theology, regards ordination in the Church as a sacrament, *i.e.* as an act of the Church whereby the gifts of the Spirit requested in the Church's prayers are bestowed by God. Ordination, therefore, does not mean the appointment, election or nomination by the congregation of persons whom it would like to fulfill a certain ministry. Neither the bishop by himself, nor the congregation by itself, can nominate anyone to a ministry in the Church, for it is God Himself who calls His servants to exercise such ministries. "And He gave some..." (Eph. 4:11). Moreover, when the laity are admitted to church-government by election or nomination, the following question arises: if certain laymen participate in the government of the Church does that really mean that God's people is participating in it? For God's people it does not matter whether the bishop governs alone or whether he is helped by lay representatives. It does not matter because in both cases the people are not exercising the ministry of witness to which it is called by God, and which is its particular ministry in church government. The people cannot transfer this ministry to representatives, because it belongs to the people as a whole, and not to separate members. Democratic principles, however perfect, have no place in the Church, for the Church is not a democracy; it is the people of God chosen by God and appointed by Him to serve Him in the Church. The activity of God's people has nothing to do either with universal suffrage or with representative government, for it depends on grace. The laity, as such, cannot govern and teach in the Church with those who have received the gifts of the Spirit, and who are called to govern and to teach in the House of God.

In order to agree with the doctrine of the Church one could follow the same course, taking one's stand however on grace and not on law. We know that the multiplicity of ministries has gradually disappeared from the life of the Church and been replaced in fact by one single ministry: the priesthood. Does not our time demand the revival by the Church of certain ministries which existed in former times, or even the creation of new ministries? Without a doubt, the new conditions in the life of the Church require new ministries. Like the ministries at the time of the apostles, these ministries should be based on the gifts of the Spirit in order to correspond to the nature of the Church. In other words, the persons to whom the Church would entrust these ministries should be appointed by the Church. If it is indispensable to create a Council for the government of the Church, in addition to the bishop, why not revive the ancient ministry of the presbyters, who would be elected by the Church and established for the ministry of government, as the members of the *Presbyterium* were in early times? If the hierarchy of the Church seeks persons to be teachers, why not revive the ancient ministry of the *Didascales*? But in the strict sense of the word both will cease to be laity, because they will be accomplishing a special ministry in the Church. By clinging to the legal sphere, we bring about a confusion of ministries, because we admit the laity who always remain what they are to ministries which are not within their competence. And according to the will of God, the ministries must not be confused, but differentiated. Furthermore, in this way we create ministries which are devoid of grace, thus introducing into the Church the notion of differentiation between the sacred and the secular — whereas in reality everything in the Church is sacred, and nothing is secular.

The revival of the ministries exercised in the early Church should go hand in hand with a revival of the ministry of witness of the whole people, for we must revert to a form of church-life in which the people participates in all its activities. In this connection we should recall the words of Cyprian of Carthage, which have been forgotten during the course of history: "From the very beginning of my episcopacy I made it a rule not to take any decision without your advice *i.e.* the advice of the Presbyters and without the agreement of the people."[8]

---

[8] *Epist.* XIV, 4.

Christians, who are living members of the Body of Christ, live in the Church. Their lives are a constant ministry, which begins as soon as they enter the Church and are established as God's kings and priests. Life in the Church means life with the Church. Hence God's people participates in every manifestation of the Church's life. If any sphere of it were closed to God's people, that would mean that there is a secular sphere within the Church, or that the faithful have ceased to be God's people.

It is in the sphere of the liturgy that the ministry of the faithful has been most actively shown; the faithful are, in the real sense of the word, co-ministers with their bishop. In the sphere of church-government and teaching, God's people is governed and taught by those who have been appointed to those ministries. In these spheres the gift of witness belongs to God's people, which testifies that the bishops appointed by God in the sacrament of order are governing and teaching in accordance with God's will. The ministry exercised by the bishop and the ministries exercised by the faithful are different ministries which cannot be confused, but which cannot exist without one another. This difference of ministries is conditioned by the diversity of the gifts of the Spirit. "Now there are diversities of gifts, but the same Spirit. And there are differences of administrations, but the same Lord. And there are diversities of operations, but it is the same God which worketh all in all" (I Cor. 12:4–6).

CHAPTER TWO

Alexander Schmemann (1921–1983)

Much can be said about Alexander Schmemann's life and legacy. He was an internationally known Orthodox priest, pastor, professor, seminary dean, theologian, and author. His life was devoted to the liturgical renewal and revival within Eastern Orthodox Church, especially the Orthodox Church in America. His books, articles, essays, and sermons have been translated into numerous languages, have been referenced by theologians in the East and the West, all the while serving as a general introduction to the Orthodox Christian faith. His life was devoted to the building up of the Church. For years, Schmemann taped sermons in the Russian language which would be broadcast to Russia through Radio Liberty. He was also the primary advisor to the Holy Synod of Bishops in the Orthodox Church in America and helped form and shape the early years after receiving the *Tomos* of Autocephaly, which allowed the Orthodox Church in America to be self-ruled.[1]

Perhaps, Schmemann's most important contribution to the Orthodox Church was his focus on the centrality of worship in the life

[1] *Editor's Note*: The *Tomos* of Autocephaly was a document granted by Patriarch Alexey I to Metropolitan Theodosius in 1970. This document allowed the Orthodox Church in America to be a self-ruled entity. For more information about the *Tomos* of Autocephaly and the Orthodox Church in America, see Constance J. Tarasar and John H. Erickson, *Orthodox America 1794–1976: Development of the Orthodox Church in America* (Syosset, NY: Orthodox Church in America, 1975) and Mark Stokoe and Leonid Kishkovsky, *Orthodox Christians in North America 1794–1994* (New York, Orthodox Christian Publications Center, 1995).

and practice of the Church. His writings reflect his passion for liturgical worship not only as an academic subject for study and reflection, but the formative factor for theological inquiry; according to Schmemann, the scriptures, doctrine, faith, practices, and prayers of the Church are expressed and fully realized in liturgy, specifically, in the Eucharist. One can see his life-long interest in the Eucharist throughout his writings, especially in his recently-published memoirs, his sermons from Radio Liberty, and his magnum opus *The Eucharist.* Schmemann personally contributed to the education of the Church by writing introductions to prayer books and booklets for feast days, as well as writing numerous articles for Orthodox newspapers, and through many public presentations, talks, and retreats throughout the United States and Canada.

The essay included by Schmemann focuses on a proper understanding of the relationship between the clergy and the laity. Earlier this century, there was within Orthodox theological circles a very juridical approach to ministry; clergy lead the prayers and the worship while the laity attended the service. Now there was much more to this thinking, but more or less Schmemann encountered a very hierarchical and juridical model of the Church when he came to the American shores in the late 1950's. In order to renew the Church in the United States, Schmemann produced an essay called "Clergy and Laity in the Church," originally published in 1953 by St. Vladimir's Orthodox Seminary Press. This essay was in the format of a small pamphlet which was distributed to local parishes in missions in what was then called the Metropolia of the Russian Orthodox Church here in North America.[2] It would take several generations for this teaching to reach the local level, but the Orthodox Church in America, at least in theory, has based its own self-description as being a *sobornal* and conciliar Church.

[2] *Editor's Note*: The current Orthodox Church in America was formerly known as the Metropolia of the Russian Orthodox Church.

For Further Reading

Mills, William. *Alexander Schmemann: On Pastoral Theology* (Chicago, IL: Hillenbrand Press/Liturgical Training Institute, 2010).

_______. "Cracking the Clerical Caste: Towards a Conciliar Church," *Logos: A Journal of the Eastern Church* Vol. 50 no. 3–4 (2009) pp. 441–458.

Plekon, Michael. "World as Sacrament: The World in Alexander Schmemann," *Logos: A Journal of the Eastern Church* Vol. 50 no. 3–4 (2009), pp. 429–440.

Schmemann, Alexander. *The Lord's Prayer*. Alexis Vinogradov trans. (Crestwood, NY: St. Vladimir's Seminary Press, 2001).

_______. *O Death Where is Thy Sting?* Alexis Vinogradov trans. (Crestwood, NY: St. Vladimir's Seminary Press, 2003).

_______. *Introduction to Liturgical Theology* (Crestwood, NY: St. Vladimir's Seminary Press, 1966).

_______. *For the Life of the World* (Crestwood, NY: St. Vladimir's Seminary Press, 1972).

_______. *The Journals of Alexander Schmemann 1973–1983*. Julianna Schmemann trans. (Crestwood, NY: St. Vladimir's Seminary Press, 2001).

_______. *The Eucharist: Sacrament of the Kingdom*. Paul Kachur trans. (Crestwood, NY: St. Vladimir's Seminary Press, 1988).

_______. *Church, World, Mission* (Crestwood, NY: St. Vladimir's Seminary Press, 1979).

_______. *Liturgy and Life: Christian Development through Liturgical Experience* (Syosset NY: OCA/DRE, 1974).

_______. *Liturgy and Tradition: Theological Reflections of Alexander Schmemann*. Thomas Fisch ed. (Crestwood NY: St. Vladimir's Seminary Press, 1990).

_______. "Problems of Orthodoxy in America I The Canonical Problem, II The Liturgical Problem, III The Spiritual Problem," *St. Vladimir's Theological Quarterly* 8:2 (1964) 67–85, 8:4 (1964) 164–185; 9:4 (1965) 171–193.

See also the website hosted by Holy Trinity Orthodox Church at http://www.schmemann.org, last accessed August 2010.

Clergy and Laity in the Church

No one would deny that the clergy-laity issue in our Church here in America is both an urgent and confused one. It is urgent because the progress of the church hindered by mistrust and conflicts, misunderstandings and frustrations. It is confused for there has been no constructive and sincere discussion, no real attempt to understand it in the light of our faith and in terms of our real situation. It is indeed a paradox for from both sides, the clerical and the lay, comes the same complaint: priests and laymen alike proclaim that their respective rights are denied, their responsibilities and possibilities of action limited. If the priest speaks sometimes of the lay "tyrannies", the laity denounce "bossism" of the priest. Who is right, who is wrong? And are we to continue in this frustrating "civil war" at a time when we need unity and the mobilization of our resources to withstand the challenge of the modern world? When Catholics and Protestants outnumber us 150 to 1, the younger generation shake in their attachment to Orthodoxy and we must count each one for the gigantic tasks that we face? We call ourselves Orthodox, *i.e* men of the true faith. We ought then to be capable of finding in this true faith guiding principles and positive solutions to all our problems.

The present way is nothing more than an attempt to clarify the issue under discussion. Although written by a priest, its purpose is not to "take sides," for in my opinion, there are no sides to be taken but a misunderstanding to be dissipated. This misunderstanding, to be sure has deep roots in a rather unprecedented situation in which we have to live as Orthodox. It cannot be cleared by mere quotations from canons and ancient texts. Yet, it is still a misunderstanding. This is what all people of good faith must understand. It requires only that we honestly and sincerely put the interests of our church above our personal "likes" and "dislikes," overcome our inhibitions and breathe the pure air of the wonderful and glorious faith which is ours.

Clarification of Terms. A major source of the misunderstanding, strange as it may seem, is terminological. The terms clergy and laity are used all the time, yet, without a clear understanding of their proper, *i.e.* Orthodox meaning. People do not realize that between such Orthodox meaning and the current one, which we find in, say, Webster's Dictionary, there exists a rather radical difference. We must begin, then, by restoring to the terms we use their true significance. In Webster, lay is defined as, "of or pertaining to the laity as distinct from the clergy" or "not of or from a particular profession." As to clergy the definition reads as follows: "in the Christian Church, the body of men ordained to the service of God, ministry." Both definitions imply, first, an opposition: laity is opposed to clergy and clergy to laity. They imply, also, in the case of laity, a negation. A layman is someone who has no particular status not of a particular profession. These definitions, accepted virtually in all Western languages, respect specifically Western religious background and history. They are rooted in the great conflicts which opposed in the Middle Ages the spiritual power to the secular one, the Church and the state. They have, however, nothing to do with the initial Christians use of both terms, which is alone the norm of the Orthodox Church.

The Meaning of Lay. The words lay, laity, and layman come from the Greek words *laos* which means people. "*Laikos,*" "layman, is the one who belongs to the people, who is a member of an organic and organized community. It is, in other words, not a negative, but a highly positive term. It implies the ideas of full, responsible, active membership as opposed, for example, to the status of a candidate. Yet the Christian use made this term even more positive. It comes from the Greek translation of the Old Testament where the word *laos* is applied primarily to the People of God, to Israel, the people elected and sanctified by God himself as His people. This concept of the "people of God" is central in the Bible. The Bible affirms that God has chosen one people among many to be His particular instrument in history, to fulfill His plan, to prepare, above everything else, the coming of Christ, the Savior of the World. With this one people God has entered into "covenant," a pact or agreement of mutual belonging. The Old Testament, however, is but the preparation of the New. And in Christ, the privileges and the election of the "people of God" are extended to all those who accept Him, believe in Him and are ready to accept Him as God and Savior. Thus, the Church, the community of those who believe in Christ, becomes the true people of God, the "*laos*" and each Christian is *laikos*, a member of the People of God.

The layman, is the one, therefore, who shares in the Divine election and receives from God a special gift and privilege of membership. It is a highly positive vocation, radically different from the one we find defined in Webster. We can say that in our Orthodox teaching each Christian, be he a Bishop, Priest, Deacon or just a member of the Church is, first of all and before everything else a layman, for it is neither negative or a partial, but an all-embracing term and common vocation. Before we are anything specific we are all laymen because the whole Church is the laity-the people, the family, the community-elected and established by Christ Himself.

Laymen is Ordained. We are accustomed to think of "ordination" as precisely the distinctive mark of clergy. They are ordained and the laity, the non-ordained Christians. Here again, however, Orthodoxy differs from Western "clericalism" be it Roman or Protestant. If ordination means primarily the bestowing of the gifts of the Holy Spirit for the fulfillment of our vocation as Christians and members of the Church, each layman becomes a layman, *laikos,* through ordination. We find it in the Sacrament of Holy Chrism, which follows Baptism. Why are the two, and not just one, sacraments of entrance into the Church? Because if Baptism restores in us our true human nature, obscured by sin, Chrismation gives us the positive power and grace to be Christians, to act as Christians, to build together the Church of God and be responsible participants in the life of the Church. In this sacrament we pray that the newly baptized be: "an honorable member of God's Church", "a consecrated vessel", "a child of the light", and an "heir of God's kingdom", "that having preserved the gift of the Holy Spirit and increased the measure of grace committed unto him, he may receive the prize of his high calling and be numbered with the first borne whose names are written in heaven."

We are very far from the dull Webster definition. St. Paul calls all baptized Christians "fellow citizens with the saints and of the household of God" (Ephesians 2:1a). "For through Christ", he says, "ye are no more strangers and foreigners but fellow citizens with the saints ... in whom all the building fully framed together groweth unto a holy temple in the Lord, in whom ye are also built together for an habitation of God through the Spirit."

The Layman in the Liturgy. We think of worship as specifically clerical sphere of activity. The priest celebrates, the laity attend. One is active, the other passive. It is another error and a serious one at that. The Christian term for worship is *leitourgia* which means precisely a corporate, common, all embracing action in which all those who are present are active participants. All prayers in the Orthodox Church are always written in terms of the plural we. We offer, we pray, we thank, we adore, we enter, we receive. The layman is a very direct way the co-celebrant of the priest, the latter offering to God the prayers of the Church, representing all people, speaking on their behalf. One illustration of this co-celebration may be helpful; the word Amen, to which we are so used, that we really pay no attention to it. And yet it is a crucial word. No prayer, no sacrifice, no blessing is ever given in the Church without being sanctioned by the Amen which means approval, agreement, participation. To say

Amen to anything means that I make it mine, that I give my consent to it . . . and "Amen" is indeed the Word of the laity in the Church, expressing the function of the laity as the People of God, which freely and joyfully accepts the Divine offer, sanctions it with its consent. There is no service, no liturgy without the Amen of those who have been ordained to serve God as community, as Church.

And, thus, whatever liturgical service we consider, we see that it always follows the pattern of dialogue, cooperation, collaboration, cooperation between the celebrant and the congregation. It is indeed a common action (*leitourgia*) in which the responsible participation of everyone is essential and indispensable, for through it the Church, the People of God, fulfills its purpose and goal.

The Place of Clergy. It is this Orthodox understanding of the "laity" that discloses the real meaning and function of clergy. In the Orthodox Church clergy is not above laity or opposed to it. First of all, strangely at it may seem, the basic meaning of term clergy is very close to that of laity. Clergy comes from "clerus," which means the "part of God." "Clergy" means that part of mankind that belongs to God, has accepted His call, has dedicated itself to God. In this initial meaning the whole Church is described as "clergy"—part or inheritance of God: "O God, save Thy people and bless Thine inheritance": (*kleronomia* or clergy—in Greek). The Church because She is the People of God (laity) is His "part," His "inheritance."

But gradually the term "clergy" was limited to those who fulfilled a special ministry within the People of God, who were especially set apart to serve on behalf of the whole community. For, from the very beginning, the People of God was not amorphous but was given by Christ Himself a structure, an order, a hierarchical shape: "And God has set some in the Church, first apostles, secondary prophets, thirdly teachers . . . Are all apostles? Are all prophets? Are all teachers? . . . Now you are the body of Christ, and members in particular . . ." (1 Cor. 12:28–29).

Historically the Church was built on the Apostles, whom Christ Himself has elected and appointed. The Apostles again elected and appointed their own helpers and successors, so that throughout the whole uninterrupted development of the Church, there has always been the *continuity* of this Divine appointment and election.

The "clergy" therefore is needed to make the Church what she has to be: the special People or Part of God. Their special function is to perpetuate within the Church that which does not depend on men: the Grace of God, the Teaching of God, the commandments of God, the saving and healing power of God. We stress this "of God" for the whole meaning of "clergy" lies precisely in their total identification with the objective teaching of the Church. It is not their teaching or their power: they have none, but that which has been kept and perpetuated in the Church from the Apostles down to our own time and which constitutes the essence of the Church. The Priest has the power to teach, but only inasmuch as he teaches the Tradition of the Church, and is completely obedient to it. He has the power to celebrate, but again, only inasmuch as he fulfills the eternal Priesthood of Christ Himself. He is bound — totally and exclusively — by the Truth which he represents and, thus, can never speak or command in his own name.

Our people in their criticism of the clergy fear the excessive "power" of clergy, yet too often they do not realize that the priest represents nothing else than the "Power" of the Church, of which they are members and not any specific "clerical" power. For it is clear to everybody that the Church existed before we were born and has always existed as a body of doctrine, order, liturgy, etc. It does not belong to anyone of us to change the Church or to make it follow our own taste, for the simple reason that we belong to the Church, but the Church does not belong to us. We have been mercifully accepted by God into His household, made worthy of His body and blood, of His revelation, of communion with Him. And the clergy represent this continuity, this identity of the Church in doctrine, life and grace throughout space and time. They teach the same eternal teaching, they bring to us the same eternal Christ, they announce the same and eternal saving act of God.

Without this hierarchical structure the Church would become a purely human organization reflecting the various ideas, tastes, choices of men. She would cease to be the Divine Institution, God's gift to us. But then "laity" could not be "laity" — the People of God — any more, there would be no Amen to be said, for where there is no gift there can be no acceptance ... The mystery of Holy Orders in the Church is that which makes the whole Church truly and fully the laos, the laity, the very people of God.

The Basis for Unity and Cooperation. The conclusion is clear: there is no opposition between clergy and laity in the Church. Both are essential. The Church as a totality is Laity and the Church as a totality is the Inheritance, the Clergy of God. And in order to be this, there must exist within the Church the distinction of functions, of ministries that complete one another. The clergy are ordained to make the Church the gift of God, — the manifestation and communication of His truth, grace and salvation to men. It is their sacred function, and they fulfill it only in complete obedience to God. The laity are ordained to make the Church the acceptance of that gift, the "Amen" of mankind to God. They equally can fulfill their function only in complete obedience to God. It is the same obedience: to God and to the Church that establishes the harmony between clergy and laity, make them one body, growing into the fullness of Christ.

Some Errors to Be Rejected. This simple and Orthodox truth is obscured too often by some ideas, that we have willingly or unwillingly accepted from the environment in which we live.

1. An uncritical application of the idea of democracy to the Church. Democracy is the greatest and noblest ideal of the human community. But in its very essence it does not apply to the Church for the simple reason that the Church is not a mere human community. She is governed not "by the people, and for the people" — but by God and for the fulfillment of His Kingdom. Her structure, dogma, liturgy and ethics do not depend on any majority vote, for all these elements

are God given and God defined. Both clergy and laity are to accept them in obedience and humility.

2. A false idea of clericalism as absolute power for which the priest has no account to give. In fact, the priest in the Orthodox Church must be ready to explain his every opinion, decision or statement, to justify them not only "formally" by a reference to a canon or rule, but spiritually as true, saving and according to the will of God. For again, if all of us, laity and clergy, are obedient to God, this obedience is free and requires our free acceptance: "I call you not slaves, for a slave knows not what his Lord does; but I have called you friends; for all things that I have heard, I have made known to you" (John 15:15) and "ye shall know the truth and the truth shall make you free" (John 8:32). In the Orthodox Church, the preservation of truth, the welfare of the Church, mission, philanthropy, *etc.*—are all a common concern of the whole Church, and all Christians are corporately responsible for the life of the Church. Neither blind obedience nor democracy, but a free and joyful acceptance of what is true, noble, constructive and conducive of the Divine love and salvation.

3. A false idea of Church property. "It is our Church, for we have bought or built it..." No, it is never our Church, for we have dedicated it, i.e., given it, to God. It is neither the clergy's, nor the laity's "property," but indeed the sacred property of God Himself. He is the real owner, and if we can and must make decisions concerning this property, those decisions are to comply with God's will. And here again both clergy and laity must have initiative and responsibility, in searching out the will of God. The same applies to Church money, houses and everything that "belongs to the Church."

4. A false idea of the priest's salary: "*We* pay him..." No, the priest cannot be paid for his work, because no one can buy grace or salvation, and the priest's "work" is to communicate grace and to work at man's salvation. The money he receives from the Church (*i.e.* from the People of God and not from "us"—employers of an employee) is intended to make him free for the work of God. And he, being also a member of the Church, cannot be a "hired" man, but a responsible

participant in the decisions concerning the best use of the Church's money.

5. A false opposition between the spiritual and the material areas in the life of the Church: "let the priest take care of the spiritual, and we — the laity — will take care of the material things ..." We believe in the Incarnation of the Son of God. He made Himself material in order to spiritualize all matter, to make all things spiritually meaningful, related to God... Whatever we do in the Church is always both spiritual and material. We build a material Church but its goal is spiritual: how can they be isolated from one another? We collect money, but in order to use it for Christ's sake. We organize a banquet, but if it is at all related to the Church, its goal — whatever it is — is also spiritual, cannot be abstracted from faith, hope and love, by which the Church exists. Otherwise, it would cease to be a "Church affair," would have nothing to do with the Church. Thus to oppose the spiritual to the material, to think that they can be separated is un-Orthodox. In all things pertaining to the Church there is always a need for the participation of both clergy and laity, for the action of the whole People of God.

CONCLUSION. Many mistakes have been made on both sides in the past, let us forget them. Let us rather make an attempt to find and to make ours the truth of the Church. It is simple, wonderful and constructive. It liberates us from all fears, bitterness and inhibitions. And we shall work together — in the unity of faith and love — for the fulfillment of God's Kingdom.

CHAPTER THREE

Sergius Bulgakov (1871–1944)

With the publication of several new translations of Bulgakov's writings, especially new English translations of *The Lamb of God*, *The Bride of the Lamb*, *The Comforter*, and the *Friend of the Bridegroom*, a new generation has been introduced to his theological vision and expression of Orthodox faith and practice. Furthermore, there has been a scholarly renaissance regarding Bulgakov's theological legacy. Recently, a session of the American Academy of Religion devoted was devoted to Bulgakov's thought, and an issue of *St. Vladimir's Orthodox Theological Quarterly* was devoted to Bulgakov's theology as well.

Bulgakov was born in Livny, in Orel Province, to a long line of clergy. After attending the local parochial school, he transferred to the theological seminary in Oriel in 1884. However, Bulgakov entered into a theological crisis after being introduced to Marxist thought and philosophy and left the seminary. Two years after leaving Oriel, he entered a university at the Lyceum at Yelets where he studied law, economics, literature and philosophy.

In his youth, Bulgakov was a Marxist and atheist, focusing his attention on social dynamics and history, but in mid-life returned back to the Orthodox Church of his childhood, and he did so with great fervor, eventually seeking ordination to the holy priesthood. As a layman, Bulgakov attended the famous 1917–18 Moscow All Russian Council. After some time, Bulgakov returned to the Church and was ordained by Bishop Feodor of Volokolam on July 24, 1918, which also happened to be the feast of the Holy Spirit. This is noteworthy because Bulgakov was very much influenced by the work of the Holy Spirit, and eventually devoted an entire book to the ministry of the Holy Trinity called *The Comforter.*

Bulgakov was a professor of theology, author, speaker, and ecumenist. His writing reflects a deep love for the Church as well as for the unity of Christians everywhere. In a brief autobiographical essay entitled "Hagia Sophia," Bulgakov reflects on the sheer beauty and importance of the famous cathedral in Constantinople dedicated to the Holy Spirit. While visiting this grand cathedral, he realized that this was the unity not only between heaven and earth but the unity of all Christians everywhere.

Bulgakov always kept this theme of Christian unity in mind, and it is a theme noted in his preaching, teaching, and pastoral care. Bulgakov ultimately saw this unity take shape in the eucharistic liturgy. In the liturgy, all of creation is represented, the entire cosmos, the living and the dead, the clergy and laity, all gathered around the one altar offering thanksgiving to God. It is this gathering in a bond of love which becomes the foundation for ecclesiastical ministry.

However, Bulgakov's theological creativity produced a backlash from more conservative groups such as the Russian Orthodox Church Abroad which condemned his writings on the notion of the divine wisdom or "sophiology." In his writings, Bulgakov emphasized that divine wisdom was not separate from God but was a feminine principle within the Godhead which was distinctly manifested in Scripture. Bulgakov's theological reflection on wisdom instigated his colleagues to have him expelled from teaching theology. Yet both Michael Plekon and Paul Valliere point out that Bulgakov himself was never condemned and his books and articles still continue to enjoy a large readership even today.

Bulgakov had many disciples and followers, one of whom was the young Alexander Schmemann. Juliana Schmemann recalls that she and the young Alexander attended the weekly Divine Liturgy every Thursday morning in a small chapel where Bulgakov presided. Towards the end of Bulgakov's life, when he was dying of throat cancer, he continued to serve the weekly Liturgy with only a handful of people in attendance. Juliana comments on these early liturgies: "he was wearing very, very light weight vestments and it was really an angelic sight. This man without a voice, who was the liturgy. I think that maybe this is when both of us-we communed in the liturgy the most."[1]

It is this image of Bulgakov as a priest, as a man of prayer, and as a celebrant of the liturgy that Schmemann would remember the most. It is this love for the liturgy and the sacraments, especially the Eucharist which is emphasized in the following essay which was published in an anthology by Roderic Dunkerley (ed.) entitled, *The Ministry and the Sacraments: Report of the Theological Commission appointed by the Continuation Committee of the Faith and Order Movement under the Chairmanship of Arthur Cayley Headlam*, SCM Press 1937. Bulgakov clearly shows that while the liturgy is celebrated by the priest or bishop, it is the people of God gathered around the eucharistic table which truly constitutes the true catholic Church in all its fullness.

The second essay entitled "The Episcopate," which was published in *A Bulgakov Anthology* by James Pain and Nicholas Zernov (Philadelphia: The Westminister Press, 1976), is a personal reflection on the tragedy and divisiveness of clericalism among the hierarchy in the Church. Bulgakov shows that ordination does not give the clergy extra or special power of authority over the laity, even though some hierarchs think otherwise. The only authority is the authority of love,

[1] Elena Silk, "The Eucharistic Revival Movement in the Orthodox Church in America: Past, Present, and Future," M.Div. thesis, St. Vladimir's Orthodox Theological Seminary, 1986, p. 26. See also Paul B. Anderson, *No East or West* (Paris, YMCA Press, 1985). Anderson reflects on Bulgakov's serving the liturgy in the following statement, "While some priests or ministers go through the prescribed readings, prayers, and sermons by rote, Father Sergei's every liturgy was an authentic renewal of the Last Supper of Our Lord. When he, with arms uplifted, faced the elements on the altar to pray that he might truly be transformed and received as the Body and Blood of Christ, it was if this was the first liturgy since that fateful Thursday when Jesus fed his disciples the bread and wine of communion" (p. 56).

which is also a theme found in Afanasiev's work. Throughout his writings, Bulgakov always points out that there is not general love, but love incarnated in human interaction with other humans. This particular essay is very poignant in a time when theologians and scholars are reflecting on the role and function of the office of the episcopacy in both East and West. Bulgakov shows that, in a *sobornal* and conciliar Church, there is no room for power struggles or abuse of power, yet unfortunately this still takes place in both East and West.

For Further Reading

Bulgakov, Sergius, trans. Boris Jakim. *Bride of the Lamb* (Grand Rapids, MI: Eerdman's, 2002).

_______. *Lamb of God* (Grand Rapids, MI: Eerdman's, 2007).

_______. *The Comforter* (Grand Rapids, MI: Eerdman's, 2004).

_______. *Friend of the Bridegroom: On the Orthodox Veneration of the Forerunner* (Grand Rapids, MI: Eerdman's, 2003).

_______. *Social Teaching in Modern Russian Orthodox Theology*. Trans. by Boris Jakim (New Haven, CT: The Variable Press, 1995).

_______. *Sophia, The Wisdom of God.* Translated by Patrick Thompson, O. Fielding Clark, and Xenia Brakevich (Hudson, NY: Lindsfarne Press, 1993).

_______. *Apocatastasis and Transfiguration.* Translated by Boris Jakim (New Haven, CT: The Variable Press, 1995).

Gallaher, Anastasy Brandon. "Bulgakov's Ecumenical Thought Part 1. In Bulgakov and Intercommunion, Part II," *Sobornost* 24:1 (2002), pp. 24–55; 24:2 (2002), pp. 9–28.

Gavrilyuk, Paul. "The Kenotic Theology of Sergius Bulgakov," *Scottish Journal of Theology* 58 (2005) pp. 251–69.

Pain, James and Nicolas Zernov (eds.). *Sergius Bulgakov: A Bulgakov Anthology* (Philadelphia, PA, The Westminister Press, 1976).

Plekon, Michael. "Sergius Bulgakov: Political Economist and Priest, Marxist and Mystic," in *Living Icons* (Notre Dame, IN; University of Notre Dame Press, 2002), pp. 29–55.

______. "Still Waiting at Jacob's Well—Sergius Bulgakov's Vision of the Church," *St. Vladimir's Theological Quarterly* 49:1–2 (2005) 125–144.

Valliere, Paul. *Modern Russian Theology: Bucharev, Soloviev, and Bulgakov* (Grand Rapids, MI: Eerdman's Publishing, 2000).

Williams, Roman. *Sergei Bulgakov: Towards a Russian Political Theology* (Edinbugh: T & T Clark, 1999).

See also the Bulgakov website with links www.byzantineimages.com/bulgakov.htm.

The Hierarchy and the Sacraments

1 **Hierarchy and the Apostolic Age.** The origin of the three degrees of Holy Orders as the basis of Church organization is one of the most difficult problems of modern ecclesiastical history. The sources at our command render its solution more or less hypothetical. The most probable conclusion, suggested by historical data, is that the threefold ministry in its present form was not known in the Apostolic and post-Apostolic Church of the first century.[2] We find evidences of it at the beginning of the second century, at the time of the first epistle of Clement, of the epistles of St. Ignatius, and later. By the middle of the second century a hierarchical organization with a more or less obviously monarchic bishop at the head came to be established.

We observe, as it were, two epochs: the apostolic and post-apostolic age, when the gifts of grace associated later with the grace of ordination were poured out freely, so to speak, over and above the hierarchical privileges, and various charismatics acted side by side with the Apostles (I Cor. 12); and, beginning with the second century, the age when the gifts of grace were regulated through hierarchy of the type of the Old Testament priesthood. There is no need to exaggerate, as Sohm does, the contrast between the two epochs, but the difference between them is obvious. And the most important point is that the actual transition from one epoch to the other eludes observation. The original absence of the three degrees of Holy Orders is a historical

[2] It is appropriate here to recall Cyprian's *in solidum:* every individual bishop has ecumenical episcopacy as such, not partly, but as a whole.

fact which cannot be disproved by Orthodox and Catholic apologists. We do not know in detail how hierarchy came to be established, nor can we say that it was founded upon direct apostolic succession recognisable by any external signs. Examples mentioned in the Acts warrant the supposition that the first bishops were ordained by the Apostles themselves, but -this is not absolutely certain. The testimony of Tertullian and St. Irenaeus about the unbroken apostolic succession in the Church of Rome, and of St. Polycarp in the Church of Asia Minor, is not sufficiently convincing, and, besides, these writers do not even attempt to show that all ordinations in all the Churches can be directly traced to the Apostles. The idea of the direct and unbroken apostolic succession is suggested, in the first instance, by the Catholic doctrine of the primacy of Peter, who continues his sojourn in the Church in the person of the Roman pontiff, and also by the theory that all the seven Sacraments were directly established by Christ Himself. This theory, adopted by the Council of Trent,[3] and also developed by Orthodox theologians,[4] does not of course allow for the fact that there was a hiatus between the pre-hierarchical and hierarchical period of Church history. History puts before us a question that requires a dogmatic interpretation; the question, namely, as to how we are to understand the principle of hierarchy in its significance for the Church, and also the general principle of apostolic succession, which is now regarded as the ideal basis of hierarchy. The Roman Catholic doctrine of the primacy of Peter and of the continuity of his apostolic dignity in the Popes has, at any rate, the merit of consistency, though it is bought at the price of the dogmatic myth of Peter abiding in the Roman Popes and the See of Rome. But even from the Romanist point of view there is no reason to speak of the *personal* succession of other Apostles. Indeed, nothing is said of it, for it is of no interest to Rome. It would be of more advantage to Orthodox theologians, but they have not as yet attempted to prove the position, and it is

[3] *Tridentin. can. canones de sacramentis in genere,* can. I. (sess. VII.).
[4] *Confessio Dosith.,* Art. XV.: *Conf. Orth.,* Pars I., Qu. 90.

doubtful whether they could. We do sometimes find them speaking of the episcopate as a whole possessing the fullness of apostolic grace. But this must not be taken literally, for the idea of apostolic dignity continuing in the Apostles' successors is utterly foreign to Orthodox theology. The dignity and the office of the Holy Apostles, who have known Christ in the flesh and been called by Him, is not transferable; the episcopate certainly has not the fullness of apostolic gifts, and in this sense is not an apostolic calling. The latter is much higher than episcopacy, which is only one aspect of apostleship, and ought not to he even compared with it- Christ's breathing on the Apostles to give them the Holy Spirit and the power to remit sins (John 20:22–23) was, as it were, their ordination confirmed at Pentecost. But the actual calling of the Apostles by Christ was not connected with or limited to any particular power. The tongues of name of the Holy Spirit that descended on the Apostles at Pentecost were infinitely more than the grace of episcopal ordination, and included all their prophetic and charismatic gifts. The Church is called Apostolic, not only because it has the apostolic succession of episcopal ordination, but also with reference to the whole fullness of apostolic tradition. And apostolic succession in this latter sense applies to the whole Church and not only to the hierarchy, just as Pentecostal gifts were given not to the apostolic hierarchy alone, but to the whole body of the Church. The Romanist tendency is to interpret Pentecost as meaning that only the first hierarchs — the Apostles — were gathered in the Upper Room in Sion, and that only through them were the gifts of grace handed down to other members of the Church. But such an interpretation is contrary to fact, for it is said in the Acts that not only the Apostles but Mary the Mother of God and many others were present during the descent of the Holy Spirit (*cp*. Acts 1:14 and 2:1, 4). And even if it had not been the case, the Apostles at Pentecost could not have represented only the hierarchy, "the teaching and the ruling Church," apart from the laity. It would be more correct to suppose that the twelve Apostles represented the whole body of the Church with all its members, *i.e.* both the clergy and the laity, not differentiated as yet, but all in unity. This is entirely in keeping with Matt. 28:19–20, where the command to baptize and to teach, directly addressed to the Apostles, is in truth intended for the whole Church. This is borne out by the fact that Baptism may be administered by laymen, and Baptism presupposes teaching. No doubt, the fullness of gifts bestowed upon the Church represented by the Apostles included hierarchical powers, but it was not limited to them. The Old Testament priesthood took its beginning from the fullness of gifts of the prophet and seer, Moses; the Apostles founded the Christian hierarchy not only in their capacity of first bishops but in all the fullness of their apostleship, which cannot as such be transferred to anyone. It cannot therefore be said that bishops alone have apostolic grace.

The Apostles founded local Churches and directed their organisation. This must not, however, be taken to mean that they created the whole system of ecclesiastical regulations, determining the structure of the Church. The divine-human nature of the Church presupposes Divine inspiration and guidance, and, in response to it, human creativeness and self-determination. This is why the Church has to undergo a process of historical development. Thus the Primitive Apostolic Church was to a certain extent formless[5] and imperfectly organised. On the other hand, it enjoyed the personal service of the Apostles, who continually visited various communities, as did the later "charismatics." This, however, was not sufficient to satisfy all the practical needs of the local communities (or *ecclesiae),* which therefore had their own bishops, deacons, or presbyters. In apostolic literature we find no indications that special persons were set apart for the celebration of the Eucharist, which began immediately after Pentecost (Acts 2:42, 46), except the Apostles themselves, who of course were not able to satisfy the liturgical needs in all the communities. This expressive silence seems to indicate that at that early stage the sacramental life had not yet received a definite hierarchical structure.

[5] This circumstance has led Sohm to believe that formlessness is the ideal norm of church life, and that ecclesiastical laws and institutions mean falling away from it.

The general idea of universal priesthood was the guide to practice. Remains of survivals of that stage can be found in the *Didache (The Teaching of the Twelve Apostles),* which speaks of the Eucharist being celebrated by evangelists, prophets, bishops, or presbyters.

2 The Growth of Hierarchy in the Post-Apostolic Age.

The direct testimony of history cannot be disproved by dogmatic postulates about the uninterrupted existence of hierarchy for sacramental purposes from the very beginning. It appears more probable that in the course of time hierarchy arose, as it were, spontaneously, in accordance with the spirit of the apostolic tradition, though there was a period when it did not exist.[6]

The fact that hierarchy is of comparatively late historical origin creates serious dogmatic difficulties, and the very discussion of it arouses much passion and prejudice. Some people think that this fact disproves the necessity for successive ordinations and is an argument for an elected ministry; others take the very recognition of the fact to be a wicked heresy, undermining the hierarchical principle in the life of the Church. Both attitudes are equally wrong in their one-sidedness, hut there is no doubt that the fact in question does require a dogmatic interpretation.

Some Sacraments have been directly established by Christ and are called evangelical; others came to be unfolded in the life of the Church in the course of historical development. This circumstance in no way detracts from their value, since they are in the spirit of the apostolic tradition, and have existed in the primitive Church in an embryonic form. Such are Extreme Unction, Marriage, in a certain sense even Penitence and, apparently, Ordination. It is, so to speak, a part of the Protestant creed that dogmatic value attaches only to that which bears the stamp of primitiveness *(Ur-Christentum),* of prehistoricity. This presupposition contains a tacit condemnation of the

[6] This does not of course preclude the possibility of direct apostolic succession of hierarchs in individual cases, as, for instance, in Rome (according to St. Irenaeus and others). But these cases are exceptions and not the rule.

historical development of the Church, which is regarded as merely a falling away from grace. But why should the early and the undeveloped institutions, as compared with the later and more developed, be alone regarded as having force? Why should the latter be deprived of the authority of the holy tradition ascribed exclusively to the former? No answer has ever been given to this question, for it was regarded as self-evident that primitive Christianity was the ideal norm of Christianity as a whole. And yet no doubt can attach to the Church tradition that in the second century, after an interval of a few dozen years separating the apostolic from the post-apostolic age, we find episcopacy and the threefold division of hierarchy. The principle of hierarchy comes to be generally recognised, and St. Ignatius, St. Irenaeus, St. Cyprian and others regard it as indubitable and self-evident. It is supposed to be in the interests of freedom or of prophetism to accept only the primitive pre-hierarchical Church tradition; but in truth it breathes the Old Testament spirit of legality in its insistence upon rules laid down once for all. The living Tradition of the Church, true to the apostolic teaching, did not remain stationary but, in its gradual development, in due season gave rise to hierarchy. The ancient apostolic practice of laying on of hands as a means of transmitting grace was adopted in ordination. The power to transmit grace was given by the Apostles to their successors (*cp.* St Paul's Epistles to Timothy and Titus). The laying on of hands had originally a varied and indefinite significance. It was only in the later tradition of the Church that definite forms of it came to imply definite—and different—gifts out of the fullness of the treasure-house of the Church. In this sense it may be said that hierarchy in its present form has been established by the Church herself. Roman Catholic and Orthodox theologians usually distinguish between institutions which are *jure divino* and *jure ecclesiastico,* that is, between absolute or divine and historically relative institutions. The three degrees of holy orders, according to the Catholics headed by the Pope, obviously belong to the first. But in truth neither category does full justice to the nature of hierarchy. The hierarchical principle, succession through the laying on of hands, is a divine institution, existing *jure divino,* but in its concrete historical existence hierarchy arises in the life of the Church, *jure ecclesiastico.* Taken as a whole it exists *modo divino-humano,* in the God-man-like action of the Church.

In the primitive Church the fullness of Pentecostal gifts was poured out abundantly, both during the lifetime of the Apostles and for some time, perhaps for twenty or thirty years, after their death. There is no direct evidence to show that in founding new ecclesiastical communities the Apostles personally ordained definite hierarchs for them. Rather, a possibility was provided for establishing a hierarchy, and this in time was done by the Church herself. Out of the fullness of her abiding Pentecost the Church created a hierarchy in accordance with the Divine Spirit dwelling in her, and with the general principle of the successive transmission of grace. In the Old Testament Church hierarchy was established at the command of God through the prophet Moses; in the Christian era hierarchy arose through the prophetic spiritual activity of the Church. The Church is logically *a priori* to hierarchy, and not *vice versa.* The conception of hierarchy as a direct and unbroken succession of ordinations beginning with the Apostles is typical of a later age — the age of Irenaeus, Tertullian, and Cyprian. It is, however, too pragmatic in character, and cannot be regarded as *historically* certain. There is no doubt that apostleship contained all the fullness and power of episcopacy given to the *whole* Church at Pentecost, but this does not mean that apostles were actually bishops of definite Churches. On the contrary, they did not remain in any one fixed place; there is no evidence whatever to show that they did. Titus and Timothy, ordained by St. Paul, were not bishops in our sense of the term. The supposition that apostles were bishops is necessary only from the point of view of the Roman Catholic conception of hierarchical succession, from St. Peter in the first instance, and of hierarchy as of a power *over* the Church, a special application of the principle *ex of ere operato.* It is supposed that the mere fact of successive ordinations establishes once for all a hierarchy which rules over the Church in the capacity of an ecclesiastical oligarchy. Although this idea is prevalent among Orthodox theologians as well, it is not consistent with the Orthodox conception of the Church as an organic unity of its different members —the union of all in freedom and love, *sobornost* or commonalty. From this point of view all gifts, including the grace of Ordination, were given to the whole Church as a body, and consequently the Church was able to differentiate various organs for the fulfillment of specific functions and to establish hierarchy. This did not require a direct succession of ordinations going back to the Apostles; such a succession is only a supposition and cannot be proved. The whole idea of hierarchy must be interpreted in accordance with the organic conception of the Church, which implies that hierarchy exists in and for the Church, and is not over it; it is an organ of the Church, endowed with special powers. The Romanist doctrine has had in this respect so much influence upon the theology of all denominations that a great effort of thought is needed to overcome it. We must accept as our starting-point the principle that hierarchical powers belong to the whole Church, and that episcopacy has arisen within the Church through the Church's own power, and was not given to it, as it were, from without, straight from the Apostles. Pentecostal gifts included episcopal grace, but did not create bishops there and then. Owing to those gifts, in the course of general Ordinations, bishops were created locally in accordance with the needs of the Church. It was perfectly natural that they should have been ordained by the laying on of hands of other already existing bishops, and that this should be called "apostolic succession." The usual interpretation of this term is that within the limits of the historical vista there is no break in the succession of Ordinations. But in the primitive Church the idea of "apostolic succession" had also another and a wider meaning of great dogmatic importance. It meant not only the succession of hierarchical Ordinations but also the enduring bond of belonging to a definite ecclesiastical community founded, directly or indirectly, by the Apostles, *i.e.* the succession of *sobornost*. This important historical fact, noted by Turner in his excellent essay on *Apostolic Succession,* shows that the early Church acknowledged the principle of *sobornost* as the unbroken unity and continuity of life in the religious community.[7] Episcopal grace is given to the community and not to a separate individual, and can only be realized by the individual in connection with the community. This means that not episcopal laying on of hands alone, but the consent and participation of the whole community, establishes hierarchy and its succession. The organic bond between the different communities means that a particular local Church is not limited and self-contained, but is vitally connected with the whole body of the Church, This connection is outwardly expressed by the fact that a bishop is consecrated by two or three bishops representing other Churches and is thus included in the life of the whole body of the Church.

This means not ecclesiastical democracy but organic unity of the Church. Hierarchy and hierarchical succession is given to the whole Church, which as a whole takes part in Ordination, doing so not merely by consent and election, but by participating through prayer in the actual Sacrament of Ordination.[8] In the ritual of Ordination the consent of the people expressed by *axios* is essential to the Sacrament. In the formula of Ordination the faithful are also called upon to pray for the grace of the Holy Spirit; in other words, Ordination takes place not solely through the laying on of hands, as a magical or mechanical

[7] *Essays on the Early History of the Church and the Ministry,* edited by H. B. Swete, *Apostolic Succession*, by C. H. Turner, pp. 105, 106, 108, 109, 129, "The Holy Church was catholic as well as apostolic It was not one line of descent, but many, which linked the church of Irenaeus and Tertullian with the church of the Apostles in brief, it was not the apostolic succession but the apostolic successions" (pp. 106–7). "Alike to Irenaeus, to Hegesippus and to Tertullian, bishops have their place in the apostolic succession only in connection with the churches over which they preside" (p. 129).

[8] Article X in *Conf. Dosith*, after stating that episcopal succession is from the Apostles, goes on to say, "Bishops are elected not by priests or presbyters nor by the lay authorities, but by the council of the ruling church of the country in which the city intended to be the future bishop's see is situated, or at any rate, by the council of the district in which he is to be. Sometimes, however, the city itself elects the bishop, but then it has to submit its election to the council."

act, but also through the prayer of the Church during Ordination.[9] Apart from their flock, or without its consent, the hierarchs cannot perform a valid Ordination.1 so to speak, *ex opere operato.* This is why the validity of the Sacrament demands that the person to be ordained should belong to a definite ecclesiastical community.

3 **Universal Priesthood and Hierarchy.** Hierarchy and the Sacrament of Ordination appears in the Church in the course of history; but inasmuch as it springs from the Church it bears the seal of Pentecost, and may be said to exist both *jure divino* and *jure ecclesiastico.* There is no contradiction in this. At first the hierarchical principle, which is of Divine origin, was realized freely and spontaneously through special inspiration, but afterwards it assumed the form of a canonical institution. Its canonical basis was interpreted both by the Western and the Eastern Churches in a narrow and somewhat legalistic sense. The chief corrective against this legalistic one-sidedness is the organic conception of the Church as the Body of Christ, Being the Body of Christ and the Temple of the Holy Spirit, the Church is hierarchical throughout, and holy orders are not the basis, but an expression, of its hierarchical character. A radical thinker like Sohm, opposed as he is to Roman legalism—as indeed all Protes-

[9] The ritual of Ordination makes it clear that the laying on of the bishop's hands (or of several bishops in the consecration of a bishop) is not a final moment in the Sacrament, but is conjoined with his appeal to the whole Church to pray for the Sacrament to take place. "The Divine Grace, which healeth our infirmities and supplieth our defects, promoteth... to the order of... *Let us pray* for him that the Grace of the Holy Spirit may come upon him." And the congregation prays ("Kyrie, eleison"), together with the clergy, that the Grace asked for may descend upon the candidate. In the Ordination of deacons it is also said, "Not by the imposition of my hands, but by the abundance of Thy mercies, is Grace vouchsafed unto those who are worthy of Thee," which means that the candidate for Ordination is regarded as elected not only by the bishop or bishops, but also by the people, and the idea of his organic connection with the Church forms part of the Sacrament of Ordination itself. The participation of both the clergy and the laity in the Sacrament is also implied in the formula of *Apostolicae Constitutiones,* viii 6. See also St. John Chrysostom, *Ad. 2 Cor. hom. 18.*

tants are—denies that canonical law can be rightly called law at all; there is an element of truth in his contention in so far as hierarchy is based not upon law but upon grace, and is an organic function of the Church and not something superimposed upon it. In the organic unity of the Church's spiritual life the idea of power loses its rigidity, and submission means here conviction.

The primary and essential function of hierarchy is to perform Sacraments, and, above all, the Holy Eucharist; to rule and to punish is only its secondary and derivative function. Hierarchy is in the first place a *eucharistic institution.* And in so far as our Lord Himself instituted the Sacrament of the Eucharist, hierarchy is included in that institution as one of the conditions of it. The celebration of the Eucharist, evidently by the Apostles themselves, began immediately after Pentecost (Acts 2); at a later, transitional stage, according to the *Didache,* it was celebrated not only by the Apostles but also by prophets and evangelists. At the beginning of the second century we find an ecclesiastical hierarchy whose duty it was to officiate at the Eucharist, we do not know exactly how this came to pass, but evidently it was the result of the instinctive wisdom of the Church. The three orders of the Church hierarchy are defined by inference to the Eucharist; the bishop and the presbyter are those who perform the Sacrament—the bishop naturally having precedence as one who ordains presbyters; the deacon is one who assists at the celebration of the Eucharist. It is remarkable that the very earliest documents which lay down the principle of hierarchy invariably base it upon the celebration of the Eucharist. Clement does so with regard to presbyters,[10] and St. Ig-

[10] "It would be no small sin," says Clement in his epistle, "if we were to deprive of episcopacy those who blamelessly and in all holiness bring gifts" (44). Christians must perform in an orderly fashion all that the Lord has ordained. He ordained that sacrifices and holy actions should be performed not casually and in a haphazard way, but at certain times and hours (40), not everywhere and at all times, but in Jerusalem, and only by the high priests together with other officiants (41). Therefore in the Christian Church, too, the Apostles have established bishops and deacons (42). And in resemblance of the Old Testament priesthood, the Apostles instituted the order of episcopal succession.

natius with regard to bishops and all the clergy.[11] This is the basis to which is superadded this or that theoretical justification of the bishops' power and importance in the Church.

The eucharistic significance of hierarchy shows, first and foremost, its communal character. The Eucharist is *litourgia,* common work, common service. According to the ritual of the Orthodox liturgy in which the prayers of the priest and the congregation mingle and intertwine, the Sacrament is performed jointly by the people and the celebrant; the power to effect transubstantiation is realized not by a magical act *ex opere operato* apart from the congregation and without their help, but as a common task, a liturgy. All other Sacraments, including Ordination, are also performed in the communion of the celebrants and the congregation. Negatively this thought might be expressed as follows: as a matter of principle a priest or a bishop by himself, without relation to the people and apart from them, cannot and must not celebrate the Eucharist;[12] the laity present at liturgy, however few in number, are representative of the Church people as a whole.

---

[11] St. Ignatius's appeal for obedience to bishops is closely interwoven with his appeal to take part in the Eucharist celebrated by the bishops, "He who is not within the sanctuary deprives himself of the Divine bread. If the prayer of two has great power, how much more powerful is the prayer of the bishop and the whole church" (Eph. v.). "And so strive to have one Eucharist. For there is one flesh of Our Lord Jesus Christ and one cup in the unity of His blood, one altar and one bishop with presbyters and deacons, my fellow-servers" (Philad iii. and iv.). "They keep away from the Eucharist and from prayer because they do not recognise that the Eucharist is the flesh of Our Saviour Jesus Christ who suffered for our sins … Apart from a bishop, do not do anything relating to the Church. Only that Eucharist may be regarded as true which is celebrated by a bishop or by his nominee" *(Smyrn.* 5–8), etc. St. Ignatius particularly insists upon a *eucharistic* conception of episcopacy, though it includes for him other elements as well. The *Teaching of the Twelve Apostles* mentions prophets as possible celebrants of the Eucharist, *as* well as bishops and deacons; the chief duty of the latter is an orderly celebration of the Sacrament (15).

[12] Such cases of course are known in practice (e.g. Bishop Theophan, the Hermit, celebrated liturgy every day in his seclusion), but then the participation of the people, i.e. of the whole Church, is unquestionably postulated.

Hierarchy, then, is of sacramental origin, and is born of the Eucharist. Other Sacraments arose from the same source, having their centre in the liturgy or taking place in the course of it; first of all, the Sacrament of Ordination itself, Confirmation, Baptism, which originally could and indeed still can be performed by laymen,[13] Marriage, which was originally celebrated in connection with liturgy, then Penitence, and, in the course of time, Extreme Unction. It must be borne in mind that all these Sacraments are, like the Eucharist, performed by the priest together with the people; the Church acts in them through the hierarchy, or rather with its necessary participation. Sacraments not performed through the hierarchy as such are regarded as something apart from the Church or as standing above it. Sacramentalism is, then, the true basis of hierarchy, and it was in this connection that the necessity for it was felt in the first instance; but, having once arisen, hierarchy affected the whole life of the Church.

This organic interpretation of hierarchy brings us up against the biblical conception of universal priesthood opposed by the Reformers to the clericalism of the Roman Catholics. Unfortunately in the sixteenth century both the conflicting sides knew only the Western formulation of the problem and were unacquainted with Orthodoxy, which alone could reconcile them through its organic conception of the Church. It must first of all be pointed out that the principle of universal royal priesthood, familiar to the Old Testament and proclaimed by St. Peter (I Pet. 2:9), is fully recognized in Orthodoxy. All Christians are priests in the temple of their own soul, which is the Temple of the Holy Spirit, and at the same time laity taking part together with the celebrants in the Divine Liturgy and other Sacraments. It should be noted in this connection that the status of laity does not imply a complete absence of royal priesthood, but indicates a particular grade or condition of it, since all Christians are clothed with the sacred rank of laymen. Laity exists only in and for the Church; Mohammedans or

[13] Because the Sacrament of Baptism may be performed by lay persons it could not serve as a sacramental basis for hierarchy. The absence of sacramental hierarchy in Protestantism does not destroy the validity of Baptism.

heathens are not laymen any more than they are priests. The Sacrament which in the case of laymen corresponds to Ordination is Confirmation, after which a Christian is admitted to all other Sacraments. It is worth observing that the conferring of the rank of layman is an episcopal Sacrament similar to Ordination. In the Western Church, it takes the form of the laying on of hands by the bishop; and although in the Eastern Church it is performed by a priest, the oil used in the Sacrament must have episcopal consecration. In that sense Confirmation is the Sacrament of universal priesthood. And so this principle, rightly dear to Protestantism, finds proper recognition, at any rate theoretically, in Orthodoxy. The whole Church in the fullness of its royal priesthood takes part in the celebration of the holy Eucharist; this priesthood, however, is not amorphous, but organized, and officiates at the altar as different members of a single body.

But I venture to point out to our Protestant brethren that the principle of universal priesthood—*sacerdotium*—in its communal, organic application, necessarily includes a hierarchy which acts not in separation from, but in vital union with the Church. Hierarchy may and must be understood as the organization of universal priesthood. The principle of universal priesthood establishes a vital connection between the hierarchy and the body of the Church, but it does not mean that all members of the Church are practically called upon to realize that priesthood. A body has different members and they are not all hands, mouth, etc. The fact that Protestantism recognizes in practice the necessity of Church organization and differentiation of organs shows that it is a mistake to interpret the principle of universal priesthood literally. A practical application of this principle leads to hierarchy, the power of priesthood being delegated to and concentrated in certain organs. The same thing is recognized, though without due consistency, in the Protestant distinction of *sacerdotium* and *ministerium.* Although the Protestants deny the hierarchical significance of the ministry, yet, as a matter of fact, it is only in it that the *sacerdotium* is realized. It is practically nil in all other members of the Church, for it is never exercised and is only expressed, if at all, in the right of election. We thus get the paradox that in Protestantism universal priesthood is realized through personal priesthood, which is theoretically denied. In other words, owing to the absence of an organic conception of hierarchy, universal priesthood remains null and void except in the person of the pastor.[14] It is recognized in theory but not in practice, since the sacramental character of Ordination is denied. The aim of the present argument is not to reject the conception of universal priesthood or to minimize its importance, but, on the contrary, to make it real instead of purely formal. This is achieved through sacramental Ordination, which is, as we have seen, a Sacrament of the whole Church, the realization of universal priesthood. If sacramental priesthood were reinstated in Protestantism this would mean, not the rejection, but the consistent adoption of the principle of universal priesthood — present in the Church not only at the given moment but at all times of its existence. Our participation in this unity of the Church life is expressed by the principle of the so-called apostolic succession, which at the present time is realized through the episcopal laying on of hands, with the general consent and prayers of the community.

Performing Ordinations in union with the Church the bishops successively realize the function of universal priesthood. Ordination is not a magical act, *deus ex machina,* and does not imply the sacramental power of one bishop over the Church; rather it is the organ in and through which the dignity of priesthood inherent in the Church as a whole is handed down in succession to separate individuals. Organized ecclesiastical life is far more consistent with the idea of universal priesthood than an elected ministry deprived of sacramental significance. Such ministry is an extreme form of ecclesiastical legalism from which the Western Church has suffered in the past. In their reaction against this legalism, the Reformed Churches went even further than their adversary. A ministry based on the ma-

[14] It should be noticed that in any case it does not include women, since they do not take part in Ordination.

jority of votes, an anti-hierarchical ecclesiastical democracy, means secularization within the Church, and necessarily leads to ecclesiastical provincialism. The principle of election by vote can ensure only an external unity of the Church. The only consistent form of this deliberate disruption of the Church is Congregationalism, or even Quakerism, with its complete rejection of hierarchy in the name of direct personal inspiration, supposed to be another form of universal priesthood. There are two extremes in this practical rejection of hierarchical organization: Quakerism and Papalism.

It may be asked whether the necessity of a hierarchy is not disproved by the historical argument that hierarchy did not arise at once, and was in a sense absent in the primitive Church. But this question may well be met by another; is the ministry of the reformed Churches a true return to the life of the primitive Church of the holy Apostles, divided from us by many centuries? Is it not rather a romantic, pseudo-historical reconstruction? It seems more reasonable to adopt the principle of practical relativity with regard to the means by which the idea of universal priesthood is carried out in the life of the Church, replenished by continual Pentecostal gifts. All that is required is to admit the supremacy of the principle of universal priesthood entrusted to the Church and realized by it in a certain form, under the guidance of the Holy Spirit. That form, hallowed by antiquity, is the hierarchy of episcopal succession, undoubtedly adopted by the Church from the first century onwards. The principle of succession includes the idea of election, so dear to Protestantism, as well as the idea, also accepted by Protestantism, of concentrating power in the bands of an elected hierarchy. But it also ensures the unity of the Church through the handing down of universal priesthood in the *sacerdotium.* All arbitrary and unnecessary deviations from the organic unity of tradition in the ecclesiastical life are a sin against love for the Church as well as a certain evil risk disturbing sacramental activity and casting doubt upon it. This was precisely the effect of dispensing with episcopal succession at the Reformation. In so far as it was based-on the idea of universal priesthood it was a misapprehension. This idea may not have been sufficiently recognized in Roman Catholic theology, with its overemphasis of the principle *ex opere operato,* but in truth "apostolic succession" means precisely the universal priesthood of God's people. And surely the time has come to reconsider in the light of the principle of universal priesthood the Protestant conception of an elected ministry and to return, in the name of that very principle, to the unity of the Church, preserved unbroken in its apostolic hierarchical succession.

4 The Sacramental Principle in its Significance for Hierarchy. We have seen that the episcopate, and the presbytery that springs from it, is of eucharistically sacramental origin and significance. In its mystical root it is a *sacerdotium,* and in virtue of this, episcopacy becomes an ecclesiastical power. Canonical right is based upon the sacramental life, the so-called apostolic succession has in the first instance a sacramental significance and exists for regulating the performance of Sacraments. All other aspects of episcopal power are derivative; they are historical and canonical superstructures on the sacramental basis. Having once arisen the *sacerdotium* was used as an organizing force in the Church and later had pragmatic interpretations, often exaggerated and one sided, put upon it by ecclesiastical writers of different epochs. This hierarchical hyperbolism began with St. Ignatius,[15] was further developed by St. Irenaeus,[16] and re-

[15] See *Tral.* iii.; *Smyrn.* viii.; Magnes. vi.; Eph. iii.; Magnes. iii. St. Irenaeus in his struggle against the Gnostics, who claimed to possess an occult tradition, lays main emphasis on preserving [he true tradition in the episcopacy of apostolic succession, which he confirms by the example of the Roman Church. *Adv. haeres.* iii. 3. See also Hegesippus and Tertuilian (*Praescr. haer.* 32, *ad Marcionem* iv. 5).

[16] St. Cyprian's conception of hierarchy is somewhat ambiguous. On the one hand he emphasises the solidarity (*in solidum*) of the episcopate as a whole, which binds the Church into a unity: on the other he accepts St. Peter as the visible centre of it (though Cyprian does not recognise the bishop of Rome as the *episcopus episcoporum*). His fundamental principle of the monarchical episcopacy, "*episcopus in ecclesia et ecclesia in episcopo,*" is also ambiguous and may be interpreted both in the spirit of Papalism and in the organic sense. But he,

ceived a final touch at the hands of St. Cyprian,[3] who formulated the principle of *episcopus in ecclesia* and *ecclesia in episcopo,* and the general theory of "monarchical episcopacy," which found its culmination in the Vatican dogma. Orthodox theologians, who like in their own way to keep pace with the Romans, not always grasping where this may land them, also sometimes speak of bishops as vicars of Christ or even as representatives of God.

These dogmatic hyperbolae overshoot the mark. It is true in a sense that a bishop or a priest while celebrating the Eucharist or other Sacraments bears the image of Christ the High Priest *in persona Christi,* but this is equally true, except of course with regard to the Sacrament of Ordination, of all bishops and presbyters as *sacerdotium* in an equal degree, so that for the sake of dogmatic exactitude it would be better to avoid these metaphors.

The principle of hierarchy is then sacramentally eucharistic and may be expressed in the words of St. Ignatius *(Smyrn.* viii.): ὅπου ἂν φανῇ ὁ ἐπίσκοπος ἐκεῖ τὸ πλῆθος ἔστω · ὥσπερ ὅπου ἂν ᾗ Χριστὸς Ἰησοῦς, ἐκεῖ καὶ ἡ Καθολικὴ Ἐκκλησία.

5 The Teaching Power of Hierarchy. Historical development of the Church favoured hierarchy, which being the centre of sacramental life, gradually became the organ of ecclesiastical unity and power. In addition to its office of *sacerdotium*, it exercised its power and influence in the offices of *magisterium* and *jurisdictio*

too, insists on the sacramental nature of hierarchy; *ut sacerdotes qui sacrificia dei cotidie celebramus* (Ep. lvii, 3), nor does he reject the idea of "commonalty" as the union of *sacerdos* with the people *(plebs), illi sunt ecclesia plebs sacerdoti adunata et pastori suo grex adhaerens Unde scire debes episcopum in ecclesia esse et ecclesiam in episcopo* (Ep. lxvi, 8). This is not contrary to his other principle that the unity of the Church is connected with episcopacy (the famous controversy about the two texts concerning St. Peter, *De Unitate* c 4, is not of decisive importance in this connection) Extremely important for the sacramental interpretation of hierarchy is St. Cyprian's contention that *every* bishop wholly and organically, *in solidum,* belongs to the episcopate, and being a part of it, represents the whole.

teaching and ruling. The latter developed, with the growing intimacy between the Church and the State, *sacerdotium* and *imperium*, the spiritual and the secular authority. The power to teach and to rule was a perfectly natural and normal consequence of the sacramental character of hierarchy, since the power to perform Sacraments is the highest that man can have and none other can be compared to it. In the West the power of the clergy as a monarchic episcopate reached its climax in papalism; in the East, by the Grace of God, the Church did not follow the same course to the end, but stopped half-way. The teaching power of hierarchy is not of course one of its charismatic gifts; there is no such thing as *charisma infallibilitatis* proclaimed in the Vatican dogma. So far from being infallible in their teaching, bishops have actually been known to err; the history of the Church shows that there have been heretics among Popes, patriarchs, and bishops. Great councils of bishops have been subsequently rejected and condemned by the Church, for example "The Brigandage of Ephesus," the Iconoclast Council of 764 and the Union Councils of Lyons and Florence. The teaching of the Eastern Church is always in danger of replacing personal papalism by the collective, and of substituting for the Vatican dogma of the infallibility of the Pope the infallibility of the collective Pope — the episcopate. To this end there has been created the fiction of unanimity among bishops at ecumenical councils and on all important occasions in the life of the Church. Those who are familiar with the history of ecumenical councils know how far from the truth this contention is. Of course after various manipulations by both the ecclesiastical and the secular powers a certain measure of unanimity was reached, though not always; take, for instance, the Third Ecumenical Council at Ephesus, but this unanimity was not necessarily a guarantee of truth, as can be seen from the instance of the Iconoclast and Florentine councils. Historical analysis shows that the decisions of the councils acquired authority not merely through being ratified by the episcopate as such, but through being accepted by the Church people as a body. As against this it is usually pointed out that ecumenical councils consisted of bishops alone; this circumstance is alleged as an argument in favour of collective papalism. But, in the first place, allowances must be made for the influence of the secular government which invited the bishops to the council, and also for the difficulties of the means of communication in those days; secondly, it must be remembered that laymen—the Emperor ("the external bishop") and his officials — were present at the councils as well as other people, for instance, a number of monks as at the Seventh Ecumenical Council, and the Pope's representatives, who were generally priests. It has never been canonically or dogmatically decreed that councils were to consist exclusively of bishops, and at the present day, when circumstances have changed, the practice may be regarded as obsolete. For instance, the Moscow Council of 1917–18 consisted not only of bishops, but of priests and laymen, and this is also the case with similar gatherings of the English Church and the convocations of the American Episcopal Church. The idea of collective papalism, *i.e.* of the unanimous and infallible decision of bishops, has a Romanist flavour and differs from Romanism only by being less consistent. To proclaim an Eastern Vatican dogma of the infallibility of the episcopate would be in glaring contradiction both to history and to present-day life. A dogmatic claim of this kind would have to be based on the Romanist idea of an external organ of infallibility, analogous to the Pope *ex cathedra.* But there is in Orthodoxy no automatically infallible seat of judgment, for, according to the Epistle of the Eastern Patriarchs, the whole body of the Church, and not only the hierarchy, is the guardian of the true doctrine. The whole of the Church, guided by the Holy Spirit, testifies to the truth. The absence of an outward seat of judgment is regarded by the Roman Catholics as a sign of weakness and helplessness, but in reality it is an advantage, for it is more in keeping with the nature of the Church in which the Holy Spirit Himself teaches every truth in His own way.

Nevertheless, in virtue of its sacramental power and in connection with it, the hierarchy naturally enjoys a special right to teach — *jus magisterii* — to preserve and to proclaim the doctrine of the Church.

This right belongs to it in the first instance in connection with the Church services, celebration of Sacraments, preaching and catechising. The bishop watches over teaching in the Church, but this teaching is in no sense a sacramental privilege of the clergy, inaccessible to the laity.[17] With the blessing of the responsible bishop laymen are allowed to preach even during Church services, to say nothing of other occasions. Besides, they have the right to pass judgment on theological matters, and in certain cases it is their duty to do so. Lay theologians were invited even to the Vatican Council for special tasks. It would be an intolerable superstition to believe that the grace of Ordination takes the place of theological knowledge, or makes up for the absence of it, being a kind of magic which turns ignorant men into theologians. The reverse rather is the case; a candidate for Ordination ought to be prepared for his office.

But apart from preaching it is the duty and the privilege of the clergy to guard the doctrine of the Church and give it authoritative utterance. Without pretending to any infallibility in matters of doctrine, bishops are, as it were, the mouth of the Church, pronouncing authoritative judgments in complete accord with it. It is precisely in this sense that at ecumenical and local councils the last word rightly belongs to the bishops, at the Moscow Council bishops had the right at special meetings to veto the Council's decisions. This right of the episcopate as a whole, and of individual bishops in particular,[18] may be called *conditional infallibility.* It may be said in practice that *judicium episcopati pro veritate habetur, donec corrigetur* or *sinon corrigetur* by the Church. This of course is still more the case with respect to actions that bear upon the teaching of the Church, and may be described as dogmatic facts. Thus at the present time the bishops are called upon to act with decision and authority with regard to the

[17] Rule 64 of the Trullan Council forbids laymen to preach publicly on matters of dogma (obviously without a direct permission or commission from the bishop), but, of course, does not in any sense forbid them teaching in general.

[18] It *is* appropriate here to recall Cyprian's *in solidum:* every individual bishop has ecumenical episcopacy as such, not partly, but as a whole.

movement for greater ecumenical unity and to make momentous decisions. The question of sacramental intercommunion, in particular, is one that directly comes within their jurisdiction. But it cannot be sufficiently emphasized at this juncture that that power can only be exercised in agreement with their flock. In a case of this sort the hierarchs cannot merely issue commands — as the history of the Florentine Council clearly shows; its decisions simply could not be forced by the hierarchs upon the people. This must be remembered at the present time in dealing with questions of ecumenical *rapprochement.* The hierarchs have no power to command that there should be a union of the Churches if the people are not ready for such a union and refuse to accept it.

In addition to all this it must be remembered that the presence of the Divine Grace in the Church is not limited to apostolic succession and the Sacraments. There exists in it *direct* and immediate reception of the gifts of the Holy Spirit, the power of prophecy which St. Paul bade us not to quench. The prophetic office cannot from the nature of the case be brought under any regulations, for the spirit bloweth where it listeth. With reference to the question of the *potestas magisterii,* it is important to note that the Church recognizes the legitimacy of the prophetic type of teaching, which is essentially not the province of hierarchy. Hence the teaching resources of the Church are not limited to its hierarchy. The first task of the latter is to proclaim the truth, to give it form, and bear authoritative witness to it.

6 Hierarchy and Jurisdiction. The hierarchy has also *potestas jurisdictionis,* the power to regulate the life of the Church, first and foremost in the sacramental sphere. This function is of course connected with the sacramental power of hierarchy, but has a purely historical origin, and exists *jure ecclesiastico.* The canonical structure of the Church at any given epoch is simply the expression of the state of things that actually obtains within the Church. This or that form of canonical structure can have no *dogmatic* foundation for it, such as Rome seeks to provide in its papal dogma. A historical instance of the two conflicting ways of interpreting the nature of ecclesiastical power is provided by the famous 28th rule of the Fourth Ecumenical Council at Chalcedon. That rule established a pentarchy of patriarchates and raised the See of Constantinople almost to the level of that of Rome. This procedure was frankly and decisively defended on purely historical, and not dogmatic or canonical grounds; it was urged that Constantinople was a "ruling city" and the political and cultural capital of the Empire. In like manner, the exalted position of the See of Rome was justified by the fact that Rome, too, was a "ruling city." The adherents of Rome, who maintained that the primacy of the papal see rested on dogmatic grounds, could not, of course, have it explained by a mere concatenation of historical circumstances which might change at any moment — as in fact they did, both with regard to Rome and to Constantinople after the fall of Byzantium. The instance of canon 28 is very instructive, and the principle it stands for is important for the present time when all the historical setting has changed beyond recognition. The sacramental bond between separate bishoprics which form a certain ecclesiastical unity finds expression in the consecration of a bishop by two or three bishops from other dioceses. This implies that they are recognized as being *in solidum* not only with their particular Churches, but with the ecumenical episcopate and the ecumenical Church as a whole. The creation of a new see or the consecration of a new bishop always transcends the local limitations of a given diocese, and for this reason alone it is wrong to speak of a *monarchic* episcopate which is either a polemical fiction or a dogmatic exaggeration. Both in its origin and in its realization episcopacy necessarily implies an organic multiplicity. The Roman see with its dogmatic proclamation of papalism presents the only consistent example of a monarchic episcopate. There is only one road to the truly monarchic episcopate, "the road to Canossa."

The sacramental necessity for intercommunion between separate bishoprics, based upon the organic unity of the Church as a whole, always required the existence of certain order, agreement, canonical rules, which were in fact laid down at ecclesiastical councils. There thus arose several stages of canonical hierarchy as a practical consequence of the "apostolic rule," the 34th, that the bishops of every nation ought to have a primate. This led to the formation of metropolitan areas and patriarchates, which are arising afresh in our own time, without the slightest reference to the ancient pentarchy. The principle of canonical jurisdiction combines with the sacramental principle, and indeed sometimes comes into conflict with it, claiming exaggerated importance for itself. In the course of history, canonical differences have created, and still create, many church schisms which interfere with the actual performance of Sacraments. This includes, for instance, various canonical prohibitions to officiate, leading to regrettable and painful divisions in the Church. There is often a lack of proper balance between what may be called the canonical logic of facts and the ambition of individual bishops or sees. The domain of the Church is different from that of an empire, but the wise rule *pas trop gouverner* has not always been observed by the hierarchs. Historical circumstances have bound canonical unities to national ones, this is the origin of nationally political patriarchates, but it must be remembered that the truly sacramental unit of the Church is a diocese which is related to the Church as a whole — Cyprian's *episcopus in ecclesia.* In view of the extreme centralisation of the huge national-state Churches, hindering the development of local life, it may well be asked whether it is not time gradually to make room for separate episcopal communities of the apostolic type, abandoning the principle of papalism in any of its forms, whether Western or Eastern, and reinstating the organic conception of the Church. Sacramentally hierarchical " Congregationalism "of episcopacies is more in keeping with the spirit of orthodoxy and the historical needs of the moment than a belated restoration of State Churches, Besides, States have long ago become secular, and want to be separated from the Church at the very time when ecclesiastical organisations want to retain and perpetuate the connection. The Constantine epoch of the connection between the Church and the

State is over, and for the Orthodox Church a new period has obviously begun since the Russian revolution.

It is instructive to consider the canonical structure of Protestant Churches. Rejecting the sacramental nature of hierarchy and transforming it into a purely elective office, Protestantism has built upon this basis a very efficient canonical organization. There is no need to discuss the principle *cuius regio eius religio* that determined the relation between the Church and the State at the period of the Reformation, or the fact that the established Church in England has a layman, the King, for its head; it is sufficient to glance at the actual organization of the ecclesiastical power. Protestantism established a complex system of ecclesiastical government in which the members of the various canonical bodies are either elected or directly appointed by the State. Thus instead of a hierarchy they have an ecclesiastical bureaucracy governing the Church. The abnormality of the whole position has been sufficiently demonstrated in present-day Germany. It may well be asked whether this system in any way corresponds to the ideal of the primitive Christian Church, for the sake of which the Reformation rejected the sacramental hierarchy? It may well be doubted whether consistories, superintendents, have much in common with the charismatics of the early times, though Protestantism does aim at being a prophetically charismatic Church. This secularization, this open and avowed caesaro-papalism, can only be overcome by discarding the revolutionary aspect of the Reformation and re-establishing sacramental hierarchy. The gloomy shadow of medieval papalism that the Reformation was so anxious to escape lies, in truth, on the Protestant secularization of the Church. The call to complete and correct the Reformation has more than once been heard in the Protestant world (*e.g.* Harnack), but hitherto this call has been understood merely as an urge to destructive criticism of Christian dogma. Is it not time, however, really to continue the Reformation and to free it from the shadow of papalism which still rests upon it, though in the negative sense? The same wish may be uttered with regard to those representatives of the Orthodox world who apparently seek to realize papalism without a Pope or, what is still worse, to realize collective papalism. Not wishing in any way to detract from the dignity of the Roman patriarchate, the great Apostolic Church of the West, we think it essential for the future of Christianity in its striving for ecumenical unity, inwardly to overcome papalism in our own midst, replacing it by the idea of ecclesiastical catholicity or *sobornost*.

The Episcopate

Like the church of Rome, Orthodoxy too, as it developed first in Byzantium and then in the Russian East of the Church of Moscow, sufferings from papalism, not consciously dogmatic, clearly responsibly formulated, but actual psychological. Orthodoxy is grounded in *sobornost*, the communality of the body of Church, and not in episcopacy, the bishop or the bishops alone, and on this account it cannot be regarded as a parody, I should say a caricature, of Roman ecclesiastical autocracy and absolutism. Nevertheless there is a peculiar kind of exaggeration prevalent in the Russian and other Slavic churches and with regard to episcopacy. Fortunately, this disease seems to be much less virulent in the Greek Church, the birth place of Orthodoxy, which indeed suffers from a certain ecclesiastical laxity offensive to our sense of piety.

I have to make this confession hoping that a voice from the grave it will carry more weight and not be vitiated by any personal considerations. In my lifetime I endure the evil in silence, and my silence is partly due to the lack of courage and partly to the aversion I feel to the petty scandal to which such a protest of a little Russian Luther would inevitably give rise. As a matter of fact it has nothing to do with Lutheranism or a desire to undermined the gracious power of episcopacy, which to me is a mystical reality as evident as daylight. My "Lutheranism" is a struggle not against but for episcopacy, a striving to reclaim its true dignity, to free it from the contamination of despotism, based on slavish psychology.

The slavishness is to be found first of all in the attitude of the bishops of secular power, in casereo-papism, the union of the church with the state, in subsitution the kingdom of this world for the kingdom of God. Such an attitude is found in Imperial Byzantium, Tsarist Russia, the Soviet Union, Polish nationalism, and various radicalism. While thus submitting to Caesar outside the Church, the bishops have demanded the same submission to themselves within the Church, not of course from the laity, who have remained free and in a sense exercise power over the bishops, but from the clerics bound by canonical obedience.

Such an abuse of pastoral power and the tendency towards despotic autocracy is psychologically made worse by the fact that, contrary to the second canon of the Sophia council, which excluded monks from episcopal office, our episcopate has been confined to monks, or rather to pseudo-monks since the vows of obedience became a step for obtaining episcopal power and lost all relation to monastic spiritual discipline.

Owing to the actual conditions of Russian Church life, taking monastic vows for the sake of an episcopal career became one of the most painful peculiarities of our ecclesiastical system; everybody knows this. The intolerable spiritual contradiction involved in this has become more and more manifest, especially in our time, when due to war and revolution secular authorities constantly supersede one another. Each new regime has its own incumbent and power elite, and the episcopacy is filled to an alarming extent by men bent on making a career. All this must inevitably lead to a purifying in the life of the church that will save it not from episcopacy, but in its name, from bishops of a certain type. St. Seraphim is said to have prophesied that such a time would come for the Russian Church.

No doubt the position of the episcopate is psychologically difficult in itself; it harbours the danger of a peculiar kind of man-worship. This has always been the case, both in the Old Testament and beyond the confines of revealed religion. It was not an accident that the high priests, Annas and Caiaphas, the whole ideological, confessional, and religious, man-deifying complex is involved in their rejection of Christ. And, alas, this type of Old Testament high priest has continued to repeat itself inside the history of the New Covenant. There is a paradox here, the high priesthood is a divine institution in the Old Testament, but historically and psychologically it is dearly paid for in its fallen humanity, frail in its sinfulness. It is wrong defiantly to reject the divine institution itself on the ground of human sinfulness, as Protestantism has done, but it is also wrong to make an idol of it and worship it slavishly. This is a peculiar tragedy of Church life.

In the Roman Church it has found expression in the anthropotheism of the papacy and in the East in the papalist tendencies to the episcopate in the dogmatic and canonical sphere and everyday life and customs. In the Russian Church one of the most important practical expressions of the tendency is the liturgical cult of the episcopacy which imparts to divine worthiness the character of bishop-worship. The people love this ceremonial, they are brought up on it in the Church and, of course are demoralized by this style of piety. The central nerve of prayerful life, the Divine Liturgy, is overshadowed by the pomp of episcopal ritual, by the decorative and therefore religiously pernicious lengthening of service. The real acting of it is only felt within the sanctuary, for the icon screen to some extent protects the congregation from the provoking spectacle, but its difficult to think and speak calmly of this introduction to decorative show into the holy of holies under the pretext of piety.

Enthusiasm for this pageantry is most frequently encountered among the less spiritual members of the episcopate, who assume the role of living icons. But, alas, the temptation is real for all, and the most difficult aspect of the matter is that all of this tragic glorification of the episcopate is based not upon recognized dogma but upon ecclesiastical psychology and is a matter of feeling. Basically everything is undamaged and as it should be, but psychologically the Church is affected by the spiritual disease of man-worship.

In any case, I must confess that for my affection and respect for the bishops with whom I had personally had contact, this ecclesiastical despotism was the heaviest cross I had to bear as a priest, and I feel guilty of passivity, of connivance. Invariably when I read in the church the Lord's severe words denouncing "Moses seat," my voice shook helplessly with secret pain. Such is the bitter truth of my priesthood.

Another bitter truth concerns what I may call my liturgical destiny. I took holy orders solely in order to officiate, chiefly to celebrate the Divine Liturgy. In my naïve inexperience was I discerned very little as to the actual position of a priest in the Church. It soon became very apparent to me that in order to officiate one had to have a church, or in any case an altar. When I became a priest I was too old to follow the usual path of a priestly career from the beginning. In addition, my ordination came at a time of bitter Church persecution in Russia, and afterwards in exile I lived among refugees who had very few churches. As a result, during the quarter century of my priesthood I never had a church of "my own" but always either concelebrated with a bishop or vicar or occasionally took a service by myself through never on great holy days. On such occasions as Holy Week and Easter my friends tried to arrange services or me in private houses, and this almost always meant a struggle in self-defense. To my knowledge, no bishop has ever sought to provide me with a church. My position in this respect was a heavy cross to bear as a priest and those near and dear to me share my personal unhappiness. I cannot think of this calmly even now, when illness has made it impossible for me to officiate unaided. The psychological source of such indifference on the bishop's part is the same as I have indicated above.

There is much in the practice and customs of Orthodoxy that gives cause for sorrow, sacerdotalism, lack of culture and enlightenment in Church life, ritualism, superstition, and ignorant formalism, in fact everything that makes our Orthodoxy unorthodox, and yet in all redeemed by the gracious gift of love for God. The fiery ordeal through which Russia is passing has brought to light both the Orthodox peoples' spiritual helplessness in their struggle with Bolshevik demonism directed against religious faith and holiness, and the special religious genus and vocation of the Russian people and their love of God. Such gifts could only be manifested in all their force and magnitude in the times by trial by which the Lord in his mercy has honored the Russian people and their Church. I thank and glorify my God for having allowed me to enter the ranks of clergy to serve him precisely in these terrible and tragic times when the Church's outer prosperity is at its lowest ebb.

All that has been said does not shake or limit my loyalty and devotion to Orthodoxy but merely frees it from all "orthodoxism" natural to the local church consciousness of its narrow provincialism which takes itself to be universal and all embracing; breathing with one lung only, or with a part of it, it feels as though it were breathing fully. "Ecumenism" as a fact means dissatisfaction with provincialism where of the Roman or Eastern Byzantine type. One may in a kind of ecclesiastical conceit imagine oneself to embrace the whole fullness of the Church, but there is bound to remain a dim conscience that this is of the case. That which was given and commanded to us has been lost in the distant past, but to this day it remains a promise, a longing, an unsatisfied desire, as an open embrace that has nothing to clasp and cannot be replaced by brandishing a fist at the "orthodox" who think differently. There should always be in one's heart a living pain at the Church's division and a sincere prayer "for the union of all," given us as a promise and set us a task in life. Till this is fulfilled there can be no ecumenical Orthodoxy. I am speaking of the catholicity or universality of Orthodoxy not of the dogmatic doctrine or the purity of tradition, but of the feeling of the Church. Hitherto, this feeling of universalism has not found adequate expression.

But I am even more conscience of another and perhaps more important divergence from "historical" Orthodoxy. It has be do with the future, with eschatology, with the tremendous expectation and longing for the coming of Christ, Orthodoxy seems somehow to have lost this, not in its dogma but in fact, under the overwhelming burden of its historical heritage. The loss is even more evident in Roman Catholicism. Tradition has ceased to be "vital" and has become the depository of the faith, to be preserved but not developed creatively. Yet

Orthodoxy demands not the more possession of the inherited wealth of faith and life but prophecy and apocalypse, a call and a promise. In this sense apocalypse implies concern for the history of the present and the future as well as that of the past. The Church has no continuing city on earth, but seeks one to come. Orthodoxy implies inspiration, the *eros* of the Church, her yearning for the Bridegroom, the feeling proper to his Bride. It is creativeness directed towards the final goal, the expectation of the End. It is not cowardly, fear of life and flight from it, but the overcoming of all giveness and the longing for a new heaven and a new earth, for a new meaning and life with Christ. All this is ineffable and sounds like music in the soul; it is like a symphony of colors, like art and poetry. It is eager expectation and promise. "Even so, come, Lord Jesus."

Much as I am "rooted" in the Church and at one with everything in it, in this feeling for her life I have remained solitary and alien to historical Orthodoxy, which has not satisfied me. Or, rather, I feel that to accept this limited sense of Orthodoxy is to betray it and to lose something vital and precious. It is almost impossible for me to put this feeling into words or to communicate it to others; it is like the reason of the heart, it brings together those lost in the sea of life and unites the in a bond of brotherhood as a Church within the Church.

I may refer to this experience as a Sophianic feeling for life which allows us to recognize the divine ground of the world under the crust of matter. I cannot say that I have been alone in this recognition, kindred spirits joined me and were near me, but so far as the institutional church is concerned, am lonely and cold in it. And yet so firm is my hope, so apocalyptic my attitude towards life, that I am supreme and joyous in my expectation. In the light of it I behold the present and foresee that which is to come; I seek the prophetic meaning of events and grasp their hidden significance, finding in them the fulfillment of the promised future.

In the light of the apocalypse, I comprehend the historical tragedy which is being unfolded before us, and especially its main chapters and themes. Two of them glow for me with particularly vivid light; the destinies of Russia, my native land, and of Israel. All that is happening in the world seems to be centered in them, and they hold a special place in my thought. I am drawn to them more than to anything else in attempting to interpret prophecies. The terrible and as it were preordained destinies of these two peoples indicate their exceptional significance in the life of mankind as a whole. At the present time they are becoming more than ever before the world's history.

I do not expect to see the fulfillment of my prophetic hopes in my lifetime. So be it, it is God's will. But this does not undermine the firmness of my faith, the certainty of the expectation, any more than it drowns the victorious cry of the heart: "Even so, come, Lord Jesus!" I am expecting a miracle in history, the revelation in it of its higher meaning, of the divine will. This can only happen through a manifestation of the fullness of biblical Christianity in the spirit and power of prayer and prophecy.

CHAPTER FOUR

Metropolitan Kallistos Ware (1931–)

Timothy Ware was born in Bath in Somerset, England, and for the first part of his life attended the Church of England. He matriculated and attended Magdalen College at Oxford University, where he pursued a degree in Classics and Theology, eventually converting to the Orthodox Faith in 1958. After his conversion and ordination, Timothy then took the monastic habit and changed his name to Kallistos. For the rest of his life, Ware has devoted himself to the understanding of the Orthodox Faith and Tradition, being a world renown Orthodox scholar, theologian, and author, but also an apologist for the Orthodox Faith and practice. His best-selling book, *The Orthodox Church*, followed later by the *Orthodox Way*, contains his deep devotion to the historical development of the Church as well as the rich liturgical and spiritual heritage of the Eastern Church. Together with Philip Sherrard and G. E. H. Palmer, Ware helped translate the entire *Philokalia*, *Festal Menaion*, and *Lenten Triodion*, into English. These books contain many of the hymns and scripture readings for the major feast days and Lenten season.

Ware officially retired from his teaching post at Oxford University in 2001, yet he still maintains an active scholarly career leading retreats, delivering keynote addresses, and participating in theological conferences. He continues to lecture at the new Institute of Orthodox Studies at Cambridge University as well as in other venues throughout the world.

His essay, "Patterns of Episcopacy in the Early Church and Today: An Orthodox View," was first published in a book entitled

Bishops, But What Kind: Reflections on Episcopacy by Peter Moore (ed.) (London: SPCK, 1982). This essay provides a penetrating view of episcopal ministry in the early Church, focusing mainly on the unifying, teaching, and liturgical role of the bishop. However, this essay is not only a historical survey, but calls into question how the Church can rediscover the teaching aspects of the episcopate as seen in the early Christian era. This essay is important because it also considers the issue of authority and unity in the office of the bishop, a topic which is of concern to modern theologians, especially within Roman Catholic and Orthodox circles. As Ware shows, the bishop was not a symbol of imperial authority and power, a mirror of the emperor, but the chief pastor and leader of the other presbyters under his care. Likewise, decision making was always done in consultation with the other presbyters, which formed the *presbyterium* or council of elders. This model of ministry, clearly reflecting a conciliar model, has broken down in many Churches today. In practice, the parish rector often functions as a local bishop due to the large geographical areas of most dioceses. Furthermore, for various reasons, including the large territories of most dioceses, few bishops surround themselves with the *presbyterium,* the council of priests or presbyters, seeking their advice on financial and other pastoral concerns. This lack of mutual accountability causes a breakdown of the sobornal nature of the Church.

For Further Reading

Behr, John; Andrew Louth, and Dimitri Conomos. *Abba: The Tradition of Orthodoxy in the West Festschrift for Bishop Kallistos (Ware) of Diokleia* (Crestwood, NY: St. Vladimir's Seminary Press, 2003).

Ware, Timothy (Kallistos). *The Orthodox Church* Rev. Ed. (NY: Penguin, 1993).

_______. *The Orthodox Way* Rev. Ed. (Crestwood, NY: St. Vladimir's Seminary Press, 1990).

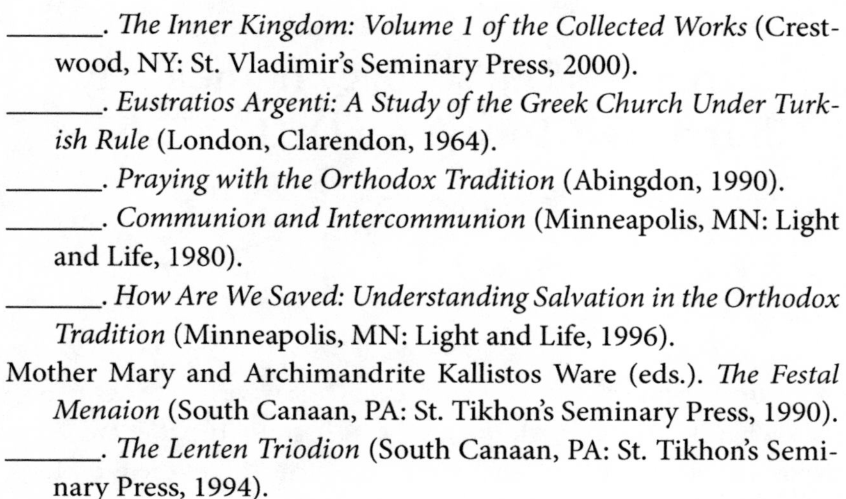

_______. *The Inner Kingdom: Volume 1 of the Collected Works* (Crestwood, NY: St. Vladimir's Seminary Press, 2000).

_______. *Eustratios Argenti: A Study of the Greek Church Under Turkish Rule* (London, Clarendon, 1964).

_______. *Praying with the Orthodox Tradition* (Abingdon, 1990).

_______. *Communion and Intercommunion* (Minneapolis, MN: Light and Life, 1980).

_______. *How Are We Saved: Understanding Salvation in the Orthodox Tradition* (Minneapolis, MN: Light and Life, 1996).

Mother Mary and Archimandrite Kallistos Ware (eds.). *The Festal Menaion* (South Canaan, PA: St. Tikhon's Seminary Press, 1990).

_______. *The Lenten Triodion* (South Canaan, PA: St. Tikhon's Seminary Press, 1994).

Patterns of Episcopacy in the Early Church and Today: An Orthodox View

1 EUCHARISTIC CELEBRANT OR COMMITTEE CHAIRMAN? What is a bishop? All too easily we assume that the answer is obvious; yet in fact the bishop's role has varied in different periods. Which is to be our model: the collegial episcopate of New Testament times, with groups of presbyter-*episkopoi in* each local church? Or the so-called 'monarchical' bishop of the second and third centuries, clearly distinguished from the presbyters, yet presiding over no more than a single congregation, the normal celebrant at the Sunday Eucharist? Or the bishop of the fourth century onwards, ruling over a diocese of not just one but dozens or even hundreds of distinct parishes?

However strongly we may be convinced that there is an unbroken continuity between these three stages, we should not be blind to the points of contrast. The pattern of episcopacy that developed, for example, in the era following Constantine's conversion (312), and that determined the debate between Rome and the Reformation in the sixteenth century, is not identical with that prevailing in the first three centuries. This is a point of crucial significance for inter-Church discussions in our own day. When the proposal is made that non-episcopal communities should 'take episcopacy into their system', it is important to ask: What kind of episcopacy? Are they being invited to accept a pastor or a prelate, a local bishop-celebrant according to the pre-Nicene model, or the type of bishop-administrator to be found in medieval and modern times?

The Church on earth moves forward, not backward, and there can be no question of reverting exactly to any earlier pattern. Yet, in so far as history has lessons to teach us, it is perhaps the second of the three stages indicated above that can prove the most illuminating for us today. We cannot hope to return to the first stage and to reproduce the ecclesial pattern existing at Ephesus or Rome in the 50's or 60's of the first century, for the simple reason that the apostles are no longer with us. While the New Testament remains always the touchstone of our church life, we have also to recognize the uniqueness of the apostolic age. It is the second generation of the Church, rather than the first, that is relevant to our present-day situation, precisely because it was a post-apostolic age like our own. St. Ignatius of Antioch can act as our guide in a way that the apostolic age cannot, because the modern bishop, in common with Ignatius, has to exercise his ministry without the presence of the apostles.

But if the second stage is closer to our contemporary conditions than the first, it is also closer to us, in at least one fundamental respect, than the third. The 'establishment' of Christianity as the official religion of the Roman Empire in the fourth century meant that the bishop became, to a lesser or greater degree, part of the central or local government, a civil servant as well as a witness to the Kingdom not of this world. Now that we are moving into a 'post-Constantinian' epoch, we have much to learn from the era before Constantine, from the experience of the second and third centuries, when there was a clear line of demarcation between the things of Caesar and the things of God. It is true that we can hardly expect to return to the pattern whereby the bishop's diocese was limited to a single worshipping community. But in other ways the modern bishop is closer to Irenaeus and Cyprian than he is to Gregory the Great, Photius, Thomas of Canterbury or Cardinal Wolsey.

Let us look, then, at the patterns of episcopacy existing during the second stage, in the years between the New Testament and the Council of Nicaea. There are three pre-Nicene authors in particular, all of them bishops, who speak to our condition today: St. Ignatius of Antioch (+c. 110), with his insistence upon the eucharistic character of the bishop; St. Irenaeus of Lyons (+ c. 200), with his view of the bishop as teacher of the apostolic faith; and St. Cyprian of Carthage (+ 258), with his understanding of the synodical nature of the episcopate.

2 The Bishop as Eucharistic Celebrant: St. Ignatius. For St. Ignatius, the bishop is primarily one who presides at the Eucharist, acting as *alter Christus* or living image of Christ, and so constituting the focus and visible centre of unity within the Church. The Church, in Ignatius' view, is essentially eucharistic by nature: there is an organic relation between the Body of Christ, understood as community, and the Body of Christ, understood as sacrament. Here he is developing a line of thought already evident in St. Paul, "The bread that we break is a communion with the Body of Christ," writes the apostle, "The fact that there is only one loaf means that, though there are many of us, we form a single body because we all share in this one loaf" (1 Cor. 10:16–17). In this text, surely the most important concerning the Church to be found anywhere in the New Testament Paul affirms not merely an analogy but a causal connection between communion in the one eucharistic loaf and membership in the one ecclesial community. Because we all eat from the one loaf, therefore we all form one Body in Christ. It is the Eucharist that actualizes the oneness of the Church. Unity is not imposed upon us from without by some exterior authority, but created from within by bur common participation in the Holy Mysteries.

This link between the oneness of the eucharistic loaf and the oneness of the Church is also prominent in the prayer of consecration to be found in the *Didache* or *Teaching of the Twelve Apostles,* late first-early second century:

> As this broken bread was scattered over the mountains and was then brought together and became one, so may thy Church be gathered together from the ends of the earth into thy Kingdom.[1]

[1] *Didache* ix.4. Possibly this is a prayer for use at the agape rather than at the Eucharist.

The ears of wheat, growing scattered on the upland slopes, are gathered together on the threshing floor, and then ground into flour and baked to form a single loaf; and, by sharing in this one loaf at the Eucharist, the scattered members of the human race are likewise gathered into the living, organic unity of the Church. Through Holy Communion the Church becomes what it is — one Body in Christ.

This eucharistic approach is taken up and developed much more fully by St. Ignatius of Antioch. His thought is dominated by eucharistic models. He sees the Church as a eucharistic society, and the bishop as a eucharistic person. When speaking of the Church he has in mind, not an abstract ideal or a world-wide organization, but the local worshipping community. His primary *ikon* or visual image of the Church on earth is this: a table; on the table, a plate with bread and a cup with wine; and round the table the gathered People of God, together offering the Eucharist. *Ecclesia,* the 'assembly' of the Church, means for him, not merely any kind of assembly, specifically the assembly of God's People 'called out' and gathered for eucharistic worship.

For Ignatius, therefore, the bishop is not primarily a teacher or administrator, but the celebrant who presides at the Sunday liturgy. As *episkopos,* 'overseer,' it is his task precisely to 'watch over' the Eucharist. Ignatius does not in fact mention the bishop's *cathedra* or throne; but, had he done so, he would have regarded it, not as a monarch's throne, a professor's chair or a judge's tribunal, but as the seat which the bishop uses when officiating at the Eucharist. By the same token, an *ex cathedra* pronouncement would have meant for Ignatius, not an arbitrary directive issued by some remote figure, but the kind of loving, pastoral advice that the bishop gives when addressing his flock during the Sunday liturgy. In a typical passage, St. Ignatius writes:

> Take care to participate in one Eucharist: for there is one flesh of our Lord Jesus Christ, and one cup for union with his blood,

> one altar, just as there is one bishop together with the presbyters and the deacons my fellow-servants.[2]

The perspective is the same as in 1 Corinthians 10:16–17 and the *Didache.* The repetition of the word 'one' indicates the manner in which Ignatius views the Church's unity, and the bishop's ministry within the one Church: "one Eucharist . . . one flesh . . . one cup . . . one altar . . . one bishop." The Church is one because its members are assembled round one altar, receiving communion from one loaf and one chalice, under the presidency of one bishop. There is one bishop, one eucharistic Body, and so one Church. The three are interdependent.

It is significant that Ignatius should speak so insistently of 'one bishop.' The New Testament appears to envisage, alongside the traveling ministry of the apostles, a twofold local ministry of deacons and *presbyter-episkopoi,* with the latter acting in each place collectively as a committee or college.[3] Ignatius, on the other hand, assumes the existence of a threefold order, making a sharp distinction between the college of presbyters, who function collectively, and the single or 'monarchical' bishop. It is far from clear how this threefold pattern evolved from the twofold scheme found in apostolic times. The threefold pattern, so it seems, was by no means universal in Ignatius' day, and perhaps did not come to prevail generally until the end of the second century.[4] At Alexandria the collegial system of

[2] *To the Philadelphians* iv.

[3] For the apparent equivalence of presbyters and *episkopoi,* see Acts 20:17, 28; 1 Peter 5:1 (especially if *episkopountes* is read in verse 2); Titus 1:5, 7. For a twofold local ministry of *episkopoi* and deacons, see Phil. 1:1; 1 Tim. 3:2, 8 (presbyters are mentioned in 1 Tim. 5:17–19, but with no reference here to *episkopoi).* Something closer to the Ignatian 'monarchical' episcopate may have existed at Jerusalem under James, the Lord's brother (Acts 21:18).

[4] In 1 Clement 42 and 44, we find a twofold ministry, consisting of deacons and of presbyter-episkopoi functioning as a college. *Didache* xv. 1 speaks only of bishops and deacons, along with wandering prophets. Polycarp, *Letter to the Philippians v.* 3, mentions only presbyters and deacons; this is the more remarkable, in that Ignatius addresses Polycarp as a 'monarchical' bishop. Hermas, *Vision* III. v. 1, taken in conjunction with Vision II. iv. 2–3, points to a twofold

presbyter-episkopoi may well have survived into the third century or even later.[5]

3 Unifying Ministry. For Ignatius, then, the one bishop — clearly distinguished from the *synedrion* or college of presbyters — constitutes the centre and sign of unity in the local Church: the whole flock is seen as recapitulated and personified in him.[6] This unifying ministry he exercises above all by presiding at the Eucharist, for it is the Eucharist that creates the unity of the Church. It should be remembered in this connection that Ignatius was writing at a time when, to use anachronistic terminology, the bishop's diocese consisted of but a single parish. There was at this period no more than one eucharistic assembly in each city. The parochial system, with which we are today familiar, only began to emerge in the second half of the third century, and did not become general until some time after the Council of Nicaea. Visiting Jerusalem in the 380's, the pilgrim Egeria found that, despite the large number of pilgrims and local Christians, there was still as a rule only one Eucharist on each Sunday or feast, celebrated by the bishop and attended by everyone.[7]

This primitive situation greatly reinforced the bishop's function as visible focus of unity. For Christians in Ignatius' day and for several generations thereafter, the bishop was not a distant administrator, but the local pastor whom they all saw Sunday by Sunday at the Eucharist. So far from being the norm, non-episcopal liturgies were a rare

---

ministry of deacons and presbyter-episkopoi. Justin and the other Apologists are not specific about the details of the Church's ministry. Thus, apart from Ignatius, there is no unambiguous evidence of the 'monarchical' bishop and the threefold ministry until Hegesippus and Irenaeus around the last quarter of the second century.

[5] See Jerome, *Letter* cxlvi. 1 (PL 22. 1194); *Apophthegmata,* alphabetical collection, Poemen 78 (PG 65.341B); Severus of Antioch, apud E. W. Brooks, *The Journal of Theological Studies* ii (1901), pp. 612–13; Eutychius, *Annales* (PG 91.982 BC).

[6] To the *Trallians* i.1; to the *Ephesians* i.3.

[7] See John Wilkinson (ed.), *Egeria's Travels* (1971), pp. 123–42.

exception. The bishop acted as centre of unity, not on an abstract and theoretical level, but in a specific way at the regular worship of the local congregation.

But, even though not regarding the bishop as a distant administrator, Ignatius certainly expected him to be obeyed. "I would as soon think of contradicting a bishop," said Dr. Johnson. Ignatius would have approved; submission to the bishop is a constant *leitmotiv* in his letters. We should "be subject to the bishop as to Jesus Christ," he enjoins;[8] "we should look on the bishop as the Lord himself."[9] The bishop, as president at the Eucharist, is *alter Christus,* the living *ikon* of Christ, and should be honoured as such. Elsewhere Ignatius likens the bishop to God the Father and the deacons to Christ, while the college of presbyters represents the apostles,[10] but the point of the symbolism is the same: the bishop presides 'in God's place':[11] union with the bishop is equivalent to union with God.

Without the bishop, so Ignatius maintains, there can be no Eucharist and no Church:

> Avoid divisions, as the source of evils. Let all of you follow your bishop ... Let no one do any of the things that concern the Church without the bishop. Let that Eucharist be considered valid which is held under the bishop, or under someone whom he appoints. Wherever the bishop appears, there let the people be, just as wherever Jesus Christ is, there is the Catholic Church. It is not lawful either to baptize or to hold an *agape* without the

[8] *To the Trallians* vi.1.

[9] *To the Ephesians* vi.1.

[10] *To the Magnesians* vi. 1; *To the Trallians* iii. 1; *To the Smyrnaeans* viii. 1. This appears to put the deacons on a higher footing than the presbyters, but that seems not to have been Ignatius' intention. The presbyters arc likened to the apostles, not because of any inferior status *vis-à-vis* the diaconate, but because they function collegially. The deacons resemble Christ, who said of himself: "I am among you as the one who serves (*ho diakonon*)" (Luke 22:27; cf. Matt. 20:28; Mark 9:35; 10:45).

[11] *To the Magnesians* vi.1.

> bishop. Whatever he approves is also pleasing to God ... He who honours the bishop is honoured by God. He who does anything without the bishop's knowledge is serving the devil.[12]

But, while insisting in this manner that the bishop is to be obeyed as God's image, Ignatius speaks also of the mutual bonds linking the bishop to the college of presbyters, to the deacons and to the Christian people as a whole: "... one bishop *together with* the presbyters and the deacons my fellow-servants," as he says in a passage already cited.[13] The presbyters are united to the bishop "as the strings to a musical instrument";[14] there is co-responsibility in the local Church, not autocracy. The bishop exercises "the ministry that belongs to the community";[15] he is not set up as a ruler over the Church, but performs a *diakonia* within it. When proposing to Polycarp of Smyrna that he should send a messenger to Syria, Ignatius does not suggest that he should decide the matter on his own, by virtue of his episcopal office, but tells him to "call a council" to discuss what to do.[16] "Where the bishop appears, there let the people be":[17] the bishop is not isolated from the other members of the ecclesial community, but depends on them, as they on him. In view of this reciprocity, the familiar phrase "monarchical episcopate" should not be applied to Ignatius' teaching without careful qualification. The mutual relationship between the people and their bishop is likened to that between Christ and the Father:

> As the Lord was united to the Father and did nothing without him, neither by himself nor through the apostles, so should you do nothing without the bishop and the presbyters. Do not try

[12] *To the Smyrnaeans* viii.1–2, ix.1.
[13] *To the Philadelphians* iv.
[14] *To the Ephesians* iv.1.
[15] *To the Philadelphians* i.1.
[16] *To Polycarp* vii.2.
[17] *To the Smyrnaeans* viii.2.

> to justify anything as right for yourselves apart from the others, but let there be one prayer in common, one supplication, one mind, one hope in love, in the joy that is without fault, that is Jesus Christ; for there is nothing better than him. Hasten all to come together as to one temple of God, as to one altar, to one Jesus Christ, who came forth from the one Father, is with the one Father, and departed to the one Father.[18]

Here, as elsewhere in the Ignatian letters, the unity of the Church is seen in eucharistic terms: "one prayer in common ... one temple of God ... one altar ... one Christ." The Church, as a mystery of diversity in unity, is seen also as an *ikon* of the Holy Trinity: "... may they be one, as we are one; I in them, and thou in me, may they be perfectly one" (John 17:22–3) — the union between the bishop and his flock reflects the union between the persons of the Godhead.

Such, then, is the Ignatian bishop: president at the Eucharist, visible incarnation of the Church's local unity. "Watch over unity, for there is nothing more important than this," Ignatius insists in his letter to Polycarp, Bishop of Smyrna:[19] the primary task of the bishop is to preserve unity. This Polycarp is to achieve above all through his intercession: "Devote yourself to unceasing prayers," urges Ignatius[20] — the bishop is to be a man of prayer. He also expects Polycarp to teach and preach: "Talk to each man personally ... speak to the sisters ... instruct the brothers.[21]

But on the whole the Ignatian letters place little emphasis upon the teaching role of the bishop. Nor do they speak of the bishop as a successor to the apostles. Whereas Ignatius' contemporary, St. Clement of Rome, had already developed a rudimentary doctrine of apostolic succession,[22] Ignatius himself does not connect his own office

[18] *To the Magnesians* vii.1–2.
[19] *To Polycarp* i.2.
[20] *To Polycarp* 1.3.
[21] *To Polycarp* i.3, v.1.
[22] *1 Clement 42 and 44.*

as bishop with the ministry of the apostles, but draws a sharp contrast between the two;[23] and in his Trinitarian similes he likens the presbyteral college, and not the bishop, to the apostles. It is not as teacher or as successor to the apostles that the bishop is important to Ignatius, but as eucharistic president. The bishop would be expected, of course, to give teaching to the people when he officiated at the Eucharist; and it would also be possible to envisage him, in his role of eucharistic president, as *alter apostolus* as well as *alter Christus*. A doctrine of episcopal *magisterium* and of apostolic succession is therefore implicit in Ignatius' eucharistic approach; but he does not choose to develop these aspects explicitly.

4 Bishop Celebrant: Bishop Bureaucrat. The eucharistic ecclesiology of St. Ignatius has had a profound and largely beneficial influence on modern Orthodox thought concerning the Church.[24] It is surely helpful for us, living as we do in a 'post-Con-

[23] *To the Romans* iv.3; to the *Trallians* iii.3. When he speaks of the bishop as "sent" by Christ, he uses the verb *pempo*, not *apostello*.

[24] See the pioneering study of John Romanides, "The Ecclesiology of St. Ignatius of Antioch," *The Greek Orthodox Theological Review* vii (1961–2), pp. 53–77. The fullest and most balanced treatment of the historical evidence is by John Zizioulas, *I enotis tis Ekklisias en ti Theia Evcharistia kai to Episkopo kata tous treis protous aionas [The Unity of the Church in the Divine Eucharist and the Bishop during the First Three Centuries]* (Athens 1965). See also his articles, "La communauté eucharistique et la catholicité de l'Eglise," *Istina* xiv (1969), pp. 67–88; "Apostolic Continuity and Orthodox Theology: Towards a Synthesis of Two Perspectives," *St. Vladimir's Theological Quarterly* xix (1975), pp. 75–108; "Conciliarity and the Way to Unity: An Orthodox Point of View," in *Churches in Conciliar Fellowship?* (Conference of European Churches, Occasional Paper no. 10: Geneva 1978), pp. 20–31. Compare Nicolas Afanassieff, "The Church which presides in love," in J. Meyendorff and others, *The Primacy of Peter* (1963), pp. 57–110 (a brilliant essay; but Afanassieff makes too sharp a contrast between 'eucharistic' and 'universal' views of the Church). For eucharistic ecclesiology in relation to levels of primacy, see A. Schmemann, "The Idea of Primacy in Orthodox Ecclesiology," in J. Meyendorff, *op. cit.*, pp. 30–56; in relation to the question of intercommunion, see Kallistos Ware, "Intercommunion: the Decisions of Vatican II and the Orthodox Standpoint," *Sobornost*

stantinian' world, to restore the bishop to his eucharistic context and to think of him, in Ignatian terms, as bishop-celebrant rather than bishop-bureaucrat, as officiant at the Holy Mysteries rather than chairman at committees. It is scarcely practicable for us today to revert to the second-century pattern whereby the bishop had charge of no more than a single worshipping community. But let his diocese at least be restricted in size—not more than a hundred or even fifty parishes—so that he may be as far as possible an accessible figure, known personally to his flock. Let us take as our model Greece or central and southern Italy, where dioceses have tended to remain small, in contrast to countries further to the north such as Germany or pre-revolutionary Russia, with their vast episcopal territories. Peter Hammond's portrait of the Greek bishop in the late 1940's indicates the kind of situation at which we should be aiming. Bishops in Greece today are as a rule less easily accessible, but the description is still substantially true:

> The Greek diocese is, by English standards, very small and sparsely populated; in some respects more akin to a rural deanery ... The bishop retains a far greater measure of direct personal responsibility, and delegates comparatively little ... The Greek bishop is commonly the most approachable of men; the sheer accessibility of the generality of the bishops of the country dioceses is a matter for wonder and rejoicing in a world fallen beneath the curse of an impersonal and irresponsible bureaucracy. Every morning, his liturgy fulfilled, the metropolitan takes his seat in his office and all the world comes to see him ... [He] sits at his desk beneath an eikon of the Pantocrator, questioning, counselling, reproving and writing letters of commendation, while a stalwart archimandrite leans against the door with outstretched arm to keep the multitude without at bay.[25]

v. 4 (1966), pp. 258–72; "Church and Eucharist, Communion and Intercommunion," *Sobornost* vii. 7 (1978), pp. 550–67.

[25] *The Waters of Marah: The Present State of the Greek Church* (1956), pp. 28–30, 34.

Here, surely, is a pastoral ideal that could well be followed in many places outside Greece. Ignatius' conception of the bishop as a eucharistic person, integrally bound to his flock and visible sign of local unity, raises important questions concerning titular and assistant bishops, and also concerning the manner in which bishops are appointed. Until the First World War, in many parts of the Orthodox world such as the Church of Greece, titular bishops were virtually unknown, except in the case of retired bishops, while assistant bishops were very rare. Unfortunately in recent years there has been a tendency in the Orthodox Church greatly to increase the number of non-diocesan bishops. This is certainly regrettable. In terms of eucharistic ecclesiology, titular bishops are an anomaly, a contradiction in terms, for they are not in any genuine sense presidents of a local eucharistic community. Equally, the multiplication of assistant or suffragan bishops is hard to justify. If the bishop is to unite the local community, then—as Ignatius insisted—there needs to be *one* local bishop, not two or more. Once the diocesan bishop's unifying function is shared with a number of assistants, his power to act as an effective visible sign of unity in the local church is drastically eroded. If the diocese is too large for one man to administer, would not the correct solution be to divide the diocese, not to consecrate a series of assistants?

It is significant that at a church council, the right to vote on matters of faith is accorded only to diocesan bishops, and not to titular or suffragan hierarchs. Why should this be, since all alike have been consecrated to the episcopate with the same sacramental rite? There can be only one answer: because a diocesan bishop is president of a local eucharistic assembly, while titular and assistant bishops are not. In the early Church it was as eucharistic presidents that the diocesan bishops were present at church councils; they proclaimed the faith with authority in their synodical decrees, not by virtue of some private and personal gift of infallibility, but because each bore witness to the traditional faith of the community over which he presided. This we shall see more clearly when we come to Irenaeus and Cyprian.

If titular and assistant bishops are hard to justify on the principles of eucharistic ecclesiology, then a multiplicity of overlapping episcopal 'jurisdictions' in the same place is even less defensible. Ignatius would have been appalled — and with good reason — by the present condition of Orthodoxy in the Western world, where in most large cities there are not one but several Orthodox bishops, each exercising authority over a fragment of the local flock. Instead of being a focus of unity, the bishops have become a sign of division. In the United States and Canada, for example, it has been calculated that "there are thirty-six jurisdictions claiming to be Orthodox, Eastern Orthodox, or Orthodox Catholic."[26] This situation, which is due to the massive and disorganized emigration from traditional Orthodox countries in the last hundred years, can at best be excused as a purely temporary expedient. Most Orthodox church leaders are in fact seeking actively for ways to end this jurisdictional pluralism.

As to the appointment of bishops, the Church's original practice seems to have been for the clergy and laity of the diocese to elect their own bishop. Such is the procedure envisaged by St. Hippolytus at the start of the third century, and by the legislation of the Emperor Justinian in the mid sixth century.[27] The bishops of neighboring sees attended in order to supervise the election, and then to consecrate the candidate; but it rested with the members of the local flock to make the actual choice of their future pastor. Such a practice conforms to the Ignatian view of the bishop as a eucharistic person, closely bound to the people as the one who leads their worship, ministering within the local community rather than exalted above it. From an early date, however, the bishops tended to take the election mainly or entirely into their own hands, perhaps to prevent the local landowners from controlling episcopal appointments. As a result the people's part was frequently limited to the

[26] D. J. Constanelos, "The Orthodox Diaspora: Canonical and Ecclesiological Perspective," *The Greek Orthodox Theological Review* xxiv (1979), p. 201.

[27] Hippolytus, *The Apostolic Tradition* ii. Justinian, *Novellae* cxxiii. 1; cxxxvii. 2 (ed. Schoell, pp. 594, 696–7).

ceremonial acclamation of a candidate already selected for them by the episcopal synod.

In the Orthodox Church today, election by clergy and people is not, as a rule, by direct suffrage but through an electoral college — still exists in some places, such as the Church of Cyprus, the Russian Archdiocese of Western Europe (Ecumenical Patriarchate), and the Orthodox Church in America the former Russian Metropolia. The Moscow Council of 1917–18 decreed that all bishops of the Russian Church should be chosen by the clergy and laity of the diocese, but conditions of persecution within the Soviet Union have so far made it impracticable to apply this decision. The more common method, however, of filling episcopal vacancies in the contemporary Orthodox Church is by co-option: the new bishop is selected either by an assembly of all the bishops of the autocephalous Church in question, as in Greece, or else by a more limited group of hierarchs who constitute the permanent 'ruling synod,' as happens in the Ecumenical Patriarchate, and also at present in Russia.

On Ignatius' eucharistic principles, any such restriction of episcopal elections to the bishops alone is much to be deplored. If the bishop is first and foremost the one who 'watches over' the Eucharist is not a distant administrator but the pastor of a local community then he ought to be a person known to his future flock and chosen by them, not a stranger imposed from the outside. Many members of the Orthodox Church today would in fact welcome a general return to the ancient practice.

Some Orthodox would also like to carry the argument a stage further. Let us, so they urge, not only restore the ancient practice of local episcopal election by clergy and people; but let us also return to the rules of the early Church by allowing married men as well as celibates to be candidates for the episcopate. The rule at present prevailing in the Christian East, whereby only monks can become bishops, dates only from the sixth century.[28] The rank of priesthood in the Or-

[28] The rule is found in the legislation of Justinian, *Novellae* vi. 1; cxxiii. 1; cxxx-

thodox Church has never ceased to be open equally to celibates and married men; a married priest, however, can only become a bishop if his wife is dead, or agrees to enter a convent, and he himself receives monastic tonsure. But, as Professor Trembelas rightly observes, this restriction of episcopal office to monks is merely administrative, a matter of discipline, not involving any question of doctrine.[29] Now that the Church is entering a 'post-Constantinian' situation, is it desirable to continue the limitation? To reopen the episcopal order to married men might benefit not only the episcopate, but equally the monasteries. Although this possibility is often raised by contemporary Orthodox, it has not as yet been discussed by the preparatory commission for the projected Great and Holy Council.

5 The Bishop as Apostolic Witness: St. Irenaeus. St. Irenaeus of Lyons, in common with St. Ignatius, treats the Eucharist as a decisive criterion in church life. "Our opinion agrees with the Eucharist," he states on one occasion, "and the Eucharist confirms our opinion."[30] But Irenaeus' conception of Church and bishop is in general less definitely eucharistic than that of Ignatius, and he is concerned to develop other aspects as well.

Because of his confrontation with the Gnostics, Irenaeus attaches particular importance to the continuity of teaching within the Church to the Church's apostolic character, and to the role of apostolic tradition and apostolic authority. The Gnostics appealed to a secret tradition handed down by a hidden succession of teachers; Irenaeus answered them by appealing to the tradition openly set forth in the four canonical gospels, and to the unbroken public succession of bishops,

vii. 2 (ed. Schoell, pp. 36–37, 594, 697), and it is confirmed by Canon 12 of the Council *in Trullo* (692). *Cf.* Photius, *Nomocanon,* tit. i, cap. 23, scholion: ed. G.A. Rallis and M. Potlis, *Syntagma ton theion kai ieron kanonon* i (Athens 1852), pp. 59–60.

[29] P.N. Trembelas, *Dogmatiki tis Orthodoxou Katholikis Ekklisias* iii (Athens 1961), p. 306; French trans., *Dogmatique de l'Eglise Orthodoxe Catholique* iii (Chevetogne 1968), p. 323.

[30] *Against the Heresies* IV.xxxi (xviii), 4 (ed. Harvey, ii, p. 205).

who in each local church constitute the official and authorized teachers of the apostolic faith.

We noted earlier that Ignatius says little about the bishop as the preacher and teacher of the faith, and nothing about the bishop as the link between the Church of the apostles and that of our own day. For Irenaeus these two connected roles of the bishop — as teacher and as preacher are fundamental. Whereas for Ignatius the bishop's *cathedra* or throne is the chair on which he sits at the Eucharist, for Irenaeus it is far closer to the chair of a professor: as he puts it, "The throne is the symbol of teaching."[31] For Ignatius, the bishop is primarily the one who unites; for Irenaeus, he is *par excellence* the one who teaches the truth. The Irenaean emphasis is preserved in the present-day practice of the Orthodox Church at the Divine Liturgy: after the consecration of the gifts, the priest prays for his local bishop, "… keep him … in health and long life, rightly dividing the word of thy truth" (*cf.* 2 Tim. 2:15). From the standpoint of Ignatius and Irenaeus, there can be no graver charges against a bishop than these: that he causes factions and divisions within his diocese, and that he teaches falsehood and tells lies. Irenaeus' understanding of the bishop's teaching authority and of the apostolic succession is summed up in a famous sentence:

> We should obey those presbyters in the Church who have their succession from the apostles, and who, together with succession in the episcopate, have received the assured *charisma* of the truth (*certum charisma veritatis*).[32]

By 'presbyters,' as the context shows, Irenaeus means 'bishops,' an interesting survival of the primitive New Testament usage. Here, then, he joins together what are for him the two distinctive marks of episcopacy: first, the bishop traces his descent, in unbroken succes-

[31] *Demonstration of the Apostolic Preaching* 2.

[32] *Against the Heresies* IV.xl (xxvi), 2 (ii, p. 236).

sion through his predecessors in the same see, back to the apostles and so to Jesus Christ; secondly, by virtue of this unbroken succession he is endowed with a special *charisma* or gift of grace, whereby he acts as the authoritative teacher of the apostolic faith in the local church, as the appointed witness to the truth that is held by all.

Outward continuity in apostolic succession serves as the sign and guarantee of inward continuity in apostolic faith. Apostolic succession is not merely a way of ensuring, in a mechanical and almost magical fashion, the preservation of 'valid' sacraments; far more fundamentally, its purpose is to preserve the continuity of doctrinal teaching, the fullness of Catholic faith and life. Treated in separation, outside the context of this fullness, questions of sacramental validity become meaningless.

Understood in this sense, apostolic succession is not something that the bishop enjoys as a personal possession, in isolation from the local community over which he presides. He is successor to the apostles because he is head of a particular local church, that is, president of a eucharistic assembly. Apostolic succession inheres, not in the person of the bishop alone, but in the local church as a whole. It is significant that, when Irenaeus constructs his succession lists, like Hegesippus his contemporary[33] he does not trace the succession through the consecrators of each bishop, as is commonly done in succession lists today, but through the throne or see, that is, through the local eucharistic centre over which the bishop in question presides.[34]

Irenaeus assumes, of course, that each bishop has in fact been consecrated through the laying on of hands by other bishops, but this is not the aspect that he is chiefly concerned to underline. What interests him is the bond between the bishop and his flock, and so the continuity of bishops in the same see. Apostolic succession means for him, not simply an unbroken succession of persons, but an unbroken

[33] Eusebius, *Ecclesiastical History*, IV, xxii, 1–3.

[34] *Against the Heresies* III.iii, 1–iv,1 (ii, p. 8–15). Cf. C. H. Turner, "Apostolic Succession," in H. B. Swete, *Essays on the Early History of the Church and Ministry* (1918), pp. 95–214.

continuity of communities; there can be no true succession of persons that is not mediated through the community.

The act of consecration, even when correctly performed by other validly consecrated bishops, is not by itself sufficient; it is also required that the new bishop shall be consecrated for a specific local church. Unless he succeeds legitimately to a throne, he has no true share in the grace of apostolic succession, but is merely a pseudo-bishop. This, indeed, is the conclusion explicitly drawn by Cyprian, "Novatian is not in the Church, nor can he be reckoned a bishop ... for he does not succeed to anybody (*nemini succedens*)."[35] Apostolic succession passes through the local church and is never independent of it.

All this is directly relevant to contemporary questions of Church unity. When looking at a church community divided from our own, it is never sufficient to inquire: "Has this body preserved the outward apostolic succession?" While this is a significant point, what matters far more is the question: "Does this body bear testimony to the fullness of apostolic faith and life?" In assessing the status of bishop, moreover, it is not enough to ask: "Who consecrated him, and with what rite?" We need to ask as well: "To what throne did he succeed?"

When we Orthodox, for example, are invited to express an opinion concerning the status of Anglican Orders, we need to pose such questions as these: Did Thomas Cranmer or Matthew Parker succeed, in a full and true sense, to the throne once occupied by St. Augustine and St. Theodore? Did the Anglican Church uphold in the sixteenth century, and does it uphold today, the fullness of apostolic tradition? The discussion of 'valid' orders becomes meaningless if it is limited solely to a consideration of minister, form, matter and intention, without embracing the question of the total faith and life of the ecclesial community involved.[36] Whereas, then, in the teaching of Ig-

---

[35] *Letter* lxix.3.

[36] I place the word 'valid' within inverted commas because its precise meaning is often unclear. Understanding the term in a somewhat different sense from that commonly prevailing in the West, many Orthodox theologians take the view that in no case can the sacraments of a non-Orthodox body be regarded as valid

natius the bishop is to the local community *alter Christus,* watching over his flock as the type and living *ikon of* Christ, for Irenaeus he is *alter apostolus,* the representative of the apostles. Irenaeus does not, however, identify the apostolic and episcopal ministries, but regards the apostles as unique; and in constructing his succession lists he treats, not the apostolic founder, but the person whom that apostolic founder consecrated, as the first bishop of each see. The first bishop of Rome, in his view, is not Peter or Paul but *Linus*;[37] the bishops succeed from the apostles rather than to them.

But, once this important qualification has been made, the bishop can indeed be legitimately described as *alter apostolus* in the sense that he embodies and expresses the apostolicity of the local church, its unbroken, living continuity with the Church of apostolic times. Between the *alter Christus* concept of Ignatius and the *alter apostolus* concept of Irenaeus there is no contradiction, but merely a difference of emphasis: the two notions are complementary. This is one of the cases where we should say 'both/and', not 'either/or.'

6 THE BISHOP IN SYNOD: ST. CYPRIAN. In the early part of the third century, St. Hippolytus of Rome continues to view the bishop primarily as a eucharistic person. This is clear from the prayer for an episcopal consecration, as given in *The Apostolic Tradition*:

---

per se and in an unqualified sense, but only as valid — under certain circumstances — by virtue of the principle of 'economy.' This applies, in their view, as much to Roman Catholic as to Anglican sacraments. On the whole subject, see E. R. Hardy, *Orthodox Statements on Anglican Orders* (New York 1946); E. Every, "The Eastern Orthodox Churches and Anglican Ordinations," *The Eastern Churches Quarterly* vii (1948), pp. 543–52; F. J. Thomson, "Economy. An Examination of the Various Theories of Economy held within the Orthodox Church, with Special Reference to the Economical Recognition of the Validity of non-Orthodox Sacraments," *The Journal of Theological Studies,* n.s. xvi (1965), pp. 368–420; Archbishop Methodios Fouyas, *Orthodoxy, Roman Catholicism and Anglicanism* (1972), pp. 99–109.

[37] *Against the Heresies* III.iii, 2 (ii, p. 10).

> Grant to this thy servant whom thou hast chosen for the episcopate to feed thy holy flock and serve as thine high priest, that he may minister blamelessly by night and day, that he may unceasingly propitiate thy countenance and offer to thee the gifts of thy holy Church.[38]

The bishop, according to the terms of this prayer, is the 'high priest' whose task is to 'minister': the Greek word used here is *leitourgounta,* 'celebrate the liturgy.' He is above all an offerer: presiding at the Eucharist, he 'offers ... gifts of thy holy Church,' the bread and wine which, through the power of the Spirit, become Christ's Body and Blood. After the passage cited above, the consecration prayer goes on to speak of the episcopal power to bind and loose. This might seem to give a more administrative emphasis to the bishop's ministry, but such an impression would be false; for the power to bind and loose applies precisely to the question of admission to Holy Communion, and is thus a eucharistic function.

The eucharistic nature of the episcopal ministry stands out in even sharper relief when we turn to the ordination prayer for a presbyter in *The Apostolic Tradition.* It is not said of the presbyter that he is to 'offer' the gifts, that is, to preside at the Eucharist, but that he is to 'govern' the people of God;[39] indeed, the power to perform the consecration at the Eucharist is apparently denied him.[40] Paradoxically by post-Nicene standards, in Hippolytus it is the bishop who is *par excellence* the celebrant at the Eucharist of the local church, and the priest who performs administrative duties. From the fourth century onwards their respective roles are reversed.

The Apostolic Tradition of Hippolytus, then, sees the bishop very much in Ignatian terms, as the 'offerer' of the Eucharist within the local community. So on certain occasions does St. Cyprian, as for instance in his much-quoted statement:

[38] *Ibid.*, iii.4 (p. 5).
[39] viii.2 (p. 13).
[40] ix.7 (p. 17).

> The Church is the people united to the priest (*sacerdoti*), the flock clinging to its shepherd. From this you should know that the bishop is in the Church, and the Church in the bishop (*episcopum in ecclesia esse, et ecclesiam in episcopo*).[41]

It is significant that in Cyprian the term *sacerdos,* without further qualification, means the bishop rather than the presbyter. When he speaks in this passage of 'the Church,' he is still thinking in an Ignatian way, and means something visible and concrete — the local worshipping congregation, the 'gathered' Church assembled round the altar under its eucharistic president. Stressing this unity of the local church in the Eucharist, Cyprian insists that 'all the brotherhood' should be present at the celebration of the liturgy, and he strongly disapproves of any arrangement that renders this impossible.[42]

Elsewhere in Cyprian's writings, however, this local, eucharistic dimension is less in evidence. What concerns him is not only the Ignatian idea of the bishop as centre of local unity, nor yet the Irenaean conception of the bishop as link with the apostles. It is true that he emphasizes both these things; in particular, he actually identifies the episcopal ministry with the apostolic, writing 'apostles, that is to say, bishops' (*apostolos, id est episcopos*),[43] in a way that neither Irenaeus nor, still less, Ignatius would have done. For Cyprian, however, the point of primary interest is the bishop's role as a bond between the local church and the Church universal. The main focus of his attention is upon the conciliar or collegial character of the world-wide episcopate, the *concors numerositas* or 'harmonious multiplicity[44] of bishops meeting in council and together reaching a 'common mind' under the Spirit's guidance.

The practice of holding episcopal synods, particularly at moments of crisis, had developed nearly a century before Cyprian's time.

[41] *Letter* lxvi.8.
[42] *Letter* lxiii.16.
[43] *Letter* iii.3.
[44] *Letter* lv.24.

A precedent for such synods can indeed be found even earlier, in the Apostolic Council at Jerusalem described in Acts 15. Even though there is no direct link between this and the episcopal synods of a later period, it provides a paradigm and standard for true church councils in every age. Gathered synodically, the apostles declare, "It seemed good to the Holy Spirit and to us" (Acts 15:28); and such exactly is the claim also made by episcopal synods. 'To *us*', not 'to *me*': collectively the shepherds of the Church, whether apostles or bishops, speak with an authority which none of them possesses individually. At every authentic council, the total is greater than the sum of the parts: together the members of the episcopate become something more than they are as scattered individuals, and this 'something more' is precisely the presence of Christ and the Holy Spirit in their midst. "Where two or three are gathered together..." (Matt. 18:20): the 'common mind' which the assembled bishops reach under the Spirit's guidance is not merely their mind but Christ's.

Episcopal councils, to judge from the surviving evidence, were first convened on a significant scale about a century after the Apostolic Council of Acts 15, at the time of the Montanist crisis during the middle of the second century.[45] A further series of episcopal councils met later in the same century on the occasion of the Paschal controversy.[46] Assemblies of bishops were a feature of African church life at least a generation before Cyprian's episcopate: around 220 a council of some 66 bishops was convened at Carthage under Agrippinus, and another around 240, attended by 90 bishops, under Privatus of Lambesis. Cyprian for his part continued this tradition by summoning an important series of councils at Carthage during 251–6.

Cyprian summarizes the principle underlying episcopal councils in an epigrammatic phrase: "The episcopate is a single whole, in which each individual bishop enjoys full possession" (*episcopatus unus est, cuius a singulis m solidum pars tenetur*).[47] The precise significance

[45] Eusebius, *Ecclesiatical History* X.xvi, 10 and 16; xix, 3–4.

[46] *Op. cit.* V.xxiii, 3–4.

[47] *On the Unity of the Catholic Church*, 5.

of the words *in solidum* has been much debated. Probably Cyprian's meaning is somewhat as follows. There are many local churches, but only one universal Church; likewise, there are many individual *episcopi,* but only one world-wide episcopate. In neither case should we think in terms of small units constituting a greater whole, or of bricks making up a wall. Each local church, as it celebrates the Eucharist, is not just a part of the Church but the Catholic Church in its fullness; for at each local Eucharist it is the whole Christ that is present, not just a part of him. In the same way each bishop possesses, not just a small fraction of episcopal grace, but the plenitude of the episcopal *charisma;* he possesses this plenitude, however, not in isolation but in union with all the other bishops. Each bishop, in other words, shares in the one episcopate, not as having part of the whole but as having an expression of the whole. And this solidarity of the episcopate is manifested precisely through the holding of a council; in reaching a common mind at a council, the bishops are in an explicit manner exercising their episcopate *in solidum.*

Yet, while emphasizing the collegial solidarity of the episcopate, Cyprian also insists upon the rights of each individual bishop. In his view the majority at an episcopal council is not entitled to coerce the minority. The aim at such a council should always be moral unanimity, not merely a decision reached by majority vote. But what, then, is to happen if one or more bishops at a church council refuse to accept the decisions reached by the rest of their colleagues? Cyprian is well aware that this may happen. He believes that each bishop gives an account of his work solely and directly to God; and so he considers that in the event of disagreement no compulsion should be brought to bear upon the dissident bishop or bishops. The Church, while still preserving unity, will be obliged to live for a time with the fact of this disagreement.[48]

[48] *Letter* lv. 21; lxxiii. 26; cf. Cyprian's inaugural speech at the Council of Carthage in the autumn of 256 *(Sententiae Episcoporum numero LXXXVII de Haereticis Baptizandis, ed.* Hartel, pp. 435–6). For a convincing presentation of Cyprian's standpoint, see P. Hinchliff, *Cyprian of Carthage and the Unity of the Christian Church* (1974).

Here Cyprian, in common with Ignatius, continues to stress the crucial significance of the local church and the local bishop. The universal Church is not a monolithic, totalitarian collectivity, in which the individual is swallowed up by the greater whole. It is, on the contrary, a family of local churches; and, within this family, each particular church by which Cyprian still means, as Ignatius does, each local eucharistic assembly — is endowed with autonomy.

Cyprian's insistence upon moral unanimity and the rights of the minority has often been dismissed as unworkable. It might be argued with some force that, just as there can be no question of returning today to the situation envisaged by Ignatius or Cyprian whereby each parish constitutes a distinct diocese, so there can be no question of returning to Cyprian's notion of episcopal independence. Indeed, from the time of Constantine, minorities at church councils have in practice usually been subjected to coercion — although it should also be remembered that, at most great councils of the past, from Nicaea I onwards, the majority has been extremely large, not to say overwhelming. There was not merely a predominance of three-quarters or two-thirds, still less a slight numerical superiority (Ephesus in 431 forms an exception). The small size of the minority, however, does not in itself justify the use of compulsion.

If force has usually been invoked, this has been in large measure a consequence of the alliance between Church and state; an authoritarian civil government naturally desires a united State Church, and in its turn a State Church has at its disposal the physical means for imprisoning or exiling dissident minorities. Living as we now do in a 'post-Constantinian' context, should we not allow more weight to Cyprian's standpoint?

Cyprian is in fact underlining a vital matter of principle. "It shall not be so among you…" (Matt. 20:26). The Church on earth is a miracle of divine grace, the living image of eternity within time, the first fruits of the Kingdom, not a secular democracy to be administered according to this-worldly criteria of what is viable. A synod of bishops, therefore, in common with church assemblies at the diocesan or parochial level, cannot rest satisfied simply with imitating current parliamentary procedure. Even if moral unanimity is an ideal of which in practice we regularly fall short, at least let us not seek to justify this state of affairs, but let us remain painfully conscious of our failure.

In what he says about councils, Cyprian has in mind primarily episcopal assemblies; for, as Irenaeus has shown us, it is specifically the bishops who, by virtue of their apostolic office and their *charisma veritatis,* are endowed with authority to proclaim the faith. But at the same time Cyprian does not forget his basic principle that "the bishop is in the Church." The bishop is not an absolute ruler set up over the local community, but exercises his ministry within it; outside the Church, divorced from the local eucharistic community, he is no longer a true bishop.

Cyprian agrees therefore with Irenaeus that authority to define the truth belongs to the bishop, not as private possession, but because he presides over a local church. If the bishop in each place is the appointed teacher of the faith, the faith as such is the shared inheritance of his flock as a whole, and in the last resort it rests with his flock as a whole to judge whether the bishop is exercising his teaching ministry in the correct way. In the words of Hippolytus, "On such as believe rightly the Holy Spirit bestows the fullness of grace, so that they may know how those who are at the head of the Church should teach the tradition and maintain it in all things."[49]

From this it follows that the episcopal synod is never to be taken in isolation from the total church community. When the bishops meet in council, each voices not just his own opinion but the faith handed down traditionally within his local church; the purpose of their meeting is precisely that each shall bear witness to what is believed by all. While the bishops are divinely appointed to act as teachers within the Church, and by virtue of this teaching *magisterium* it is their responsibility formally to proclaim the truth in synod, the conciliar decrees need also to be accepted by the Church at large. The significance of this

[49] *The Apostolic Tradition* i.5, p. 5.

'reception' of a council by the whole Church has been much emphasized in modern Orthodox ecclesiology.[50] Cyprian for his part takes it for granted that the clergy and the Christian people or *plebs* will be present at an episcopal assembly,[51] as they were at the Apostolic Council (Acts 15:12). While it would be anachronistic to expect from him a developed theory of conciliar 'reception,' some such doctrine is manifestly implied by his principle of *episcopus in ecclesia.*

7 **Geometrical Symbols.** Such are the patterns of episcopacy to be found in three leading pre-Nicene witnesses; and the same patterns continue to be applicable to the Church of our own times. Complementing one another, each of the three emphasizes a particular aspect of the Church's nature:

Ignatius underlines the eucharistic essence of the Church: the basic ecclesial structure is the local worshipping community, united through the celebration of the Eucharist under the presidency of the bishop.

Irenaeus draws attention to the apostolic character of the Church, and sees the bishop as guarantor and teacher of the apostolic tradition.

Cyprian makes explicit the conciliar nature of the Church. Each bishop exercises his episcopal ministry in union with all the other bishops, and this he does above all by meeting them in council. Yet the parts are not swallowed up in the whole, for as head of a local church each bishop preserves his independence.

To use a mathematical analogy:

For Ignatius the episcopate is a geometrical point: the bishop is the centre of unity in the local eucharistic assembly.

For Irenaeus the episcopate is a vertical line: the bishop is the link between the apostles and the local church over which he presides.

For Cyprian the episcopate is a horizontal line: he thinks in terms of the college of bishops, dispersed in many places throughout the world, yet manifesting their solidarity by gathering in council.

---

[50] See Kallistos Ware, "The Ecumenical Councils and the Conscience of the Church," *Kanon* ii (Jahrbuch der Gcsellschaft das Recht der Ostkirchen: Vienna 1974).
[51] *Letter* xiv.2.

So the bishop is at one and the same time:

—the centre of unity within the local church;

—the link uniting that local church and the apostles;

—the bond of unity between that local church and all the other local churches.

CHAPTER FIVE

Kyprian Kern (1900–1960)

Archimandrite Kyprian (Constantine) Kern was born near St. Petersburg, and his father served as a professor of forestry at the local university, or Lyceum, in St. Petersburg. He received his early education at the famous Alexander Lyceum in St. Petersburg; however, when the school closed due to financial problems, Kern left for Moscow seeking to enter the famous Moscow Academy. As a layman, he attended the famous All Russian Council in Moscow in 1917–18, which was influential in his decision to leave the pursuit of law and turn to theology. It is noteworthy that Sergius Bulgakov, Anton Kartashev, and Nicholas Berdiaev were also in attendance at the council and would later be reunited together in Paris as they worked together at the St. Sergius Theological Institute. In 1925, Kern left his Russian homeland to live in Belgrade, Serbia, which by then had a formidable Russian community. He was one of the earliest members of the Brotherhood of St. Seraphim of Sarov, which was established in Belgrade. He finished his theological studies in Belgrade, eventually writing his doctoral dissertation on the theology of St. Gregory Palamas.

In 1927, he entered into the monastic ranks, changing his name from Constantine to Kyprian, and began teaching at the Faculty of Theology in Bitola in southern Serbia. After being ordained to the holy priesthood, Kern was nominated to the Serbian episcopate in 1933; however, he declined such an appointment. His primary love was theological studies, and he wanted to remain as a professor of theology. Actually, on a trip to Belgrade, Fr. Sergius Bulgakov invited

Kern to teach at St. Sergius, but Kern wanted to hone his theological skills in Belgrade. He turned down the offer, only to accept it later.

From 1928–1930, Kern was sent to administer the Russian Missionary Society in Jerusalem, taking over the missionary work there which was started in the mid 19th century by Fr. Anthony Kapustin. After several attempts at refusing such a post, Kern eventually accepted the position. During his time in Jerusalem, Kern wrote a history of the Russian Mission and the ministry of his predecessor Anthony Kapustin.

In 1936, Kern left his Serbian home and left to take up teaching at the St. Sergius Theological Institute in Paris. There he began teaching Patristics, Church History, and Liturgics. Metropolitan Evlogy (Georgevitsky), the spiritual leader of the Russian community in Western Europe, assigned Kern to be the chaplain for one of Mother Maria's houses of hospitality at rue Lourmel. However, since Mother Maria was difficult to get along with, he soon left and took up residence at St. Sergius. In addition to his teaching post, Kern also served a small Orthodox community dedicated to St. Constantine and Helen in nearby Clamart, a suburb of Paris, where Nicolas Berdiaev and his wife also lived.

While a professor of theology at St. Sergius, Kern was reacquainted with Sergius Bulgakov whom Kern met previously in Belgrade. Kern also worked alongside Nicholas Afanasiev, Anton Kartashev, and Geroges Florovsky. Eventually, Kern and Afanasiev established the Fraternity of St. Seraphim of Sarov, an association of faculty and students who came together for prayer and fellowship. Kern also became the teacher and mentor for the young Alexander Schmemann and John Meyendorff, who later spoke very highly of Kern's influence on them.

Kern's work on the Eucharist was so influential in the life of Alexander Schmemann that Schmemann dedicated his doctoral dissertation to Kern. In 1953, towards the end of his life, Kern established the famous "Liturgical Weeks" at St. Sergius which gathered together clergy, laity, scholars, and theologians from across the Christian divide in order to discuss various aspects of Church life, especially the liturgical and sacramental worship. These Liturgical Weeks still meet during the month of June in Paris.

In addition to his work on patristics and liturgy, Kern was also interested in pastoral theology and eventually authored a book on the subject. In it, he traces the history of pastoral care in the Russian theological tradition, highlighting particular priests and bishops who exhibited what he considered to be good pastoral ideas. Kern was adamant that the leader of the faith community be highly educated, familiar with literature, politics, society, and culture.

For Kern, it was the eucharistic gathering where both clergy and laity gathered around the one table of the Lord to offer their prayer and praise. He had no time for clericalism or the abuse of power and authority by the clergy over the laity, which is a theme that runs throughout his writing and which is also a theme in several of his writings, especially "Two Models of the Pastorate Levitical and Prophetic," where he shows that the prophetic priest is one who is seeking God's will in life and will risk his own stability and comfort for the preaching of the Gospel. This he contrasts with the Levitical type of the priesthood which is best exemplified in the Old Testament image of the Temple and the Levitical priests who serve there. These priests, Kern says, exemplify a rigid formalism and ritualism which suffocate. They are too worried about rules and regulations and have no time for creativity and freedom. He finishes his essay by saying that these two forms of priesthoods exist today in constant tension with one another.

Kern identifies a healthy pastorate which does not identify solely with the clergy but with the entire people of God who gather around the eucharistic table for praise and prayer. While the clergy lead the community in prayer, the entire people offer the Eucharist, where the true Church is revealed. Kern also speaks about the importance of pastoral formation, focusing primarily on the spiritual and intellectual education of clergy. While Kern lived a monastic life, he was in many ways a monk of the world, enjoying art and music, as well as what some would call secular literature. He enjoyed visiting art museums and engaging in local cultural events, always engaging in the world around him.

This chapter, "Pastoral Christian Ministry," was a chapter in his book *Orthodox Pastoral Theology*, which was originally published in 1947 in Russia and recently translated into English.

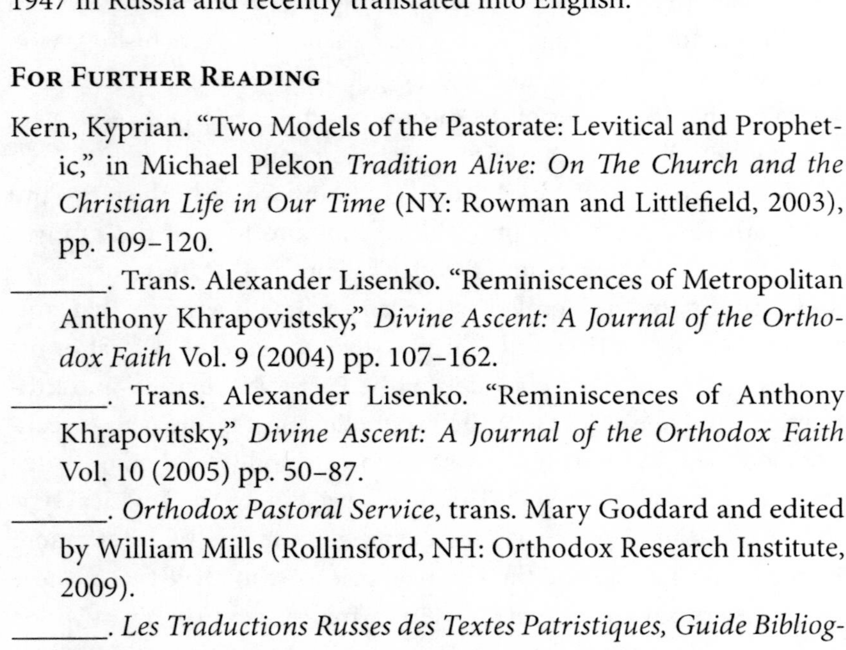

For Further Reading

Kern, Kyprian. "Two Models of the Pastorate: Levitical and Prophetic," in Michael Plekon *Tradition Alive: On The Church and the Christian Life in Our Time* (NY: Rowman and Littlefield, 2003), pp. 109–120.

_______. Trans. Alexander Lisenko. "Reminiscences of Metropolitan Anthony Khrapovistsky," *Divine Ascent: A Journal of the Orthodox Faith* Vol. 9 (2004) pp. 107–162.

_______. Trans. Alexander Lisenko. "Reminiscences of Anthony Khrapovitsky," *Divine Ascent: A Journal of the Orthodox Faith* Vol. 10 (2005) pp. 50–87.

_______. *Orthodox Pastoral Service*, trans. Mary Goddard and edited by William Mills (Rollinsford, NH: Orthodox Research Institute, 2009).

_______. *Les Traductions Russes des Textes Patristiques, Guide Bibliographie* (Chevetogne, 1957).

Pastoral Christian Ministry

Let us briefly review the foundations for pastoral ministry, which does not emanate from a void, but flows in the world and among people. The world is the sum total of hostility toward God and goodness, it is a domain that lies in evil, yet the world, like the empirical creation, is not itself evil. Man, even if fallen is still the image of God: "I am the image of Thy ineffable glory, even as I bear the ulcer of transgressions." There may be a whirlpool of sin in the depths of man's soul, nevertheless man remains God's loved being, whom the pastor cannot help but love, as he cannot help but love the world — the empirical creation.

Pastoral actions and passions, which some pastors philosophically compare to salvation, are the results of man's inner consciousness of God's kingdom. This consciousness of Christ's kingdom, this new creation of Christ, is, of course, a battle against the kingdom of evil, evil that is present in all of us. But goodness and evil cannot be understood without, as previously mentioned, a free will. Goodness, to which the pastor summons us, is only goodness freely accepted. Forced goodness is no longer goodness. Goodness is only goodness when it is not distorted by evil, force, compulsion or threats of terrible torments. Behind such a so-called goodness, one that is tied to a feeling of fear may easily be perceived as being the reflection of inquisitorial bonfires.

These, then, are the ideological preconditions of pastoral service. They require a most thoughtful maintenance of the pastor's own inner attitude. Viewing this subject in a historical setting, it becomes clear that the quality of the Orthodox Christian pastoral counseling differs from other types of non-Christian services.

There exists a predominant type of sacred priesthood in paganism. The priest, shaman, or sorcerer appears to be the chief mediator between man and Divinity. He offers sacrifices, he exorcizes, mollifies the angered God, he casts spells to cure human ills and guards man against evil fate. The highest point of pagan religious consciousness is reached when man rises above the primitive level of religious experiences and awakens to mystical religious feelings. At this point an even stronger belief in the leadership of the pagan priest in the sphere of mysticism manifests itself, a sphere other religious authorities cannot attain. Mystic, sorcerer, diviner, the priest could fathom the secret spheres, spheres that were not open to the common man and the ordinary pagan. At the height of pre-Christian religious consciousness a yearning for a genuine spirituality emerged, a yearning, which could not be fulfilled by the then popular religious culture. Exorcism and esoteric rituals were typical in paganism. In the mystical cults of priesthood and its ordination the coming of authentic revelations was keenly and deeply felt and thirsted for. But even for the pagan priest the requirements for spiritual leadership are rather small. In paganism, the understanding of pastoral ministry had not yet matured.

The Old Testament presents a considerably higher understanding of pastoral ministry. The cultivation of the priestly code, especially in the post-captivity period of Israel's history, in the majority of cases stood side by side and was tied to other responsibilities, unknown in paganism, responsibilities which represented only a partial characteristic of its priestly class. By far a greater cultivation of ethical norms is inherent in the Old Testament. Even before Christ, the most perfect moral code was well known to the biblical priest. The Old Testament developed an understanding of holiness, absent from other religions of the ancient world. The biblical religious ideal gave a definite understanding to righteousness, expressing itself in the fulfillment of the instructions of the law. These laws, these norms were predominant in the Old Biblical consciousness. They were elevated above any other ancient ethical conceptions, yet they carried within themselves their own weakness. The law, the sum total of the commandments, had to be fulfilled for justification, yet did not itself give the power for fulfillment of these commandments. Above all the law left man hopeless, constantly pointing out to him his weaknesses, imperfections and iniquities, "Weakness of the Law" is the theme of Pauline apostolic sermons. Weakness of man could not be filled by the weakness of the law. Man remained, in the face of the ideally righteous law, just as remote from God as an unrighteous one. The law did not empower the sanctification of man's spirit and did not impart the means for attaining that holiness to which it so clearly pointed.

The law taught goodness, yet at the same time exposed man's sack of goodness, leaving him hopelessly seeking this goodness and exhausted under the burden of regulations of this law. Israel knew no compassion for the sinner. The Prophet Elijah, who zealously and with complete fervor is seeking God, hates not only sin, but also the sinner. He is merciless to man and creature, he command the elements, even death, yet feels no mercy for the fallen.

The priesthood of the Old Testament is powerless before God and cannot bring comfort to the sinful man. The massive written rabbinical directions about the impurity of man and animals in many situations of life gave rise to a detailed code of various oblations, sacrifices, mollifying and burnt offerings, all of which failed to ring man nearer to God or God nearer to man. The strict understanding of selectivity and circumcision, as a sign of a covenant with God resulted in alienation from other people. In the sphere of the Old Testament's moral and religious concepts, it is the priest who performs the religious rites. All Israel is considered the essence of God's sons and people, yet the understanding about the adoption of man as God's creation did not exist in the ancient religious ideas.

Only the good news of the New Testament brought new revelations about priesthood and real pastoral ministry. The Gospel of Christ the Savior taught new about God's adoption. Every man is the son of God and may call God "Father." The sermons of the apostles gave man hope to be in communion with God. These sermons were later expanded upon by the theology of Athanasius, Gregory the Theologian, Gregory Nazianzus, Maximus the Confessor, Simeon the New Theologian, and Gregory Palamas, developing into the final study of deification, the beginnings of which reach back to Plato and Plotinus. The Gospels gave mankind faith that in Christ we are a new creation. The transformation of humanity into the image of God and the ascent of our essence to be above the established angelic order inspires man in his Christian self-awareness. Christian humanism, as opposed to pagan and revolutionary humanism, ennobles man's understanding of self. In Christ all the limits and confines that were insurmountable for pagans and Jews, have been overcome. In the realm of the Gospel "there is neither Jew nor Greek, there is neither slave nor free, there is neither male or female, for you are all one in Christ Jesus" (Galatians 3:26–28). Christianity brings glad tidings, a full acceptance of the world, creation, nature, and of course man, the best creation, created in the image of the Creator.

Because of this, the substance and quality of Christian priesthood and pastoral ministry are quite different from the pagan and Jewish Levitical priesthood. The Christian priest is the builder of Mysteries, builder of the Body of Christ. He is called — and through him others also, to build a new blessed kingdom.

The Christian priest is called upon to propagate man's adoption by God; to gather all the dissipated children of God into the transfiguration of the world and mankind. Obviously, neither the moral perfection of the Gospels nor the cultivation of dogmatic truths compile the most important elements of Christianity. The most important element — that is God incarnate Himself. "Great is the mystery of Godliness" (Timothy 3:16). The mystery of God's humanity underlies the very foundation of Christian propagation, our Eucharistic life, our ascetic God-likeness of similarity, our mysticism. God is not only man's and the world's primary reason of life, but also its final goal. God's Material process, mentioned in the writings of Vladimir

Soloviev, is the propagation of world-wide perfection, which only He dared to teach, Who is the Creator. This predetermines the relationship of the Christian pastor to the world and to man.

Man, in whose society the priest is called to serve, was, is, and will always be, in spite of all his sins and degradations, God's beloved creation. For this reason the Orthodox priest must be inspired by faith in man, his predestination in the everlasting assembly, communication with god Incarnate, his kin in the flesh, according to the words of Simon the New Theologian. To that end the priest's most important means of communication must be based upon the Good News of salvation, universal faith in this salvation and worship, instead upon the premise of hellish torment.

Characteristically, pastoral counseling should strive to overcome the evil in the world and in man with goodness and love rather than with accusations and condemnations. He must be more concerned with salvation than with anticipation of Judgment Day and condemnations of all heretics, sinners, and dissidents. He must remember, based on the history of all the saints that a complete righteous man and a complete sinner do not exist. From the heights of holiness degradation can occur, yet repentance and rebirth are possible even from those depths of degenerations that seem hopeless. The pastor must particularly keep in mind that man's moral destiny is first of all governed by freedom. Freedom always holds the dangers of evil and sin, yet in freedom there also lies goodness, which will overcome evil and sin. Christianity is God's message about freedom, which, as mentioned earlier, is quite different from propagations of revolutionary, political and mutinous freedoms. It is a spiritual freedom. Therefore the pastor should worry less about his inviolate authority but more about his persuasiveness about truth. The criterion of truth is in the truth itself. Compulsory authority is not characteristic of Orthodoxy. The pastor must call for acceptance of truth, for submission of self to the superior Christian freedom.

In his "Admonitions To Chastity," the monk Evargius says: "God created heaven and earth.. There is no angel who could not sin and not a demon who is evil by nature. God has created the one and the other and gave both a free will.

1 Preparation for Priesthood. Occupying the central focal point throughout Christian history for the theological writers and ascetic teachers was the question of preparation for the future priest. For the sake of clarity, this question must be divided into several, more specialized subjects of pastoral study courses. Mainly, it is divided into two parts. Is the preparation for the highly-valued priestly service necessary, or must all such matters be entrusted to God's grace, which fills all and heals all? What should this preparation consist of, if it is declared necessary? In the latter case, this question will take its place alongside these special themes: spiritual preparation, intellectual preparation as well as external preparation, and so forth.

By taking a routine look at this question, one may see two opposite opinions. According to one theory, no human science, specialization or skill can, nor should, take place where the bounty of the Holy Spirit is sought; it is omnipotent, and therefore sufficient. The other theory is exactly the opposite. Preparation is essential, therefore it should be painstaking, elaborate and extensive. If, according to one opinion, the priest should comply with the most necessary and simple requirements of commonly and primitively understood liturgical piety, then, according to our wise and observant Bishop Porfiri Ouspensky, it would be limited to the "censer and the sprinkling brush", since, as many tend to think, "for the sake of humility", more would not be required; yet according to the other opinion, the preparation of the future priest should be broad enough to impose upon him a duty to understand the simple households of a village as well as medical disciplines and other various practical subjects, the sports of today, the ability to lead youth camps as well as modern social concerns.

Pastoral study must therefore find the well-known equilibrium and discover that middle royal golden road, so that the priest could avoid primitivism and obscurity, yet would not be excessively absorbed by completely uncharacteristic pastoral concerns.

After these introductory remarks, we must now turn to the first question, namely is preparation for priesthood necessary? The answer suggests itself to be on the affirmative. This is instilled into us by the entire history of priesthood and the collective experience of the church. It is true that in the past ages of Christianity religious schools did not always exist—yet a pastoral preparation for the understanding of a priest's high future calling was always required. On the other hand, at a time of great tranquility in the life of the church, its hierarchy begrudged the emergence of systematic education. History acknowledges the famous schools of Alexandria, Odessa, Constantinople, Rome and many various other places in the first centuries of the church's existence. The age of great religious debates and the emergence of heresies provided the church with a keener sense for the necessity of preparation. If in the first three centuries a systematic religious and pastoral education was not in existence, so, from the time of recognition of Christianity as a free state religion, its education became more and more organized and was vastly improved.

It did not always have the same forms: monasteries were for a long time the center of education; occasionally prominent individual hierarchs or pastors assembled around themselves future priests; such was the priestly preparation in the period of enslavement of the church by Tatars and the Turks and in neglected and remote countries, removed from the main centers of civilization. But it may definitely be asserted that the church had never given up paying attention to this question, cautiously admitting young candidates to priesthood by the laying of the hands and requiring of them a sound, knowledgeable and multifaceted preparation.

Among the widespread misunderstanding about Christianity, there undisputedly exists the most dangerous notion of all, one that depicts Christianity as a religion of simpletons, ignorant and uneducated people. This was maintained by the Emperor Julian the Apostate and the famous Celsius, stemming from their hostile feelings toward Christianity and a desire to humiliate it, yet the works of St. John Chrysostom, Gregory the Theologian, Basil the Great, Photius and many others are full of quotations from a great variety written sources, such as Ecclesiastes, Saints as well as pagan writers. People of our time, devoted Christians, also love to maintain this notion, but instead of preserving Christianity's purity, simplify and bedim it.

As was pointed out earlier, the baby Jesus was visited not only by simple shepherds, but wise men from the East, seeking God, bearing God's highest truth beyond the world of Christianity. If, on the one hand, the Savior called simple fishermen, so on the other hand, among the people who most of all spread Christianity, was Apostle Paul, an educated man of his time. Very early on Christianity recognized intellectuals and defenders, such as the holy martyr Justin the Philosopher, Athenagoras, Clement of Alexandria, not to mention the abundance of ecumenical teachers and pastors of the golden age of the Church.

It should be remembered that Apostle Paul, author of three Pastoral Epistles, relentlessly put many great requirements upon his students and coworkers and issued guiding instructions for the appropriate examination of those who sought ordination at the hands of a bishop. The apostle warns: "do not lay hands on anyone hastily" (1 Timothy:5–22); he demanded that besides moral qualities, the bishop should also "be able to teach" (1 Timothy 3:2); and requiring that they "be tested" (1 Timothy 3:10). The clergyman has to constantly admonish "with all authority," (Titus 2:15), "in season and out of season" (2 Timothy 4:2); "to continue in the things you have learned and been assured of" (2 Timothy 3:14), "holding fast the faithful word as he has been taught, that he may be able, by sound doctrine, both to exhort and convict those who contradict" (Titus 1:9), "these things command and teach" (1 Timothy 4:11), "take heed to yourself, and to the doctrine."

If we proceed from the apostolic writings to the works of the teachers of the classical period of our theology, we will quite easily find confirmation about the above-mentioned writings. Those advocates who vainly seek to oversimplify and obfuscate Christianity, allude to examples of some Christian pastors, like Bishop Sevier — a former mill worker, and Alexander — a coal miner. These cases do not represent the accepted rule and are the exceptions from the common majority, and are, therefore, difficult to find in the history of priesthood. The church demanded something else. The lessons learned from the mouths of the church's best and most experienced teachers direct the priest, and especially the bishop, not only to practice piety, but to study and acquire wisdom from reading, a practice that will become, with the passing of years and the growing dangers for the church, a greater and deeper experience. It must always be kept in mind that the direction of the ship of the church was corrected at its most critical, troubled times of heresies and schisms, by the hands of loyal, experienced and wise helmsmen. Yet the temptations of primitivism and obfuscation were apparently always hovering around the priesthood. Not in vain did many prominent writers of the church warn those seeking the priesthood about the difficulties of this art, elevating it above sciences and human wisdom. There exists an interesting legend about an episode in the life of Pope Leo the Great who had a vision shortly before his death, in which the Apostle Peter announces the forgiveness of all his sins, save one: the sin of rash and careless ordinations of priests. Then, in a second vision, after the Pope's special prayers, forgiveness for this sin is granted as well.

It is, therefore, quite natural that the great teachers and priests of the ecumenical church repeatedly uttered words of warning or reproach for careless treatment of admittance to priesthood to those who sought it and to those who administered the laying of the hands. To such luminaries as St. John Chrysostom belong the famous "Six Books of Priesthood," to St. Ambrose of Milan "The Responsibilities of the clergy" and to Blessed Jerome "About the Life of the Clergy," works that are revered as guiding and warning instructions for future pastors of the church. Pope Gregory the Great wrote also about the responsibilities of priests. Brilliant words on the same subject came also from St. Ephraim the Syrian and Gregory the Theologian, who, as is well known, was forced into ordination by his father and, fearing the high calling of priesthood, withdrew into the wilderness. His

42nd, or defensive letter, represents an explanation of his flight and at the same time a confession about how he views the life and activities of a priest; therefore this letter can and should serve as a highly edifying guide for priests.

This is what St. Chrysostom writes: "... accept ignorant men as priests and appoint them to oversee property for which the Son of God paid with His Blood." "We pervert priesthood by entrusting it to inexperienced people". There is an often-heard opinion that preparation hinders piety, holiness, humility and so forth, therefore it would not be remiss in this instance to cite the words of Blessed Jerome: "ignorant and simple priests consider themselves holy, because they do not know anything." St. Gregory the Theologian (3rd letter) warns: "first one must gain wisdom, then teach wisdom," or "one cannot be a worthless model for other painters"; "we do not have an established boundary between teaching and studying"; "it is one thing to be a shepherd of sheep and bullocks, and quite another thing to direct human souls." In subsequent years, those teachers and archpriests who understood the dangers of quick and untested ordinations would not still their voices. St. Tikhon of Zadonsk as well as Holy Father John of Kronstadt wrote about preparation and it was extensively covered, as mentioned in the first chapter, in Pastoral Theology courses. It should also be remembered that certain pastoral teachers, Metropolitan Anthony (Khrapovitsky), for one, while denying the necessity of the so-called calling, transferred the center of gravity to the question of preparation. In pre-revolutionary Russia, the general education for priesthood consisted of ten years, four years of religious school and six years of seminary; those desiring a higher level of preparation had to go through another four-year course at a theological academy, so that the full education was acquired over the span of fourteen years. The Catholic world also recognizes their lesser seminaries and greater seminaries and faculties, corresponding to our theological academies. In some particular cases, such as in a post-war period, in times of upheavals or in for-flung regions, it was necessary to revert, as a last resort, to shortened pastoral courses, but this was only the exception to the general rule. Returning to the question of what comprises pastoral preparation for the priest's future activities, we must breakup this subject into three parts.

A) ***Spiritual Preparation.*** The priestly candidate, the future pastor, is preparing to embark upon a spiritual path, or, according to Russian terminology, enter the priesthood. This word alone commits us to a great deal. It does not fully cover its similar terminology in other languages; *sveshtenstvo* (Serbian); *Klir, Clergé,* or clergy (Greek, French, and English), but corresponds more to the German understanding of *Geistlicher,* from *Geist*, spirit. First of all, the clergy must be spiritual. It signifies a belonging to the kingdom of the Spirit, not to the kingdom of social commitments, the domain of materialistic calculations and interests, political desires, and so forth. This, before all else, means the education of self in the Spirit of God's Kingdom, of creation of it within self, for this Kingdom is not somewhere, in some earthly dominion, but in us. The Kingdom of God is not a theocratic idyll, but a category of our spirituality. This is the first requirement on the path of spiritual education, a spirit, which, it is sad to say, is often absent in the clergy, a clergy that is inflamed with passions of national and political aspirations, or even weighed down with cares about the daily bread and with seeking material goods. This spiritual growth does not occur all at once, but is acquired by long-standing inspirations, spread over ones whole life: spiritual self-education from early childhood and a decisive choice of directing ones aspirations — to the earthly kingdom or to that which is not of this world.

Two elements in this choice become clear — a negative and a positive element. The first one leads to a decisive rejection of all things that are of this world and draw us to it; the sin of seeking earthly gains, career motivations, notional political biases and so forth. This does not at all denote an aversion for cultural and social participations, but rather a release from all attractions of this world, its evils, it's non-spiritual impulses. This means not being a slave to worldly concerns, to all that is sinful. The positive element consists of accumulating all that is spiritual, all that is characteristic of the grace of the Kingdom. It must be developed; it stands at the forefront of this goal. According to St. Gregory the Theologian, the pastor must be heavenly, that is, he must not be involved with worldly sins and be a prisoner of its material goods. The pastor must be holy, yet this does not mean some pseudo-spiritual puritanism or some dried-up, anemic spirituality, memorizing special buzzword and church-Slavonic expressions, sanctimonious parading and hypocrisy, but a genuine spirituality, that is, striving for God's adoption and nurturing this spirituality and devotion in self and others, in order to be able to rise to a higher ideal of Orthodox asceticism. The pastor must be kind and compassionate, which does not at all mean sentimentality, but the ability to assimilate into himself the joys, sins, sorrows and suffering of others. The pastor must be venerable, that is, becoming like Christ, who is the perfect ideal of the Good Pastor. The pastor must be prayerful, that is, loving the activity of prayer in all its manifestations, especially the private prayer, especially the Jesus prayer, praying in church and most of all the services of Divine Liturgy. A priest without prayer, incapable of praying, not willing to explore the elements of prayer, not attracted to liturgy and in every way, under all plausible and implausible pretexts avoiding it, is a contradiction to himself and an unproductive administrator of spirituality. The pastor must be humble, that is, devoid of a sense of pride, arrogance, conceit, ambition, vanity and egoism. Humility is not expressed by low bows before others and not at all by signing ones name with the designation of humble priest so-and-so, nor by putting self into the center of the whole world, self-admiration, etc, but in a genuine liberation from all egocentrism.

The list of goals for which the priest must strive could be extended, but in the main, this is enough. All of the above may be reduced to a single condition — spirituality — that is — freedom from the power of any sin as well as any worldly, nationalistic and political ambitions. Now we should turn to the means of this spiritual education.

It would not be incorrect to state that the most powerful means to attain spirituality is in prayer. It alone is the very sphere of spiritual life, and besides, thanks to prayer, other spiritual blessings, previously lacking, may be obtained in prayer. The candidate must learn how to pray during his seminary formation. By observing whether the future priest loves the Divine Liturgy or avoids it, the directions of his striving can be judged accordingly; will the act of prayer be borne as a heavy burden or will the time spent in prayer become the best minutes of his life. This should not be generalized, since the ability to pray is a very individual matter. For some, prayer in church, conventionally arranged and ascetically more attractive, seems closer to the soul, while for others the public church prayer is much harder than a private, innermost prayer of the heart.

Therefore, the step to be taken next is: reading the Holy Scriptures, memorizing them, reflecting upon them, deepen the mind through understanding of the scriptures, familiarizing oneself with expository literature, literature of the holy Fathers as well as contemporary literature. Moreover, to cultivate spiritual growth, a general knowledge of the works of the Holy Fathers, mainly in their ascetic forms is required and should be used as a guide to moral perfection, because these works were written not from theoretical opinions, but from many years' experiences of desert and monastic life. To accomplish this goal, there has to be a gradual hierarchical reading preparation, beginning with the simpler writings, such as those of St. Abba Dorotheus, St. John of Kronstadt, Theophan the Recluse and Ignatius Brachaninov; the letters of Ambrose of Optina, and others gradually advancing to more difficult study, as, for example, The Philokalia, Isaac the Syrian, The Ladder of Divine Ascent, Simeon the New Theologian and Palamas.

A vital means for spiritual self-preparation to priesthood could take the form of frequent confessions, spiritual debates with knowledgeable people, the reading of famous ascetics' biographies and prayer books. The Western world is familiar with certain lengthy exercises in prayer and contemplations, practiced in monasteries. Such solitary and private, concentrated exercises of fasting substantially edify and build-up the spiritual wealth of the soul.

Participation in the course of spiritual self-preparation may include some of the following: visiting the sick, helping the suffering humanity and generally come to the aid of any one who suffers and is in need of compassion. It may be helpful to focus ones thoughts not on this transient, beautiful world, but on the elements of death, eternity and life after death. The reading of the Psalter over the deceased also may greatly enhance the young candidate's preparation for the priesthood.

Summarizing all of the above: it is imperative in the process of fostering the spiritual growth of the priest, to involve the cultivation of those traits that are helpful in renouncing compulsory laws and customs of this world, and to obtain the virtues that are conductive for the future priest to become spiritual and holy. All this contains within itself a special discipline, known as pastoral asceticism.

B) ***Intellectual Preparation.*** First of all, the harmful and deeply ingrained prejudice, that the pastor is in no need of intellectual preparation as well as the claim that such preparation is allegedly harmful and can even interfere with humility, life of prayer and spirituality, must be overcome and resolutely renounced. This is one of the most dangerous delusions in society as well as among the clergy, a clergy that is the primary guides of future priests. Here we have intentionally raised the matter of the three points of preparation in hierarchical order: spiritual, intellectual and external, so that we may first of all and once and for all resolutely declare that without spiritual preparation and spiritual aspiration the priest is merely an empty name, a self-contradiction, false and unworthy. Therefore, in this given context, we insist once more: without doubt the pre-eminent place belongs to spiritual self-preparation and after that comes everything else. At this point it is necessary to emphasize that spiritual self-preparation in no way impedes other intellectual and external developments; modern-day reality insistently demands the highest pastoral preparation possible and the widest intellectual range of interests as well as common courtesy and other general skills. The objection to the statement that any intellectual and external preparation which comes in contact with culture and service can harm and even destroy the pastor's spirituality is bolstered by the fact that such spirituality is insignificant and not worth a great deal. It must be remembered that the Orthodox spirituality is not as fragile as many fear.

Turning once more to history, past examples provide rich material to bring this matter to a favorable resolution. In fact, the fathers of the classical epoch of Orthodox theology—Athanasius, the Cappadocians, Maximus the Confessor, Patriarch Photius, John of Damascus and many other, were representatives of a very wide intellectual culture of their time. They represented the highest elite strata of their era. Their writings are full of evidence that their intelligence derived not only from scripture and the Holy Fathers who preceded them, but from expert testimony of pagan writers as well. They were perfectly familiar with philosophy, rhetoric, mathematics and music, that is, all that which, in the academic world of that day was known as the seven arts or *trillium* and *quadrillium*. What is also quite amazing, is that at no time did they fear that by giving the undisputed precedence to spiritual preparation and piety, secular education could somehow interfere with their piety and spirituality. Indeed, neither was their humility, faith nor prayer life impeded by their familiarity of Plato, Aristotle, Homer, Virgil, among others. Those who would dwell even a little deeper into the study of patristic writings and read the Holy Fathers, could not help but wonder at the high level and standard of education of those whom they would present as simpletons and obfuscators. Obfuscators and simpletons is exactly how the enemies of Christianity, such as Lucian, Celsius and Julius the Apostate wished to present them, yet the Holy Fathers surprised even the pagans with their external, that is, intellectual preparation. The biographies of saints and ascetic anthologies were not the only works preserved in monastic libraries. For example, it is interesting to note that Athanasius, a sophisticated Hellenist and expert on his own language, used expressions found only in the seldom-read works, such as studies on Euripides and Aristophanes. In order to remember such subtle linguistic points, these books must be read with great attention, which perhaps today would be considered out of place for monastic reading. Inferences may be made even in our own time from familiarity with the times of Plutarch and Plotinus. Knowledge of modern philosophy, literature, sciences and arts can only elevate the pastor's stature in the eyes of those of his flock who wish to learn from the priest about one or another cultural phenomenon. For the priest such knowledge can be quite useful an ammunition in his missionary and apologetics work. Only then can the pastor influence his flock, when he knows its heartbeat and what most attracts it. The priest's spirituality will not suffer from his familiarity with modern philosophical and literary currents. The price of that spirituality, which can suffer from contact with philosophy or be diminished by knowledge of literature, is not very great indeed. All intellectual preparation first of all implies a deep and genuine spirituality on the part of the priest. Intellectual preparation in no way should be a pretext for pastoral worldliness.

It is imperative to remember the potential cultural influence upon society. A society that is left by its pastor to its own devices and chances of fate in its growth and educational opportunities, becomes an easy prey to outside pressures and matures without the rewarding and guiding influence of a priest. No genuinely cultured person will turn to a priest who either knows nothing about modern matters or looks contemptuously away from anything that does not represent his narrow specialty of liturgy, required duties of the church and elementary sermons. People expect from a priest authoritative and well-thought-out answers, wise and knowledgeable, that spring from a well-educated mind. The Orthodox clergy, by virtue of many historical and social reasons, could not, or quite often did not know how to create this influence or how to stay ahead of the cultural process. In France the clergy was the creation of this cultural class and listened to it. For the three hundred years of the French Academy's existence, it counted 120 immortals, (105 before the revolution in 1789 and 15 afterward). Among these 120 'immortals,' the Academy counts 15 Cardinals, 33 bishops and archbishops, 13 Oratorians, 1 Dominican (La–Cordeur), several Jesuits and the rest — mere priests.

The Russian Academy of Science did not, in truth, exist for 300 years, but it had admitted such personalities as Metropolitan Filaret, Metropolitan Makary Bulgakov, and Platon Levshi as well as some priests such as Koschetov, Archimandrite Policarp Goitannikov and Geracim Pabsky. This, of course, viewed as a purely formal indication, cannot limit the cultural-educational factor among the clergy. Yet, even by expanding these parameters, the same experienced guidance in cultural matters, such as is exhibited in the countries of Western Europe, cannot be observed in the Orthodox clergy.

These examples can, without putting an undue stress on memory, only attest to the fact that enlightened priests were not at all the last ones in promoting the movement of spiritual progress and pastoral care. It is sufficient to remember such thinkers as Archpriest Theodore A. Golubinsky, Archimandrite Theophan Avsenev, and Arhbishop Nikanor Brovkivich, famous Sinologists such as Archimandrite Avakum the Sanctified and Palladin Kafarov; the Hebraist Father Gerasim Pavliky, Bishop Porfirius Uspensky, and Archimandrite Anthony Kapustin — all great Russian Byzantium scholars and leading experts of Greek and Russian languages. Archimandrite Anthony and his brother Platon Kapustin, one of the famous Moscow priests of his time, were astronomers, and Fr. Platon wrote articles on higher mathematics. The last protopresbyter of the Uspensky Cathedral in pre-revolutionary Russia, Fr. N. A. Lubimov, held a master's degree in Russian literature, teaching at the famous Fisherov Gymnasium. Fr. I. Foudel, a great friend of Constantine Leonteff and a man of letters, also taught law at this Gymnasium; our priests, living in foreign lands, became members of the major Academic Societies of Germany, Sweden, Spain and England.

Serving as an example in the Russian past is Archimandrite John Mihaelovich Pervushin, prior of the Village Church in Mehonsk, in the Perm province (+ June 16, 1900), a humble and prayerful priest, a kind and thoughtful pastor, who, besides all this, was also a remarkable mathematician, famous in the academic mathematical world. Upon graduation from the Kazan Theological Academy, he went to a rural church, where he spent the rest of his life. Gifted with exceptional mathematical ability, he began to send his work to the Academy of Sciences and was acquainted not only with the prominent mathematicians of Russia, but with those of the western world as well. His mathematical and numerical theories were rewarded by our Academy and were registered in the Mathematical Congress in Chicago and the Neapolitan Physics/ Mathematical Society. The numerical theories did in no way prevent him from being a good priest.

If desired, the list can be expanded, but it is important to remember that neither a title as a member of Academic Sciences, studies of astronomy, philosophy and or Byzantium, nor any other display of erudition and education can impede a spiritual individual to be liturgical, an excellent pastor and a humble monk, whose main calling is to exert a great spiritual influence upon his flock.

It is also imperative to remember that in times such as ours, when the enemies of the church are mobilizing all their forces to fight against her, the presence of enlightened, steeled by scientific schooling pastors who are always ready to answer to our hope, according to Apostle Peter, is more than appropriate. The pastor is expected to fearlessly and therefore humbly, confess his own incompetence, yet to use the words by power forcefully and with authority. Since our clergy are not accustomed to, nor wishes to be leaders in these matters, it is not surprising that those seeking guidance in live, turn to persons who are far removed from spirituality and the church. Intelligentsia's inherent lack of spirituality may be cured to a considerable extent by spirituality's approach to its strivings and interests.

Turning once more to modern reality, it must be remembered that the great influence exerted upon society by Metropolitan Anthony, Sergius Bulgakov, Alexander Elchaninov, and G. Spassky is explained by the fact that they had an excellent knowledge of secular literature and kept up with arts, sciences and current thoughts.

Throughout history elements that may be helpful or harmful can be found within all secular education. From Plato and Homer the Church Fathers extracted those elements that could bring enlightenment to their time, but avoided those in pagan education, which were unnecessary and confusing. This matter is not solely a concern of this or any other century; the danger is not confined to the present or ancient times. The Moscow Metropolitan Philaret wrote at the time (August 27, 1858): "They wage war against contemporary ideas, yet are not the ideas of Orthodoxy and morality the essence of contemporary ideals? Have they only remained in the past? Are all of us pagans? The time is not at fault; immoral and unorthodox ideas, circulated by some people, are. Thus the fight must be directed against unorthodox and immoral, not contemporary ideas." (Collections of views and opinions. Book IV, chapter 344. " It is futile to yearn for the past, since no escape from the perils of the present time can be found there " Metropolitan Philaret wrote to the Superior of the Trinity Monastery, Archimandrite Anthony on March 29th, 1838: "The nineteenth century cannot be transformed into the fourth or fifth century, any more than the Vologod province can be converted into Fivaid province" (Letters to the Superior of the Monastery, Book 1, chapter 315). In any case, our great prelates understood the benefit of education and were always able to defend Orthodoxy from attacks and accusations of obfuscation. To the Metropolitan Isidore of Novgorod, he wrote: "In vein does the critic think that the Christian faith is hostile to knowledge because it is not in union with ignorance" (Collections of opinions and beliefs," Book V, chapter 48).

The pastor, of course, has to be very well aware of the dangers that lie in his path. With enthusiastic desire to be cultured and erudite, the priest may easily yield to the temptation of secularization and, imperceptibly, put the wrong appraisal on intellectual values. When the pastor begins to lose his main and only need, when literature, philosophy and a compassionate attitude for his flock are disrupted, the pastor has lost his way. Therefore involvement with the secular must always be tempered by a degree of a prayerful, pastoral frame of mind and purely spiritual aspirations. The goal of priestly life and actions is to create spirituality in himself and in those close to him; intellectual and secular educations may only be used as a means for pastoral influence as well as to enhance his own inner wealth. The pastor should not fear education, but must in every way possible beware of being distracted by it to the detriment of his spirituality, because achieving perfection on the spiritual level is much harder than on the mental, artistic and scientific levels. Besides, the only correct course of action is the middle of the road and is only possible when one is in full harmony and balance with all the other competing forces.

2 **Ordination.** The most important and the most awesome moment in the life of every priest, a moment which shall remain in his memory for the rest of his days, even unto his death, is when the bishop lays his hands upon his head for the great service of priesthood. In the previous chapter there was enough said about the more or less protracted scholastic preparations for pastoral work. The future priest must carefully examine his frame of mind, so that in the last days of his earthly life it may be in accord with his high calling and may enable him to draw nearer to the very mystery of priesthood.

In his last academic term the candidate is faced with the crucial question about his future parish, that Altar to which the church will appoint him as its pastor. Although this question is not a part of pastoral science's framework, but rather a canonical matter, it is nevertheless imperative to utter a few words about these formal administrative details, since they cannot help but be of concern for the future protege.

There are three known methods in the history of Christianity. The protestant approach, which, basically should not even be mentioned, since it has neither ordination nor priesthood nor any sign of a formal church, an approach, which is deviating into one extreme. Dissidents from Rome confine themselves to one selected community. This is sufficient in the eyes of those who acquired their freedom from the Roman prelate and the distorted teachings of the church by buying delusions of sanctification of self and others with the price of Presbyterian anarchy, where the blessed elements are completely dismissed. This is the extreme democratization of the Church.

The Roman Catholic approach went to the opposite extreme, by way of utter suppression at least in principle, with very few exceptions, of affirmation of individuality, the source of the world and its very people. In the Roman understanding, the church is concentrated in its hierarchy. That royal priesthood, which is chosen by the people and of which speaks both the Old and the New Testaments was not forgotten in early Christianity, yet has been completely obscured in the consciousness of the high ranking Roman prelates. The people do not take part in the elections of its clergy. The ancient practice of electing the Roman pontiff with the participation of the people has been transformed into an electing conclave of a special group of cardinals, a practice unknown in the pre-eminent church. It is also the case in the life of the parish and the diocese. The people are deprived of their participation in the selection of their pastors. This is not, however, all bad. The Roman Catholics are spared the many temptations that afflict those who possess the knowledge of Orthodox Christianity because there certainly is a kind of corruption in the life of the church. It must be noted here, however, that the Roman rite of ordination has kept one detail, alas forgotten by us, namely the laying of the hands on the candidate not only by one bishop, but by other presbyters also. The ordination is not performed only by the archbishop, but by the whole assemblage of the church.

Orthodoxy has strived, and is still striving, although not always successfully, to take the middle road, avoiding one extreme appearance of Western Christianity and abstaining from excesses of another. From time immemorial Orthodoxy has preserved the principle of electing a priest and a bishop by the people. However, it remains to be seen how this matter will be resolved by historians; New Testament and canonical scholars; will they be able do demonstrate with absolute conviction the fundamentality of this or some other choosing system; did the apostles, in consultation with the "people" choose their proteges; can Christ's words be completely ignored; "you did not chose me, but I chose you" (John 15:16); words which denote the choosing is to come not from below, but from above; generally speaking, does this choosing system conform to the spirit of the Gospel, that is, can we extract from a few factors of apostolic history general deductions; is there an undisputed advantage and an invariable correctness of choosing by the required actions of the so-called "people–guardians" of piety? All these questions cannot help but be reflected in the attitude of the priest in his parish and his relations with his flock.

Understandably, this third aspect mitigates the first two extremes: Presbyterian anarchy and Latin papism. Yet not everything in this tradition is undisputable and flawless. The participation of the people in the choosing of their pastor is not, *per se*, a bad beginning, but it does not guarantee its rightness. Those people, who are reared within the church's strict framework and who are true to its canons and traditions, can more or less properly exercise their right. But in the absence of these qualities, the flock's liberal tendencies for independence may well prove to be a restraint on those who do the choosing, the "people–guardians of piety," especially if the priest's character is somewhat weak.

Be that as it may, the principle of being chosen by the people, or, more to the point, the people's participation in indicating to the authorities which candidate appears to be the more suitable, was, by and large, widely practiced in the east. The ancient Russian custom used the principle of "the prince will elevate the people". The council affirmed this statute for ordinary churches, while palace courtiers conducted the selection of priests in the prestigious churches. A formal "note of order" was issued, attesting to the desire on either side not to overstep the conditions of the agreement; this aspect brings a certain foreign spirit to the element of pastorship. It is unlikely, due to the shortage of properly prepared candidates, that it would somehow occur to the bishop to exercise his right of a "veto". Under the auspices of the synod provisions of the Russian church, the principle of appointing the clergy by election fell into disuse and the desire for its restoration was only expressed at the workshops of the synod assemblies.

More recently, in the 18th and 19th centuries, the principle of clergy election was practiced to a certain extent in the Orthodox populated regions of the Austro-Hungarian Empire: Voevodina, Boukhovina, and the Chemovitz and Dalmatian dioceses.

Without a doubt, some positive aspects in the election of clergy by the people may be perceived. Each person is granted the right to choose for oneself the spiritual leader and to entrust to him, and to no one else, one's conscience and one's soul. Nevertheless, in priesthood and pastorship, the "patronymic" principle of seniority holds sway. The pastor and his flock form, what the Old Russian proverb called "the penitent family." In a family, as well as in a patronymic social order, a crucial element of obedience and penance has to be present. The principle of clergy election carries within itself a certain lack of humility as well as a somewhat juridical and democratic elements.

It is now time to put aside these issues and turn our attention to the most important matter—ordination—its meaning and substance. The priest, whether chosen or appointed by the personal power of his future diocesan bishop, still has to face, at a certain moment of his life, this mysterious and awesome hour of ordination. Symbolically speaking, the following parallels may be drawn: election by the flock is somewhat akin to a courtship, but ordination—that is his wedding with the flock. This symbolism is fortified by common rituals and by one or another sacrament: walking around the lecturn or altar, singing the psalms, "Rejoice, O Isaiah a Virgin is With Child," "O Holy Martyrs"... At this point, certain conclusions can be drawn: the union of the priest with his flock is a lasting union, just as the principle of marriage; neither can be dissolved. Therefore the transfer of a priest from one place to another should have no place in the principle of this union, as well as, or, if not to a greater extent, the transfer of a bishop from one cathedral to another. In essence, the priest is irremovable. But there is yet another, a more important characteristic to this sacrament: priesthood—as taught by Roman Catholics, is ingrained. The Greek theologians held the same opinion. Metropolitan Philaret had a different view. Essentially, the grace bestowed by the bishop to perform the solemn sacrament of liturgy cannot be removed by any power on earth. To consider that any conservatory act could deprive a person of the grace of the Holy Spirit seems to be a theological aberration. Neither baptism nor priesthood is removable or indelible. Even the sin of apostasy does not erase the grace of baptism. The most frightful sin that can be committed by the priest, which leads to disenfranchisement from the Holy Orders, cannot, by itself, deprive the priest of grace. It would seem to be necessary, in case of some judicial error in defrocking a priest who is subsequently found to be innocent, to re-ordain him, which action, of course, even the strictest and most inflexible person dare not suggest. What should be declared as being even more frightening and blasphemous is the so-called "sacramental defrocking", practiced in the Russian and Serbian churches. A well-known case of such defrocking involved Bishop Varlaam Smolensky during the rein of Emperor Alexander 1. The condemned was led by the people from the chancel in full regalia, then, at the doors facing west, all the while proclaiming "anaxios," his priestly garments were taken off piece by piece and as a final act he was chased out of the temple with a rod. These proceedings bring to mind the inside-out structure of the "black mass." The Greek acknowledge the life-long loss in denying the priest to serve, but by no means do they advocate the "loss of rank". As is well known, the Catholics have developed a complete set of instructions in the study of a so-called "sacramental character", that is, the indelible seal of the two sacraments — baptism and priesthood.

In 1899, the Serbian Synod deprived the archpriest Milan Djourich of his priestly rank for making an attempt on the life of king Milan Obrenovich. He was subsequently convicted and sentenced to 20 years of hard labor. The stripping of Holy Vestments was performed in church while proclaiming "unworthy" (Prof. G. Voskrecensky, "from the Church Life of Orthodox Slavs," in "Theological Bulletin" in March of 1900, p. 530). The book of Serbian Metropolitan Michael "Orthodox Serbian Church In the Kingdom of Serbia" (pp. 213–215) includes this "Rite of Expulsion From Priesthood."

With these preliminary considerations in mind, we may now turn to the main theme of this chapter — the very priesthood. In addition to all else mentioned in the previous chapters about the calling, pastoral gifts and the multifaceted preparation for his future service, a priesthood candidate should never forget about the endurance of the gift of priestly service, which separates the ordinary layman from the blessed celebrant at the altar; the one who performs the sacrament, the liturgist, the intermediary between God and the world, who, by the grace of the Holy Spirit leads his flock to spiritual perfection, to worship. After ordination, he is no longer merely a man, but a clergyman. He is no longer the chosen one, chosen by his flock—if such choosing took place—but the bearer of grace. The right-hand ordination by the bishop, introducing him to the parish clergy, does not tear him away from the flock nor lock into some kind of priestly caste, but organically ties him to those who from now on will be one with him.

After engaging time and again in rigorous self-examinations and being finally convinced, as far as is humanly possible, that he does not want to look back, the candidate at last decides to accept the grace of priesthood, according to the rite of Melchizedek. Our pastoral theologians usually advise the candidate not to postpone the ordination for too long a time after the conclusion of his studies. This is probably due to the fact that each unnecessary delay does not strengthen but rather dampens the enthusiasm, brings more and newer doubts and destroys the unity of the soul. Besides, there is probably another consideration.

According to Metropolitan Anthony, God must be given all of ones fervor, to "light a whole candle in the presence of God, not offer God a good-for-nothing candle-end, spent on trivial worldly vanities." Yet the same Metropolitan Anthony advises, as far as it is possible, to separate the time of ordination from the time of marriage. As a matter of fact, the ambience of youthful enthusiasm and passion adds little to ones ability to retain that inner self-possession, so essential for the moment of ordination and even more so for the priest's first steps into pastorship. It's time to settle down.

It may be well for the candidate to withdraw for a short time, perhaps a few days before the very ordination and move away from all worldly noises and concerns. Retreating into a monastery, be it ever so small and insignificant, will help the protege to withdraw into his inner world, to pray better and with greater ease. Fasting, prayer and abstention from all that is worldly will aid the candidate to approach the awesome hour of ordination.

The eve of ordination has arrived. The protege fulfills all the required formalities, wastes no additional time in paying attention to the formality of his attire nor any other necessary preparations; signs his priestly oath in the conservatory, an oath which he must treat with utmost seriousness and awe, and finally, with the requisite papers from the bishop and the conservatory he goes to his confessor, or, if there is such a one, to the confessor of the clergy for a so-called "candidate's confession." This is a new and last control of the protege conscience before ordination. This confession is for an entire life. Of course, each confession should be viewed as a last, before death, confession, for at any given hour one must be prepared to face death and the judgment of God. But this confession is a particularly strict examination of all that was committed by the candidate over the span of his lifetime, things that could have been forgotten in previous confessions, or, due to human weakness even hidden and never confessed. With a reconciled conscience, a pure heart, a full awareness of his own worthlessness and imperfections, but not, however a stylized "disparaging humility, beyond pride," yet a truly contrite heart, the candidate, in the presence of his witness, the confessor, bring his confession to God and asks God to bestow upon him the purity of priesthood.

Through forgiveness, the signature of the confessor or by the act of the conservatory, attesting to the fact that no canonical obstacles for ordination were found, the candidate awaits the next day's ordination. St. Gregory the Theologian says in his apologetic address: "I am ashamed of other, who, with unwashed hands and unclean souls take the most holy office before they are worthy, enter the priesthood, storm into the sanctuary, push and shove around about the Holy Table, performing its office not as an example of virtue but merely as a means of making a living. Not as a service with its underlying responsibilities, but performing the duties of said office autocratically and without giving account." He further adds: "One first must cleanse himself before cleansing others; become wise before imparting wisdom, become holy before enlightening others, come nearer to God, then lead others to Him, sanctify self, then bless others."

Quite often, just before ordination, those who are weak or overly judgmental, or perhaps excessively self-demanding possessing a so-called over-scrupulous conscience, succumb to the well-known condition of faint-heartedness and the desire to run without a backward glance, lest the burden they take upon themselves will prove to be overly excessive. Such a tempting voice deserves a decisive answer. One must not, in these last minutes before ordination, hesitate and vacillate, remembering that a "double-minded man is unstable in all his ways" (James 1:8). For those who find these last minutes so painful and agonizing, the firm hand of the confessor, the encouraging voice of a real friend can and must supply help to the weakening conscience of the candidate. Here it is imperative to point to the grace of the Holy Spirit, "which healesth that which is feeble and fills that which is wanting."

These last hours may be safely compared to a personal Gethsemane, a temptation to forsake God. One of the prominent pastors spoke of "dying" before his ordination, "It seemed as if each day was a long-drawn-out agony, bringing with it new experiences of suffering, sufferings which are impossible to describe" (Fr. S. Bulgakov, "Autobiographical Notes," p. 41).

During these hours a kind of self-impoverishment takes place, as if one is saving all the viewpoints and perspectives for the Kenosis of the Son of God. The priest is called upon to duplicate the priesthood of Christ, to become like Him, to begin to imitate Him in every thing. In ordination a new birth of a person takes place; the layman becomes "the new creation in Christ."

There occurs in this unique and incomparable moment of life man's committal of obedience to Christ. The protege proclaims the awesome vows of his special love for the Superior Pastor and the

Church, uniting himself to them for eternity, not by losing self or his personality, but opening self to the mystical unity with the Body of Christ, being led and filled by Its Spirit and raised into heaven.

Every moment of this solemn performance is significant and awesome; the initiations into the first stages of priesthood—reader, subdeacon, the passing for the first time through the Royal Doors, as if through some fiery barrier, walking around the Altar, accompanied by the chanting of wedding hymns, touching the Altar for the first time, the bending of knees and the sensation of the heavy brocade omophorion upon the head, the right-handed bishopric blessing, and perhaps the most awe-inspiring words of the bishop, spoken in an undertone into the ear of the protege: "raise your eyes into heaven and ask God for forgiveness of your sins and the bestowing upon you the purity of priesthood." These words, like lightening from heaven, pierce the person's soul, like a fiery sword, they cut off all the sinfulness from him, like a thunder-clap or perhaps like a "cold, thin voice", they grasps the hearer with the words of prayer: "Oh, divine grace, which always healesth that which is ailing and completes that which is wanting, vouch for the most devout deacon, (name) to be a presbyter; let us pray for him, and bring down upon him the Grace of the Holy Spirit."

The most staggering—writes Fr. S. Bulgakov—was, course, the passing for the first time through the Royal Doors and approaching the Holy Altar. This felt as if I was passing through fire, a fire that singes, enlightens and regenerates. This was like entering into a different world, a Heavenly Kingdom. For me this was the beginning of my new existence, my permanent home, where I have resided from that time on, even until now."

Not only are the Royal Doors now open, but the deacon's doors also, as a sign to signify the relationship with the worshipers, a closer link with the people—destined to be a more spontaneous act than other sacraments. All of this is keenly felt in the repeated "axios" during each part of priestly vesting, chanted at the altar by the servers and the clergy, that is, by those who, with their chants express the feeling of the people.

The final moment at last: the handing to the new priest the discos with a particle of the Holy Lamb with these words: "receive this pledge, bear its agonizing existence until the day of the Terrible Coming of Our Lord Jesus Christ." Now the new priest is no longer a mere layman, he is a liturgist and a celebrant of Sacraments. This is no longer someone who is merely bearing the title of father, but is in fact Father. He must, according to St. Gregory the Theologian, "stand with the angels, give glory with archangels, offer up the sacrifice on the rock of the Sacrificial Altar and perform the Holy Rite with Christ, recreate creation, reclaim the image of God, work in the mines of the world and above all to be like God and create gods.

From this moment on begins not a just an existence, but a saintly life; not merely conversations, but sermons, not the feebleness of a long-standing weakling, but the boldness of Christ's friend, "forgetting those things which are behind and reaching forward to those things which are ahead" (Philippians 3:13), the Kingdom of grace, eternity and crucifixion of Christ.

CHAPTER SIX

Metropolitan Maximos Aghiorgoussis of Pittsburgh (1935–)

Metropolitan Maximos was born on the island of Chios on March 5, 1935, and raised in a priestly family. As a youth, he studied at the famous Patriarchal Theological School of Halki, which is located in present-day Istanbul, Turkey, where he received his degree in Orthodox Theology in 1957. He was later ordained a deacon in Halki on April 28, 1957, and ordained a priest in Chios in 1959. He pursued graduate studies at the University of Louvain, Belgium, where he received a Doctorate in Theology and Baccalaureate in Philosophy in 1964. In 1966, he arrived in the United States and was appointed Professor of Systematic Theology at the Holy Cross School of Theology in Massachusetts, where he remained until May 1979. In addition to St. Vladimir's Seminary, both Holy Cross and St. Vladimir's are the two most well known Orthodox seminaries in the United States. During his tenure at the school, he also served as Vice President of Hellenic College and Academic Dean of the Holy Cross School of Theology. From September 1979 to June 1985, Metropolitan Maximos was also a visiting Professor of Systematic Theology at Christ the Saviour Theological Seminary in Johnstown, Pennsylvania, a seminary of the Carpatho-Russian Orthodox Church in America. In addition to his pastoral duties, Bishop Maximos is also a trustee of St. Vladimir's Theological Seminary in Crestwood, New York. He is currently the spiritual leader of the Metropolis of Pittsburgh and is active in ecumenical dialogues between the various Christian churches as well as non-Christians.

The essay by Metropolitan Maximos, "The Parish Presbyter and His Bishop," *St. Vladimir's Theological Quarterly* 29:1 (1985), is a historical and liturgical explanation of the relationship between the local parish presbyter (*priest*) and the unifying and teaching role of the bishop. His essay emphasizes the conciliar nature of the Church where the bishop, priest, and laity work together for the building up of the entire body of Christ. The priest and bishop must work alongside one another as coworkers with Christ and not in competition with one another. Metropolitan Maximos also highlights several very practical and pastoral concerns in parish life, such as poor relations with fellow clergy colleagues, strained relations with one's bishop, and the lack of generosity and collegiality among clergy. Furthermore, he also alludes to problems such as isolationism and parochialism which exacerbate the usual tension and struggles between presbyters and bishops.

For Further Reading

Metropolitan Maximos. *In the Image of God: Studies in Scripture, Theology, and Community* (Brookline, MA: Holy Cross Press, 1999).

The Parish Presbyter and His Bishop: A Review of the Pastoral Roles, Relationship and Authority

"You know that the rulers of the Gentiles lord it over them, and their great men exercise authority over them. It shall not be so among you, for whoever would be great among you must be your servant, and whoever would be first among you must be your slave; even as the Son of man came not to be served, but to serve and to give His life as a ransom for many" (Matt. 20:25–28). And again we hear: "You call me Teacher and Lord, and you are right, for so I am. If I, your Lord and Teacher, have then washed your feet, so ought you to wash one another's feet. For I have given you an example, that you should do as I have done to you. Truly, truly I say to you: a servant is not greater than his master; nor is he who is sent greater than the one who has sent him. If you know these things, and if you do them, blessed are you" (Jn. 13:13–17).

Since Holy Week is where both of these sayings of the Lord are highlighted, they are sayings of which we are particularly mindful. These sayings are the proper ground upon which to base the position, role and authority, and relationships of and between Christ's disciples, including bishops and priests. As Orthodox theologians who are discussing the topic of the parish presbyter relative to his bishop, it is important to realize from the very beginning what is the nature of this position, role and authority. Then we may discuss the inter-relatedness as well as the distinctiveness of this particular position, role and authority, as exemplified in the two major offices of Christian ministry, the episcopate and the presbyterate. In fact, the holy diaconate, the third of the offices, should likewise be a key part of our consideration of our Christian ministry, so I will also treat the role of the deacon here.

Our holy Church takes great pride in its history. "*Historia magistra vitae*" history is the master of life, is the way an old Latin saying puts it. This applies to the Church's life in a very special manner. So, let us allow history to be our teacher, as we try to establish what—from an Orthodox point of view-should be the right kind of relationship between the bishop and the parish presbyter (priest) in our Church today.

Many questions are raised today, not only in our Orthodox American context, but also in the other Christian traditions regarding the role of the parish presbyter relative to the bishop. A good, prime example is the much-celebrated and discussed ecumenical document of "convergence," the *Baptism, Eucharist and Ministry* (BEM) report which has been developed by the World Council of Churches' Faith and Order Commission. In the BEM report, we read: "In general, the relation of the presbyterate to the episcopal ministry has been discussed throughout the centuries, and the degree of the presbyter's participation in the episcopal ministry is still for many an unresolved question of far-reaching ecumenical importance."[1]

Actually, aside from the importance that the question has in itself and in terms of the Church's ministry in today's world, the same question has been debated by theologians in terms of the possibility of a mutual acceptance and recognition of one another's "ordained ministries."[2]

Nevertheless, the scope of this presentation is not to discuss the ecumenical implications of the questions which we have under consideration here. We will limit ourselves to some conclusions and reflections concerning the role, position and authority of the parish presbyter relative to the bishop, in terms of the effective ministry of

---

[1] *Baptism, Eucharist and Ministry;* Faith and Order paper no. 111 (WCC, Geneva, 1982), p. 25.

[2] *Ibid.*, p. 32. See also Raymond E. Brown, S.S., *Priest and Bishop; Biblical Reflections* (Paulist Press, Paramus, New York/Toronto 1970), pp. 82–6.

the Church in today's world — and, more specifically, in terms of the Church's service in ministering to the holy People of God.

We deem it necessary to discuss the scriptural background of the question, together with the developments that followed in the Apostolic era and the early Church; the Church's canonical tradition; the ecclesiological principles underlying the issue; concrete situations in the USA and Europe; and some conclusions which will be proposed regarding the direction in which our Church should be going, in terms of a more effective ministry toward God's people.

1 **Scriptural Background.** By quoting the Lord at the outset, I intend to indicate that Christ is *the* model of the Christian priesthood, established by Him as a life of service to God and to the Church. Christian priesthood, in all its orders, is a life of service in imitation of the Teacher, Christ, the "Servant of God" (*Ebed Yahve*).[3]

It is characteristic that the New Testament antecedents of our Christian priesthood are not "cultic." The word "priest," in terms of *hiereus, sacerdos,* which — by the time of Eusebius (*History of the Church,* 10.4.2) — is fully applied to the Church's ministry, is completely absent as a designation of the Christian priesthood in the New Testament. It only applies to the Old Testament priesthood and to the High Priestly role of Christ Himself.

According to Karl Hermann Schelkle, the word "priest" comes from the Old Testament and from world religions. It meant "the servant of the Deity" who stood between the Deity and the people, with the exclusive function of mediating reconciliation or salvation, and who did this particularly through a ritual sacrifice and by acting as a mantic oracle. Since the New Testament rejects this current word for 'priest,' it is clear that there was no priesthood of this kind in the

[3] According to K. H. Schelkle, *Diakonia* (service) "is the all embracing and essential term for 'office' in the N.T." K. H. Schelkle, "Ministry and Minister in the NT Church," *Concilium III,* 5 (1969), p. 8.

New Testament community.[4] However, according to Schelkle, the New Testament "does use the word 'priest' in a very significant way. In the Epistle to the Hebrews (2:17; 4:14; 5:10), Christ is called the true High Priest, *archiereus,* who fulfills the Israelite tradition of the high priesthood.[5] Also, "priestly" attributes—applied to the whole Church of God as a "people set apart," a "holy and royal priesthood," echoing Exodus 19:6—are found in I Peter 2:5, 9. The expression "priests before God" is applied to the faithful, both collectively and individually, in Apocalypse 1:5; 5:10; and 20:6.[6]

A *sacrificial* and *cultic* priesthood, which is the priesthood of the Old Testament, cannot be applied to the Christian ministry in the New Testament context, in the estimate of Raymond E. Brown. It is only later, toward the end of the 1st century and the beginning of the 2nd, that Christians began to apply the term priest as such to the Christian ministry. This is due to the perception of the Holy Eucharist as a sacrifice, as in *Didache* 14: "first confess your sins, that your sacrifice (*thysia)* may be a pure one." To quote Brown: "Just after the end of the 2nd century, Tertullian (*De Baptismo* 17) can speak of the bishop as the *summus sacerdos* and Hippolytus of Rome (*Apostolic Tradition* III. 5) can refer to the 'high priestly spirit' of the Bishop.[7]

However, the New Testament does provide important antecedents of the Christian priesthood which immensely enrich the Christian ministry, such as: the Disciple, the Apostle, the Presbyter/Bishop, and the One who presides at the Eucharist, the *proestos* of *Didache.*[8] It is important to regain the idea of discipleship especially in terms of imitating Christ and His ministry. It is important to recapture the spirit of apostleship, which includes the service of ordinary work, of collecting money and goods in support of the Church's ministry, of "unceasing prayer," of suffering, and of correction—all of which

[4] *Ibid.*, p. 5.
[5] *Ibid.*, pp. 5–6.
[6] *Ibid.*, p. 6.
[7] *Op. cit.*, p. 19.
[8] *Ibid.*, pp. 13–45.

we see exemplified by St. Paul the Apostle. The minister/priest of the Church always was and should continue to be a disciple, an apostle, indeed a missionary of God's work among God's people.

If the apostle is the missionary, the Presbyter–Bishop is the *local* Christian teacher, or — if you will — the local bureaucrat and administrator. The two words, Presbyter and Bishop, are used interchangeably in the earliest Church writings. Most of the time they are in fact identical, with the possible exception of III John.[9] It is only at the end of the 1st century and the beginning of the 2nd, and certainly by the time of St. Ignatius of Antioch, that the differentiation is established. It is important to keep in mind the fact of a non-differentiation at the New Testament level, as perceived in the general opinion of scholars, between Presbyter, the Old Testament elder, and Bishop, secular episcopos or overseer. It is of great significance for the question of the relative positions, roles and authority of Bishop and Presbyter in the Church today.

Finally, as Brown argues, "the One who presides over the Eucharist" is one of the important elements and antecedents of the Christian priesthood. Later, the priesthood and priestly ministry came to be primarily identified with the celebration of the Holy Eucharist. During the New Testament times it is not always clear who presides over the Eucharistic assembly. The evidence leads us to assume that, when present, the Apostles were the presiding celebrants, or — in their absence — the Presbyters/ elders and Bishops/overseers whom the Apostles had appointed. However, in at least one case — the letters of St. Paul to the Christians of the Church in Corinth — there is no mention made of elders or overseers in the community. Who was the presiding celebrant of the Eucharist prior to the appointment of Presbyters/Bishops? We do know that a "hierarchy" had definitely been established by the time St. Clement of Rome wrote to the Corinthian church. Schelkle is of the opinion, based on the Corinthian case in point, that Christians today therefore may celebrate "the

[9] *Ibid.*, p. 35, footnote 20. See also Schelkle, *op. cit.*, p. 8.

liturgy of the word," though not the Eucharist, in the absence of a priest or bishop.[10]

Brown, in the book *Priest and Bishop,* has examined the New Testament antecedents of our Christian priesthood in terms of the question of Apostolic succession. The Presbyters/Bishops, he observes, are traditionally seen as successors to the Apostles. How much of that is fact? The answer depends on first, what is meant by "Apostle," and, second, what is meant by "succession"?

Regarding the first, Brown considers two kinds of apostleship. One is the Lucan apostleship, which is a residential type, according to which the Twelve Apostles themselves—with one or two exceptions—were not really missionaries. The second is the Pauline type, according to which an Apostle is essentially a missionary, and St Paul was the exemplar of this model. Presbyters/Bishops were residential persons in a particular place, appointed by the Apostles to head and administer the various Christian communities. Their succession to the Apostles" is primarily functional, rather than juridical—this last term signifying a succession carried out through ordination, or the laying-on-of-hands.[11]

In conclusion, looking at the original system in place, there is essentially no differentiation to be made between Presbyters/elders and Bishops/episcopoi/overseers. The Presbyters/ Bishops were appointed by St. Paul and eventually some other Apostle (s), and *they succeed to the Apostles "functionally"*—*i.e.*, as Pastors in God's service and in ministry to His people, rather than primarily in terms of a mere tactile chain of unbroken ordinations. It is this latter, simplistic understanding of Apostolic priestly orders and ecclesiastical continuity which raises the major objections to the institution of Christian priesthood as such.

2 **Post-Scriptural Era.** What is the development of the Christian priestly ministry in the life of the early Church?

[10] *Ibid.*, pp. 6–7.

[11] Brown, *op. cit.*, pp. 47–81.

St. Clement of Rome speaks, at the end of the 1st century, of the succession to the Apostles and their ministry: "They preached in country and town, and appointed their first-fruits, after testing them by the Spirit, to be bishops (*episcopous*) and deacons (*diakonous*) of those who were going to believe. And this was no novelty, for indeed a long time ago the Scripture had mentioned bishops and deacons, for there is somewhere this message: 'I will set up their bishops (overseers) in righteousness and their deacons (ministers) in faith' [quotation from Isaiah 60:17]."[12] What is significant and obvious is that, since the two are interchangeable terms for him, St. Clement does not distinguish between bishops and presbyters.[13]

The turning point is perceived in the actions of St. Ignatius of Antioch, martyred 115 AD. According to Brown, by approximately 110 AD, "in many communities one bishop had emerged as the head of a college of presbyters. Ignatios' directives pertinent to the authority of the bishop would make the most authoritarian bishop of our times blush-for in Ignatius' view episcopacy, like cleanliness, was next to godliness! "You have only to acknowledge God and the bishop, and all is well; for a man who honors his bishop is himself honored by God (*Smyrneans* 9:1)."[14] The Bishop's authority in Ignatius' view, is extolled in many other passages quoted by Brown.[15] Regarding the distinction between Bishop and Presbyter, St. Ignatius says: "... being perfectly united in obedient submission to the bishop and the presbytery, you may be satisfied in all respects..." (Ephesians 3). And again, in Ephesians 4: "for your reverend presbytery, which is worthy of God, is tuned to the bishop, as strings are to the lyre: and thus, in your concord and harmonious love, Jesus Christ is sung..."[16] A very

[12] Clement of Rome, *[First] Epistle to the Corinthians,* 12; quoted by Bettenson, *The Early Christian Fathers,* col. I (Oxford Univ. Press, London-Oxford-New York, 1969), p. 32.

[13] See *Ibid.,* p. 32, note 4.

[14] R. Brown, *op. cit.,* pp. 36–39.

[15] *Ibid.,* p. 39.

[16] St. Ignatios of Antioch, *To the Ephesians,* 3–4, quoted by Henry Bettenson in *The Early Christian Fathers* (Oxford, 1969), p. 40.

important, in fact crucial understanding here is *that there is essentially a harmony between the Bishop and the presbytery,* the presbytery being attuned closely to the Bishop's own ministry and pastoral care. Also: *the presbytery is integral to the episcopate,* for obedience to the presbyter is due as much as obedience to the Bishop.

Taken out of context, however, the Ignatian view of the episcopacy could lead to a Bishop becoming as overbearing as "the rulers of the Gentiles" whom Christ noted "lord it over them." In the same letter to the Ephesians chapter 6, Ignatius states that the bishop occupies the place of the Lord: "Clearly, then, we should regard the bishop as the Lord Himself."[17] But we read in the letter to the *Magnesians:* "I advise you, *be eager to act always in godly accord:* with the bishop presiding as the counterpart of God, the presbyters as the counterpart of the council of the Apostles, and the deacons (most dear to me) who have been entrusted with a service (diaconate) under Jesus Christ [or 'the ministry of Jesus Christ' (who 'came not to be ministered to, but to minister (*diakonisai*),... Let there be nothing among you which will have power to divide you, but be united with the bishop and with those who preside, for an example and instruction in incorruptibility."[18] In this text, yes, the Bishop occupies the central place, even of God Himself. However, a threefold, interdependent ministry is emphasized, as the presbyters are given the envious place of the "Council of the Apostles," and the deacons imitate Christ's example as "Servant of God" (*diakonon*).

In the same letter the faithful of the community of Magnesia are instructed: "Thus, as the Lord did nothing without the Father... so you must do nothing without the bishop and the presbyters."[19] And again: "Be eager to be firmly established in the precepts of the Lord and of the Apostles with your right reverend Bishop and worthily-woven chaplet of your presbytery, and with the godly deacons. *Be submissive to the Bishop and to one another,* as Jesus Christ was to the

[17] *Ibid.,* p. 40.
[18] *Letter to the Magnesians, ibid.,* p. 42.
[19] *Ibid.,* p. 42.

Father, and the Apostles to Christ and to the Father, *that there may be a union both of flesh and spirit.*"[20]

In the letter to the *Trallians,* obedience to the Christian priesthood is emphasized for the sake of unity and as a warning against schism: "When you are submissive to the Bishop as to Jesus Christ, it is clear to me that you are not living as ordinary men but according to Jesus Christ ... It is therefore necessary that you should do nothing without the Bishop; and that is your practice. Submit yourselves also to the Presbytery, as to the Apostles ... And those who are deacons of the mysteries of Jesus Christ must please men in all ways ... Likewise let all men respect the deacons as they reverence Jesus Christ, just as they must respect the Bishop as the counterpart of the Father, and the Presbyters as the council of God and the college of the Apostles: without those no church is recognized."[21]

In the same letter, the warning is given in the following terms against deception as well: "Be on your guard against such men (*i.e.*, the Docetic heretical party). And this will be your case if you are not self-assertive and if you are inseparable from Jesus Christ and from the bishop and the institution of the Apostles. He who is within the sanctuary is pure; he who is outside is not pure; that is, he who acts independently of bishop and presbytery and deacons. Such a man is not pure m his conscience."[22]

The always-present danger of schism is likewise emphasized in St. Ignatius' letter to the *Philadelphians:* "All who belong to God and Jesus Christ are with the bishop; and all who repent [that is, of schism] and who come into the unity of the Church will also belong to God ... If anyone follows a man who causes a schism, he 'does not inherit the Kingdom of God.'"[23]

Unity, based on the love and service which Christ exemplifies in the Eucharistic assembly, is a constant Ignatian theme. Again in the

---

[20] *Ibid.*, pp. 43–44.

[21] *To the Trallians, 2* and 3; *ibid.*, p. 44.

[22] *Ibid.*, p. 44.

[23] *Letter to the Philadelphians,* 3; *ibid.*, p. 47.

letter to the Philadelphians the Saint links bishop, presbyters and deacons to and within the common celebration of one Eucharist, which he clearly perceives to be the center of the Church's unity: "Take great care to keep one Eucharist (among you), for there is one flesh of the Lord Jesus Christ and one cup to unite us by His blood. There is one sanctuary, as there is one bishop, together with the presbytery and the deacons, my fellow servants, that all of our acts may be done accordingly, to God's will."[24]

In the letter to the *Smyrneans,* he emphasizes three points: the importance for God's people to submit to the ministry of the Christian priesthood, if the unity of the Church is to be preserved; the right acceptance of the archpastoral authority of the Bishop; and the fact of the Bishop's delegation of his authority to celebrate a valid Eucharist to those whom he has appointed that responsibility, namely the Presbyters:

"Shun divisions, as (they are) the beginning of evils. All of you follow the bishop as Jesus Christ followed the Father and (follow) the presbytery as the Apostles. Respect the deacons as the ordinance of God. Let no one do anything that pertains to the Church apart from the bishop. Let that be considered a valid Eucharist which is under the bishop or one whom he has delegated. Whenever the bishop shall appear, there let the people be, just as wherever Christ Jesus is there is the Catholic Church. It is not permitted to baptize or hold a love-feast (the Eucharist) independently of the Bishop. But whatever he approves, that is also well-pleasing to God; (in order) that all your acts may be sure and valid."[25]

In evaluating these strong assertions by St. Ignatius, one of the foremost Fathers of the post-Apostolic Church, we agree with Brown that he uses the respect due the Bishop as a strong weapon "against disunity and budding heresy." Also, we should notice the context in which the Saint was speaking: "... Ignatius was speaking to small lo-

[24] *Ibid.,* 4, p. 47.

[25] *Letter to the Smyrnaeans* 8; *ibid;* p. 49.

cal churches; we may compare the Ignatian bishop and presbyters to a modern-day pastor and curates in a one-parish town. Authority exercised in such a small area had a good chance of being humanized by intimacy and friendship.

In the words of R. Brown: "Within the institutional framework of the later Church, when the bishop ruled a greater area and (the prevailing) social customs rendered him more remote from his people, the type of emphasis that Ignatius put on episcopal authority would easily lead to (the abuses of) a hierarchical absolutism. As a corrective to this development, we recall that the various antecedents of the historical priesthood are capable of nullifying each other. Precisely because the priesthood is heir to the role of the Presbyter-bishop, there is a place in the priesthood for a hierarchy of authority. But because the priesthood is heir to the role of the disciple of Jesus, all authority must be modified by the ideal that one disciple is not to lord it over another or seek the first place in the manner of worldly institutions. This modification of authority was recognized already in New Testament times in the very history of the presbyterate-episcopate, for the author of I Peter 5:1–3 instituted that the presbyters had the duty of overseeing (*i.e.*, being Bishops over) the flock, but he warned them that this gave them no right to be domineering."[26] One more significant development in the history of the presbyterate-episcopate is to be found in the *Apostolic Tradition* of Hippolytus of Rome. A clergyman of the Roman Church, Hippolytus wrote this work *c.* 215 AD. However, according to Gregory Dix, the *Apostolic Tradition* actually reflects the situation within the Roman community in the years following 180 AD.[27]

According to Hippolytus' account, the bishop is ordained after "he has been chosen by all the people. When he has been named and shall please all, let him, with the presbytery and such bishops as may

[26] R. Brown, *op. cit.*, pp. 39–40.

[27] Gregory Dix, *The Ministry in the Early Church, c.* AD 90-410, translated in French under the title *Le Ministère dans l'Eglise Ancienne,* (Delachaux et Niestle, Neuchâtel-Paris, 1955), pp. 25–26.

be present, assemble with the people on a Sunday. When all give their consent, the bishops shall lay their hands upon him, and the presbytery shall stand in silence. All indeed shall keep silent, praying in their heart for the descent of the Spirit. Then one of the bishops who are present shall, at the request of all, lay his hand on him who is ordained bishop, and shall pray as follows, saying…"[28] There follows the prayer of consecration, in which the bishop is described as having the priesthood in continuity with the Old Testament priesthood, but likewise in continuity with the royal authority pertaining to princes and priestly authorities.

A "royal spirit" (*principalis spiritus, pneuma hegemonikon*) is given to the bishop, that same Spirit which was bestowed upon Jesus Christ by the Father and that he in turn "bestowed on His holy Apostles." The responsibility of the Bishop is seen as that of: (1) feeding the flock of Christ; (2) serving as "high priest without blame, ministering night and day"; (3) propitiating God's countenance "without ceasing," offering Him the gifts of His holy Church.

"By the spirit of high-priesthood," the Bishop has the "authority to remit sins according to God's commandment"; "to sign the lots" according to God's precept; "to loose every bond according to the authority" that God gave to the Apostles; and to please God "in meekness and purity of heart," all the while offering to God "an odor of sweet savor."[29] Outside the consecratory prayer, the Bishop is described in the *Apostolic Tradition* as "the One who presides over the Eucharist" (*proestos*), the one who confers the Chrismation (confirmation), the only one who has the right to ordain, and the visitor of the sick.[30]

The Presbyter is ordained by the Bishop. The Bishop lays hands upon the Presbyter's head, "while the Presbyters touch him." The presbyteral prayer of ordination asks God to grant to the Presbyter "the

[28] Hippolytus of Rome, *The Apostolic Tradition,* trans. Burton Scott Easton (Archon Books, Ann Arbor, 1962), p. 33.

[29] *Ibid.*, p. 34. See also G. Dix, *op. cit.*, pp. 32–36.

[30] *Ibid.*, pp. 36–37, 38, 47–48, 52–53.

Spirit of grace and the counsel of a true Presbyter, that he may sustain and govern God's people with a pure heart." The Presbyter, however, is not given the "royal spirit" or the "spirit of high-priesthood" which was given to the Bishop. His, rather, is the "spirit of grace and counsel," for he has the responsibility to counsel the Bishop and to help the Bishop in the administration of the Church (*ut adiuvet et gubernet*).

Allusion is made to Moses, who laid hands on the "presbyters" (elders), in order that the Spirit of God which had been imparted to him might be imparted to those whom he chose to govern God's people. In the same manner, the Christian Presbyter receives the Spirit by the laying-on of hands, making him worthy of his office, so that he may minister "in simplicity of heart," praising God.[31]

Outside the ordination prayer, the *Apostolic Tradition* describes the Presbyter as a liturgist as well, concelebrating the Eucharist along with the Bishop, or celebrating in his stead, and celebrating the sacrament of baptism.[32]

It is important to recognize the difference between a Deacon and a Presbyter, for this also reflects on the relation between the Presbyter and the Bishop. According to the ordination prayer, the Deacon does two things: first, he ministers to the material needs of the flock under the guidance of the Bishop, after he receives from the Bishop the "Holy Spirit of grace and care and diligence"; and, second, he offers to the Bishop the gifts of God's people which are offered to God and consecrated during the holy Eucharist.[33]

In the canonical note that precedes this prayer of diaconal ordination, the following statement differentiates between Presbyter and Deacon:

> "But the deacon when he is ordained, is chosen according to those things that were said above, the bishop alone in like manner laying his hands upon him, as we have prescribed. When the

[31] *Ibid.*, pp. 37–38.
[32] *Ibid.*, pp. 45–47, 49.
[33] *Ibid.*, pp. 38–39.

> deacon is ordained, this is the reason why the bishop alone shall lay his hands upon him: he is not ordained to the priesthood but to serve the bishop and to carry out the bishop's commands. He does not take part in the council of the clergy; he is to attend to his own duties and to make known to the bishop such things as are needful. He does not receive that Spirit that is possessed by the presbytery, in which the presbyters share; he receives only what is confided to him under the bishop's authority. For this cause the bishop alone shall make a deacon. But on a presbyter, however, the presbyters shall lay their hands because of the common and like Spirit of the clergy. Yet the presbyter has only the power to receive; but he has no power to give. For this reason a presbyter does not ordain the clergy; but at the ordination of a presbyter he seals while the bishop ordains."[34]

And, in conclusion, Hippolytus also makes here a clear-cut distinction between the Presbyter and the Bishop. The Bishop is the chief administrator and the chief celebrant of the sacraments (*mysteria*). The Presbyter — particularly in the time of Hippolytus — shares in the administration of the Church and is counselor to the Bishop, along with his fellow presbyters (a "presbyterium," meaning council of presbyters). Always under the authority and in the place of the Bishop, he also celebrates the sacraments of Baptism and the Eucharist. According to the *Apostolic Tradition*, the Presbyter very clearly has only the "power to receive" authority at the hands of the Bishop, and therefore he is unable to ordain, for "he has no power to give" outside of the Bishop's delegation.

3 The Canonical Tradition and the Liturgy of the Church. Reflecting the above described practice and teaching of the early Church, *Apostolic Canon* 39 says: "Let Presbyters and Deacons do nothing without the consent of the Bishop. For he is the

[34] *Ibid.*, p. 38. See also Gregory Dix, *op. cit.*, pp. 55–66.

one entrusted with the Lord's people, and it is from him that an accounting will be demanded with respect to their souls."[35]

This canon takes the spirit of the Ignatian letters one step further with regard to the Bishop's position and authority. It implies that the presbyters and deacons are accountable solely to the Bishop, whereas the Bishop is solely accountable to God, and thus it moves strongly in the direction of a monarchical episcopate and an episcopal absolutism.

Still, the above canon is neither an isolated case nor an aberration in the life of the Church. Canons 14 of the 7th Ecumenical Council; 57 of Laodicea; and 6, 7, 41 and 50 of Carthage, all corroborate the doctrine found in Apostolic Canon 39.

For example, canon 57 of Laodicea states "that in villages and small towns and country districts, Bishops are not to be appointed, but circuitors *(periodeutes),* who, however, having been pre-appointed, may do nothing without the consent and approval of the Bishop."[36] *Periodeutes*, circuitors, is the same as *chorepiscopos*, country, or auxiliary, bishop. By this time, the anomaly of the so-called auxiliary bishop was being created so that the ruling bishop might be able to serve the wider needs of his expanding diocese, most specifically as it relates to geographical growth. Auxiliary, or country, bishops as described in this canon were for all practical purposes no more than glorified presbyters with extra duties.

The early 5th century Council of Carthage compiled a lengthy series of canons—close to 150 in number—in relation to and resulting from the extremely prolific canonical legislation emanating from the African churches. Among these canons, numbers 6, 7, 41 and 50 refer to the issue of the relationship and relative positions of Bishop and Presbyter:

a) *Canon 6* stipulates: "The application of Chrism and the consecration of virgin girls shall not be done by Presbyters; nor shall it

[35] St. Nicodemos and Agapios, *The Rudder*, trans. D. Cummings (The Orthodox Christian Educational Society, Chicago, 1957). p. 59.

[36] *Ibid.*, p. 574.

be permissible for a Presbyter to reconcile anyone at a public liturgy. This is the decision of all of us the African bishops.[37] St. Nicodemos of Mt. Athos[38] interprets this canon actually to mean that a parish Presbyter may not: 1) prepare and consecrate the holy Chrism (*myron*); 2) consecrate nuns; or 3) publicly absolve those serious sins which involve excommunication. All these are the prerogatives of the Bishop alone according to the historic Churches of East and West. "By the permission of the Bishop," however, "even a Presbyter can reconcile penitents," St. Nicodemos pointed out. Also see *Apostolic* Canon 39 and Canon 19 of the 1st Ecumenical Council.[39]

b) *Canon 7* states that: "If anybody is in danger and demands to have recourse to the sacred Altar for reconciliation when the Bishop is absent, the Presbyter naturally ought to ask the Bishop, and then allow the one in danger to have recourse thereto, in accordance with the Bishop's orders."[40] This canon is in continuity with and expands upon the preceding one, in that the Presbyter is given permission to forgive sins *in extremis*, but always in behalf of, in the stead of and with permission from his Bishop.

c) *Canon 41* says: "It has pleased the Council to decree that Presbyters shall not sell any property of the Church in which they were ordained if it be without the consent and approval of their own Bishop: in like manner as it is not permissible for Bishops to sell any lands of the Church without the knowledge of the Synod or of their own Presbyters. There being therefore no need or necessity, neither is it permissible for a Bishop to misappropriate or embezzle anything out of the funds, or title, of the ecclesiastical treasury, or matrix."[41]

[37] *Ibid.*, p. 608.

[38] The interpretation given to the number one prohibition by St. Nicodemos, is not completely accurate: the priest, according to the Western tradition represented by the council of Carthage, is not allowed to celebrate or "apply" the holy chrismation (or confirmation). According to the Western tradition, this is also one of the exclusive privileges of the Bishop.

[39] *Ibid.*, p. 608.

[40] *Ibid.*, p. 609.

[41] *Ibid.*, p. 629.

For a change, the canon is even-handed in correcting financial discrepancies; not only can the Presbyter, or anyone else, according to other canons of the same and other councils, not dispose of church property, but neither can the Bishop do as much without the consent of the Synod of Bishops or even the Council of his own Presbyters. A warning is also given to Bishops who misappropriate or embezzle church funds or property.

d) Finally, canon 30 states: "It is decreed that penances be fixed in respect to time by judgment of Bishops in accordance with the difference in sinful deeds. But no Presbyter may release a penitent from his penance without the consent and approval of the Bishop, except if necessity drive him to do so in the absence of the Bishop. As for any penitent whose offense is public knowledge and noised about, as one agitating the whole Church, let the (Bishop's) hand be laid upon him before the apse."[42]

The canon is related to canons 6 and 7, with more specifications regarding both the condition of the sinner and the episcopal absolution of his (her) known public sin. In the case of such a public sinner, the immediate attention of the Bishop is required. The Presbyter has no authority to reconcile this public sinner with the Church, except in the absence of the Bishop, and — it is understood — in the stead and on behalf of the Bishop. On this basis, one can understand the development of the Western tradition regarding reserved sins, that can only be absolved by the Holy See.

In spite of the Western flavor of some of these canons, they also witness to a constant development in the life of the Church, clearly distinguishing between the role, position and authority of the parish Presbyter relative to the Bishop. This position becomes clearly subordinate and derivative, in continuity with St Ignatius' monarchical episcopate.

One more, of the many other canons, will be considered in the context of the question we discuss. It is *Canon 14 of* the 7th Ecumenical Council (787). The canon reads: "It is perfectly plain to everybody

[42] *Ibid.*, p. 633.

that order reigns in the Church, and that it is pleasing to God for the transactions of the Priesthood to be maintained with rigorousness. Since, then, we behold some persons receiving the tonsure of the Clergy from infancy and without imposition of hands, and reading from the pulpit at the *synaxis,* but doing so in an uncanonical fashion, we forbid the doing of this from now on. The same rule is to be observed also with reference to monks. As for the appointment of an Anagnost, or Reader, by imposition of hands, each abbot is given permission to do this but only in his own monastery, provided that hands have been laid upon that very same abbot himself by a Bishop to enable him to have the presidency of an Abbot—that is to say, more plainly speaking, if he is a Presbyter or Priest. Likewise also in accordance with the ancient custom, auxiliary Bishops may only with the permission of the Bishop appoint Anagnosts, with imposition of hands.[43] What this canon makes clear is that any ordination, whether to the so-called major or minor orders, in which the tradition of the Church includes the Readers (Anagnosts), is the sole privilege and responsibility of the Bishop. If there is an exception to be made, the Bishop will allow an Abbot that he has appointed to ordain Readers for his own, and only in the confines of his own, monastery. This can be done, provided that the Abbot is a Presbyter himself. Auxiliary Bishops (*chorepiscopoi*) fall in this same category, being under the absolute authority of the ruling Bishop, and thus allowed, with permission, to appoint Anagnosts with the laying-on of hands.

The Liturgy of the Church is in continuity with what we find especially in the *Apostolic Tradition* of Hippolytus. The continuity is more direct in the Western Church, where similar expressions with the consecratory prayer of a Bishop are found in the Tradition and the contemporary Roman Liturgy. The prayer in today's Roman Liturgy is simplified and readjusted; however, in essence it is identical with that of the *Apostolic Tradition.*[44]

[43] *Ibid.*, p. 443.

[44] See episcopal consecration rites in today's Roman Church: Cardinal: Father of our Lord Jesus Christ, merciful God, bringing comfort to all, from your heaven-

Reference is made to the Old Testament Priesthood, and to its continuation in the Church. An invocation of the Holy Spirit follows, calling upon the Spirit — whom God gave to His beloved Son and whom He gave to the Apostles — to come and consecrate the new Bishop. His duties are delineated as in the Apostolic Tradition: feed the flock, reconcile with God, offer the Holy Eucharist, and forgive sins.

Finally, in the liturgy of the Eastern Orthodox Church, the ordination prayers of the three orders also reflect the tradition of the early Church:

a) The new Bishop is elected by a council of Bishops, who give their consent for his ordination. The Bishop is elected for a given church, to be in the tradition with the "ordinance of degrees and ranks unto the service and divine celebration of the august and all-spotless Mysteries upon the Holy Altar," established by the "all-laud-

---

ly home you look with care on the lowest of your creatures, knowing all things even before they come to be. Your life-giving revelation has laid down rules for your Church, the just people of Abraham upon whom you had set your mark from the beginning. In that Church you have established a government and priesthood, so as not to leave your sanctuary without its liturgy; and from the beginning of the world it has pleased you to be glorified by the ministries that you have chosen.

The following part of the prayer is recited by all the consecrating Bishops, their hands joined:

Now pour out upon these chosen ones that power which flows from you, the perfect Spirit whom you gave to your beloved Son, Jesus Christ, the Spirit whom he gave to the apostles, who established the Church in every place as the sanctuary where your name would always be praised and glorified.

Cardinal: Father, you know what is in every heart. Inspire the heart of your servants whom you have chosen to make bishops. May they feed your holy flock and exercise the high priesthood without blame, ministering to you day and night to reconcile us with you and to offer gifts of your Church. By the Spirit of this priesthood may they have the power to forgive sins, as you commanded. May they assign the duties of the flock according to your will and loose every bond by the power you gave the apostles. May their gentleness and singleness of purpose stand before you as an offering through your Son Jesus Christ. Through him glory and power and honor are yours with the Holy Spirit in the Church, now and for ever. See *The Rites of the Catholic Church,* Vol. 11 (Pueblo Publishing Co., New York, 1979), pp. 94–96.

able Apostle Paul." These "degrees and ranks" are those of "Apostles, Prophets, and Teachers." The Bishop receives the Spirit, through the laying-on of the hands, in order for him to be in continuity with the "anointed Kings and consecrated Bishops." The Bishop is made worthy to pray for the salvation of his flock, and exercise his office "without stain or blame" (Petitions). In the second part of the consecratory prayer, the Bishop is described as the teacher of his flock, the one who offers "sacrifice and oblations for all the people" of God (Eucharist) and the good shepherd who gives up his life for the sake of the flock. He is a leader of the blind, a lamp in the darkness, a teacher of the young, and a reprover of the unwise. His staff is given to him for two purposes: to be "a staff of support unto those who are obedient," and "unto correction, gentleness and unto obedience" of the "disobedient and the wayward; and they shall continue in due submission."[45]

b) The ordination prayer of the Presbyter is much more simple. After the invocation of the Holy Spirit and laying-on of hands, the Bishop prays for the new Presbyter whom God deemed "worthy to serve the word of His truth in the Divine ministry of this degree." God is asked to "be favorably pleased to grant unto him the great grace of Thy Holy Spirit, and make him wholly Thy servant, in all things acceptable unto Thee, and worthily exercising the great honours of the priesthood which Thou has conferred upon him by Thy prescient power."

In the second prayer, more concrete reference is made to the gifts of the Holy Spirit to the new Presbyter, in order for him to: 1) worthily stand in innocence before God's holy Altar; 2) proclaim the Gospel of God's Kingdom; 3) minister the Word of God's truth; 4) offer to God spiritual gifts and sacrifices, and 5) renew God's people through the laver of regeneration. Overall, the Presbyter/priest is expected to be a good steward and to «receive the reward of a good Steward in the degree committed unto him, through the plenitude of (God's)

[45] See I. F. Hapgood, *Service Book of the Holy Orthodox-Catholic Apostolic Church* (Syrian Antiochian Orthodox Archdiocese, Brooklyn, (1965), pp. 329–31.

goodness."[46] Then, as the Bishop hands down to him the Holy Eucharist, he says: "Receive this (Holy Eucharist) which is handed down unto thee, and preserve it until the coming again of our Lord Jesus Christ; for at that time so will He demand it of thee."[47]

c) At the Deacon's ordination, the first prayer speaks of two diaconal responsibilities, consonant with the *Apostolic Tradition* account: 1) service to the Church in general, and 2) helping in the administration of God's "spotless Sacraments." The Deacon's calling in ministry is essentially that of St Stephen, the first Deacon and Martyr. Make the ordainee worthy, the Bishop prays, of the degree of ministry "which it has seemed good to God to confer upon him. For they who minister well prepare for themselves a goodly degree." God is asked to prove the new Deacon to be "wholly His servant." The following prayers extol especially the responsibility of service, quoting the Lord: "Whoever wants to be first among you, let him be your servant" (Matt. 20:26).[48]

One can readily discern the continuity in the Church's tradition, as it is expressed in the liturgical texts of both East and West. The Bishop, in essence, has full administrative, teaching and liturgical authority and responsibility, in which—according to their respective orders—both the Presbyter and the Deacon participate. In the current liturgy of the East, the Presbyter is depicted as sharing primarily in the Bishop's teaching and liturgical responsibility, while it is the Deacon who is charged with assisting the Bishop administratively.

4 **Ecclesiological Principles.** Some of the ecclesiological principles that underline the issue of distinctiveness and interrelatedness of the office of the Bishop and Presbyter are the following: a) the ministries of the Bishop and Presbyter are the ministries of the Church, having their origin in Christ; 2) these ministries are of apostolic origin and succession, and 3) the Church is fully present in each

[46] *Ibid.*, p. 317.

[47] See original Greek in *Archieratikon* (Apostoliki Diakonia, Athens, 1971), p. 86.

[48] Hapgood, *op. cit.*, p. 313.

one of the local communities, as it is present throughout the world. On the basis of these considerations we will discuss the ministries of Bishop and Presbyter as relating to the Church and its mission in the world.

A) ***Ministries of the Church.*** In my estimation, K. H. Schelkle is right when he states that, "the New Testament taught and practiced the universal priesthood of the Church. The fathers still know about and speak of this priestly dignity of the whole Church. Although in their teaching and activity they build up the ecclesiastical hierarchy, they nevertheless stressed the unity of the Church in the class distinction of priests and laity. In a letter St. Cyprian, Bishop of Carthage, wrote (66, 8; *cf.* 33, I): "The Bishop is in the Church and the Church in the Bishop. The Bishop is not the Church but he represents it, just as the people are represent in the Bishop."[49] Schelkle quotes St. Augustine, saying that the power of forgiving sins is given to the entire Church, clergy and laity together; and St. John Chrysostom, who says: "The Eucharist is common to all. It is not only celebrated by the priest but by the people together with him, for he begins only after the faithful have given him their consent by proclaiming it is right and fitting..."' (*Homily on 2 Cor* 18:3; PG 61, col. 527). Schelkle concludes: "The Fathers were therefore convinced that the whole Church mediates grace, the whole Church remits sins, sanctifies, conveys life in truth. Throughout antiquity and in the Middle Ages there is evidence that the sacraments are not only dispensed by the ecclesiastical officials, but involve the intercession of the whole Church in the sacramental action."[50]

BEM is aware of this principle, that ministries in the Church are the ministries of the *entire* Church; for its section on Ministry begins with "the Calling of the Whole People of God," being a calling to carry out the mission of Christ and the Church. Consequently, *BEM* discusses the "ordained ministry" in the ecclesiological context, indicat-

[49] K. H. Schelkle, *op. cit.*, p. 10.
[50] *Ibid.*, p. 10.

ing that the following are the "guiding principles for the exercise of the ordained ministry in the Church": The "ordained ministry should be exercised in a personal, collegial and communal way." BEM explains what is meant by each of these aspects of Christian ministry: "It should be *personal* because the presence of Christ among his people can most effectively be pointed to by the person ordained to proclaim the Gospel and to call the community to serve the Lord in unity of life and witness. It should also be *collegial,* for there is need for a college of ordained ministers sharing in the common task of representing the concerns of the community. Finally, the intimate relationship between the ordained ministry and the community should find expression in a *communal* dimension where the exercise of the ordained ministry is rooted in the life of the community and requires the community's effective participation in the discovery of God's will and the guidance of the Spirit."[51] Each of these three aspects should be kept together, for each of them is an integral part of Christian ministry.

B) *Apostolic Origin and Succession.* The ministries in the Church are all of Apostolic origin and succession or at least they should be. R. Brown is right in tracing the succession of ministries from the Apostles to the Bishops of St. Ignatius at the beginning of the 2nd century.

Brown asks the question: "Are the Bishops successors of the Apostles?" His answer is negative, if by "succession" we understand an "uninterrupted chain of ordinations" going back to the Apostles. Brown distinguishes between the Lucan picture of the Twelve Apostles and the Pauline picture of missionary Apostles. According to the Lucan picture, the twelve Apostles — with the exception of one or two, particularly Peter — are not real "apostles," *i.e.* "missionaries, nor are they local church leaders, nor men who ordained others or passed on powers to them." To the contrary, "in Luke's description … the Twelve emerge as a type of Council, presiding over the multitude when meetings are called affecting the destiny of Christianity."[52]

[51] *BEM*, pp. 20–21, 25–26.

[52] R. Brown, *op. cit.*, pp. 55–59.

For St. Luke, the Twelve Apostles "were the Apostles *par excellence* because they were Jesus' chosen companions during his ministry." According to this criterion, St. Paul could not be an Apostle. However, another criterion for Apostleship, according to the same St. Luke, is to be an eyewitness of the Resurrection of Christ. St. Paul was an Apostle according to this criterion, for he saw the Risen Lord on his way to Damascus (Acts 9:3–6). Conscious of his Apostleship, St. Paul develops his own criteria of true apostleship, like his own: a) to see the Risen Lord and be called by Him; b) to be sent on a mission to the Gentiles; and c) in one's own life to imitate the death and resurrection of the Lord.

According to the Lucan picture of apostleship, the Bishops cannot be successors of the Apostles except in a remote way: they are not companions of Christ, nor witnesses of His Resurrection. It is not clear if the Twelve ordained more than the seven deacons (Acts 6: 6). Neither are the Bishops successors to the Pauline type of an Apostle. However, they succeed to Saint Paul's ministry, for it was his practice to appoint local leaders to the communities he was establishing.[53] Brown concludes as follows:

> And so the affirmation that all the bishops of the early Christian Church could trace their appointments or ordinations to the apostles is simply without proof—it is impossible to trace with assurance any of the presbyter-bishops to the Twelve and it is impossible to trace only some of them to apostles like Paul. The affirmation that the episcopate was divinely established by Christ himself can be defended in the nuanced sense that the episcopate gradually emerged in a Church that stemmed from Christ and that this emergence was (in the eyes of faith) guided by the Holy Spirit. Personally, I do not think that tracing the appearance of the episcopate more directly to the Holy Spirit than to the historical Jesus takes away any dignity from bishops;

[53] *Ibid.*, pp. 59–72.

> and I suggest that, upon reflection, these conclusions will be scandalous chiefly to those who have never understood the real import of our oft-repeated boast that Christianity is a historical religion.[54]

Even though it is difficult to establish a linear succession to the Apostles, in the way suggested by St. Clement of Rome, there is no difficulty in seeing "Apostolic succession" in the light of "Apostolic tradition," *i.e.* as a succession that can be called "functional"[55] and "sacramental," of the Ignatian type.[56]

Apostolic succession involves the entire Christian community as an "Apostolic community," keeping the apostolic doctrine and life, continuing the Apostolic ministry, giving the Apostolic witness to the world. Historical continuity with Christ and His Apostles through ordination is only one of the elements of this succession, and it is to

---

[54] *Ibid.*. p. 73.

[55] *Ibid.*, pp. 73–81. After discussing the various aspects of "functional" apostolic succession, whether of the Twelve or the Pauline type, as found in the Presbyters/Bishops of the NT and the immediate post-NT era, R. Brown concludes: "Many other aspects of functional succession to the apostles could be discussed, but the few instances mentioned exemplify well the conflicts caused by the fact that local bishops have been made heirs to the quite diverse activities of the Lucan and Pauline types of apostles. Perhaps as a result of a better historical understanding of why there are difficulties, Catholics shall be able to modify an often too simplistic concept of the bishops as successors of the apostles and in so doing enable the bishops to serve more effectively and realistically as the formal representatives of an apostolic succession that must be shared more broadly" (*ibid,* p. 81).

[56] *BEM* (p. 29) makes the following statement concerning the two kinds of "successions":

> "In the early Church the bond between the episcopate and the apostolic community was understood in two ways. Clement of Rome linked the mission of the bishop with the sending of Christ by the Father and the sending of the apostles by Christ (Cor 42:44). This made the bishop a successor of the apostles, ensuring the permanence of the apostolic mission in the Church. Clement is primarily interested in the means whereby the historical continuity of Christ's presence is en-

be understood in the context of the others. We can certainly rejoice to see that BEM sees "apostolic succession" in this light.[57]

c) ***Where Is the Church?*** The Christian ministry — a ministry of the Church, in the Church and for the Church — continues to be exercised throughout the ages and up to our days in continuity with the Apostolic Community. Now, where is that Church in which this ministry is to be exercised?

The question is not out of place, for reputable theologians are discussing whether the Church that Christ founded is to be fully and completely found at the local or at the universal level.

The well-known Eucharistic ecclesiology, with the late Fr. Nicholas Afanasieff as the main exponents wants the Church to be found fully at the local level, where the Eucharist is celebrated. The Church of God is fully present in any of the local communities where one finds all the elements of apostolicity, including "apostolic succession" in the narrow sense, thus guaranteeing continuity with the Apostolic Community. "One plus one is still one in ecclesiology," Fr. Afanasieff said.[58] This ecclesiology I sured in the Church thanks to the apostolic succession. For Ignatius of Antioch (*Magn* 6:1, 3:1–2; *Trall* 3:1), it is Christ surrounded by the Twelve who is permanently in the Church in the person of the bishop surrounded by the presbyters. Ignatius regards the Christian Community assembled around the bishop in the midst of presbyters and deacons as the actual manifestation in the Spirit of apostolic community. The sign of apostolic succession thus not only points to historical continuity; it also manifests an actual spiritual reality." (Commentary 36) would normally exclude the idea of a primacy of one church in a group of churches, for each one of the churches is the complete Church, thus independent from the others.

The so-called universal ecclesiology, of a Roman type, would allow this primacy to exist, for the various local churches around the world exist in interdependence with one another. The late Fr. Alexan-

[57] *BEM*, pp. 28–30.

[58] N. Afanasieff, "The Church which Presides in Love," in *The Primacy of Peter* (The Faith Press, London, 1963), p. 75.

der Schmemann showed the need for such an inter-dependence and the need for an Orthodox primacy, even if this primacy is seen not as a primacy of power, but as a priority among the other churches, a primacy of authority and a primacy of service.[59]

Thus, to the question “where is the Church?”, the answer is that *the* Church is fully present in each local community where the Eucharist is celebrated; but it is also present throughout the world, for the local communities exist in interdependence.

The next question is: where is the local Church, that fully manifests the Church of Christ? This question may also be debated. According to some, this local Church is the Diocese; according to others, this Church is the local parish. There are arguments that go both ways. Let us review these arguments:

Those who believe that the local Church is the parish believe so because there the liturgy is duly celebrated. This indicates that all the ecclesial values needed for this celebration at the parish level exist. One can touch upon the Holy Kingdom of God breaking through during that Eucharistic celebration. The parish is the workshop of God’s Holy Kingdom, of which the Church is the inauguration. The argument from the early tradition of the Church that the Presbyters/Bishops were presiding over the Eucharist of the local community, that community being the equivalent of today’s parish, is certainly a very strong one that favors this position.

To the argument that the Bishop is needed for the Eucharistic celebration and that the Bishop is absent at the parish level, the supporters of the parish as the local church respond by saying that the Bishop is actually present, through his throne (or *Synthronon),* which indicates the dependence of the parish upon him; through the *antimension* that the Bishop consecrates and which becomes the link between the priest and the Bishop during the celebration of the Eucharist; through the commemorations of the Bishop’s name at the

[59] A. Schmemann, “The Idea of Primacy in Orthodox Ecclesiology,” in *The Primacy of Peter,* pp. 30–56.

Liturgy; and finally through the parish Presbyter, who is the representative and the Bishop's real presence at the parish, especially at the Liturgical celebration.

Others may argue that the local Church is the diocese. For it is only at the diocesan level that the fullness of "ecclesial values" exists, including the presence of the Bishop and of the fullness of priesthood. Only the Bishop can celebrate all the sacraments and provide for the needs of the local communities. The local parishes cannot exist independently, for they cannot be self-sufficient. They cannot provide themselves everything that is needed for them to be fully the Church of Christ without the Diocese.

In my estimation, these apparently competing positions can be readily reconciled. It is true that the full Church of Christ exists where the episcopal office exists, *i.e.* at the Diocesan level. It is true that the parishes need the diocese, to take them out of their isolation and lead them to interdependence with a greater family of Churches. It is true that "parochialism" is the danger of parishes that feel self-sufficient and become separatists. But at the same time the Diocese cannot exist *in abstracto,* or at the Diocesan headquarters only. The Diocese is present in each one and all of the parishes which constitute it, for the Bishop is present fully in each one and in all of the Presbyters who represent him at the parish level, especially in the Eucharistic celebration and communion.

In conclusion, today *the local Church is the Diocese, which is manifested in each one and all of its parish communities, constituting the Church "in that place."*

5 **Inter-Relatedness, Interdependence, and Distinctiveness of the Episcopal and Presbyteral Office.** As the Parish and the Diocese constitute the one and only local Church, so the Bishop and the Presbyter constitute the one priestly office established by Christ in His Church. To quote the joint statement *On the Pastoral Office* of the Orthodox-Roman Catholic Consultation/ USA (ORC/USA): "In accord with the development whereby the

presbyterate is explicitly included in the pastoral office of the bishop under virtually all aspects, the presbyter is viewed as having the same relationship to Christ as the bishop. Both are seen directly to represent Christ before the community and, at the same time, to represent the church, as confessing believers, in their official acts."[60]

The two offices are inter-related and interdependent, for both of them depend on Christ whom they represent and manifest to the community. They are also distinct from one another, the same way the Parish and Diocese are distinct. Let us once more quote the *Pastoral Statement*:

> The offices of bishop and presbyter are different realizations of the sacrament of order. The different rites for ordination of bishop and presbyter show that a sacramental conferral of office takes place by the laying on of hands with the ordination prayer which expresses the particular significance of each office.

While both bishop and presbyter share the one ministry of Christ, the bishop exercises authoritative leadership over the whole community. The presbyter shares in the pastoral office under the bishop.[61]

As we have seen, historically, "the bishop gradually emerges everywhere as the center of unity of his own local church and the visible point of contact with other local churches. He is responsible for faith and order locally.[62] On the other hand, also historically speaking, and following the developments stated above, "the presbyterate comes to share in the exercise of more aspects of the pastoral office in subordination to the Bishop. This subordinate role is seen especially in presbyteral ordination, which is reserved to bishops.[63] Presbyters and Bishops share together and according to their own degree in a min-

[60] "The Pastoral office: a Joint Statement," in *Toward Reunion,* ed. by Edward Kilmartin (Paulist Press, New York, 1979), p. 81.
[61] *Ibid.*, p. 82.
[62] *Ibid.*, pp. 80–81.
[63] *Ibid.*, p. 81.

istry which is personal, i.e. distinctive, unique and incommunicable, but also collegial and communal. To quote *BEM*:

> The ordained ministry needs to be constitutionally or canonically ordered and exercised in the Church in such a way that each of these three dimensions can find adequate expression. At the level of the local eucharistic community there is need for an ordained minister acting within a collegial body. Strong emphasis should be placed on the active participation of all members in the life and the decision-making of the community. At the regional level there is again need for an ordained minister exercising a service of unity. The collegial and communal dimensions will find expression in regular representative synodal gatherings.[64]

At the local eucharistic community, the ordained minister who acts within a collegial body may be the Presbyter acting with his helpers, assistant pastor or parish council. At the regional level the ordained minister exercising a service of unity is certainly the Bishop.

The Bishops, as they exercise their duties to "teach aright the word of Truth," to preside over all the sacraments and administer discipline as prescribed above,[65] depend very much on their Presbyters, in order for the work to be done at the level of the local Church, *i.e.*

---

[64] *BEM*, p. 26.

[65] See Hippolytus, *Apostolic Tradition,* and *Liturgy,* quoted above. Also, cf. BEM, p. 26, number 29:

> "*Bishops* preach the Word, preside at the sacraments, and administer discipline in such a way as to be representative pastoral ministers of oversight, continuity and unity in the Church. They have pastoral oversight of the area to which they are called. They serve the apostolicity and unity of the Church's teaching, worship and sacramental life. They have responsibility for leadership in the Church's mission. They relate the Christian community in their area to the wider Church, and the universal Church to their community. They in communion with the presbyters and deacons and the whole community, are responsible for the orderly transfer of ministerial authority in the Church."

the local parish. They count on their Presbyters for their cooperation in accomplishing the common task, *i.e.* fulfilling the mission of the Church in today's world, in all of its aspects. They count on their Presbyters in terms of both a personal *symbouleia* (counsel) concerning the needs of the local church and the way to meet them, and also in terms of a collective counsel, through the collective wisdom of the Presbyters Council.

On the other hand, the Presbyters as they do the hard work at the grass roots,[66] as they labor day and night to teach, counsel on a one to one basis, visit the sick, bring the sacraments to the shut-ins, celebrate the sacraments, be family men, work for the salvation of their own family and the family at large, which is the local church, they need the support, love and care of their Bishop. They are certainly accountable directly to the Lord from whom they expect their just reward. They may not expect rewards from the Bishop. They certainly expect his love, compassion, understanding, and full support in their everyday hard work in the parish. Just as they pray for him at the Eucharist and in a personal way, so they may expect him to do as much for them and their families.

We have tried to describe the healthy relation between the Parish Presbyter and the Bishop as they exercise their role and responsibility more than authority in the life of the local church. Let us now spend a moment with some problematic situations in our contemporary church life regarding unhealthy relationships between Presbyters and Bishops.

---

[66] See also BEM's description of the role and responsibility of a Presbyter: "*Presbyters* serve as pastoral ministers of Word and Sacraments in a local eucharistic community. They are preachers and teachers of the faith, exercise pastoral care, and bear responsibility for the discipline of the congregation to the end that the world may believe and that the entire membership of the Church may be renewed, strengthened and equipped in ministry. Presbyters have particular responsibility for the preparation of members for Christian life and ministry" (p. 27).

6 **Some Contemporary Problems.** When we speak of contemporary problems, we do not always expect them to be new problems. Some of them are very old, and persist up to our days.

On the side of the Bishop, one of the possible problems may be episcopal absolutism, known as despotism. It is the very problem that the Lord addressed with His disciples, that we quoted at the beginning of this paper. The Bishop may not be a true father to his priests and their families, insensitive to their needs and problems. The Bishop may not always support his priests when they need him. He may at times side with the parish council, and be ultimately unfair to his own close co-worker, who is supposed to be his presence in the parish. These problems have to be solved in the best interest of all involved, if the Bishop wishes to be efficient in doing his work and enabling others to do a better job. There is no reason for despotism, for the form of Church government is participatory, communal, collegial, as it is also personal.

If the Bishop takes his role seriously as a father to his Presbyters and to their families, he will be sensitive to their needs and problems. The Bishop will always be supportive of his priests, always keeping the channels of communication open, giving them not only his counsel, wisdom, and support, but he will also "lay down his life" (Jn. 10:11, 15) for them.

On the side of the parish Presbyter, some of the common illnesses are isolationism, parochial spirit, lack of interest toward his parishioners and especially towards the youth and the young adults, party spirit, undermining of the work of the Bishop and of the Diocese, non-participation in diocesan programs, compromises and alliances with the parish council, lack of courage, lack of cooperation with other colleagues and fellow-Presbyters and with the Bishop, etc.

What is needed to cure the situation is the persistence, love, understanding and compassion of the Bishop, as well as peer pressure from the "college of Presbyters." A good spiritual father who will actually be available to hear the confession of our Presbyters, and who is not necessarily the Bishop, may be of great help to the parish Presbyter. A spiritual center, or a monastery, where the Presbyter may spend some time to rebuild himself and recharge his spiritual batteries may be in order.

Another very common problem is stress. Hopefully our Dioceses will organize themselves in such a way that they may be of service to the entire people of God, beginning with the good workers in the Lord's Vineyard, the parish Presbyters and their families.

7 **Conclusions.** Some brief conclusions come to mind at the end of this "exploration into ministry," focusing on the relative positions, roles and authority of the Bishop and the parish Presbyter:

1) The basic principle is that all ministries in the Church have their origin in the Servant of God, our Lord Jesus Christ, who came not to be served but to serve, and who gave His life as a ransom for many. Presbyter and Bishop alike derive their authority of service from Christ, making it their respective responsibility to imitate His life and ministry of service.

2) In New Testament times, the term "priest" is not applied as such to our Christian priesthood and ministry, because the classical pagan and Jewish temple priests were cultic figures only, and not pastoral. It is only later that the Church accepted the term "priest" (i.e., *hiereus, sacerdos*) for its sacred ministry, arising from a time when the Holy Eucharist was perceived as a "sacrifice" (*thysia*).

3) The antecedents of the Christian priesthood in the New Testament are primarily those of Disciple, Apostle, Presbyter/ Overseer, presidency of the Eucharist, and the Good Shepherd (*poimen, pastor*) ministering to the People of God.

4) During the New Testament times, Bishop/Overseer and Presbyter/Elder are seen to be interchangeable.

5) A development toward distinguishing between the position, role and authority of Bishop and Presbyter occurs immediately after the New Testament era, that is, at the end of the 1st century and the beginning of the 2nd. St. Ignatios of Antioch is an important witness and exponent of this development, so that he is often perceived as the advocate of a "monarchical episcopate."

6) One of the main reasons why St. Ignatios so vigorously advocated such an understanding of the Episcopacy, with the Presbyterate closely intertwined in its support and counsel, was to defend the Faith against heresy and to preserve the Church's unity. This was the same basic rationale for the convening of regional and ecumenical synods (i.e., episcopal councils) in the ensuing years of the Church's history.

7) Another important development is the *Apostolic Tradition,* authored by Hippolytus of Rome between the years 180–217 AD. This document reflects in particular the life of the Roman Church towards the end of the 2nd century, but it basically serves as a source of ecclesiastical life and general norms for the early Church. It speaks of the Bishop as having the "royal spirit of Christ and of the Apostles," whereas the Presbyters have the "spirit of counsel." Nevertheless, it also clearly delineates the Presbyters' participation in the governance of the Church (though always together with and under the Bishop), and the Presbyters' celebration of the Eucharist and Baptism in behalf of the local Bishop.

8) The *canonical tradition* of the Church reflects the Ignatian doctrine concerning Bishops, Presbyters and Deacons. Apostolic Canon 39, along with Canons 57 of Laodicea, 6. 7, 41 and 50 of Carthage (419 AD), and 14 of the 7th Ecumenical Council, mandate that Presbyters do nothing in their ministry without their Bishop.

9) The Church's Liturgy, both in the East and the West, is in fundamental continuity with the doctrine of the *Apostolic Tradition* (Hippolytus). In fact, the Roman Liturgy echoes almost word-for-word the Hippolytan prayer of episcopal consecration. The Orthodox Byzantine Liturgy is very much parallel to it. Both affirm that the Bishop has from God the fullness of authority and responsibility for teaching the truth, celebrating the Eucharist and Sacraments, and administering the life of the Church. The Presbyter shares in certain of these responsibilities of the Bishop.

10) The ecclesiological principles which underlie the relative roles and responsibilities of Presbyter and Bishop are: (a) all ministries, including those of the Presbyter/Bishop, are the ministries of

the Church; (b) all ministries are Apostolic in origin and denote a real, not merely a "tactile," Apostolic succession; (c) the Church of God is both Parish and Diocese. The Bishop shares with the Presbyter (parish priest) the same pastoral office, manifesting the same Lord, with whom both the Bishop and the Presbyter have a personal relationship and responsibility together in ministry. Nevertheless, on the basis of the distinction between Parish and Diocese, the Presbyterate and Episcopate are also distinct.

11) Their relationship is interdependent. The Bishop exercises leadership over the community, whereas the Presbyter — with and under the Bishop — shares in the governance and administration of the Church. The Bishop depends on the Presbyters for an effective ministry of the local church, and he needs the counsel and support of the Presbyters, both on a personal and on a collegial level.

CHAPTER SEVEN

Georges Florovsky (1893–1979)

Georges Florovsky was born and raised in Odessa, the son of a priest. Florovsky's theological career took him to Paris in 1925, where he was professor of Church History. He was ordained to the priesthood in 1932 and became the dean of Saint Sergius Theological Institute, where he taught Church History and Patristics. He was active in ecumenical activities and was a longtime member of the Sts. Sergius and Alban Fellowship, a local ecumenical effort between the Orthodox and Anglican Churches,. He moved to the United States, where he taught and lectured at St. Vladimir's Orthodox Theological Seminary, Holy Cross Greek Orthodox School of Theology, Princeton, Harvard, Columbia, and Union Theological Seminary.

Florovsky was instrumental in the early days of the World Council of Churches, attending the first World Council of Churches meeting in Edinburgh 1937, and in numerous national and international ecumenical meetings. He wrote hundreds of essays, books, and book reviews for a variety of theological and ecclesiastical journals, many of which were published in ecumenical journals. Florovksy's theological research was devoted mostly to Church History and Patristics, which has often been called a "neo-patristic synthesis." Florovsky was one of the early Orthodox thinkers to return back to the writings of the Fathers of the Church to regain their patristic vision of theology.

The essay included in this volume first appeared in an ecumenical volume of essays devoted to the role of the diaconate in the Church called, "The Problem of the Diaconate in the Orthodox Church," in

Richard T. Nolan (ed.), *Diaconate Now*, Washington, DC: Corpus Books, 1968. In this essay, Florovsky takes a historical look at the diaconate within the Eastern Church and identifies some problems with the current role of the deacon within the Orthodox Church and looks to seek ways how to realign the diaconate to more of a liturgical and ministerial role in the Church. For the most part, the order of the diaconate as a full and vibrant ministry of the Church has all but been lost, especially in the Eastern Church where is role is generally limited to assisting at the divine services. In the West, the role of the deacon has expanded, and deacons can also bury parishioners as well as preach at Mass. In the East, the role of deacon is more limited in scope, and due to work schedules, most deacons have a full-time job outside the parish.

For Further Reading

Blane, Andrew (ed.). *Georges Florovsky: Russian Intellectual — Orthodox Churchman* (Crestwood, NY: St. Vladimir's Seminary Press, 1993).

Florovsky, Georges. *Bible, Church, Tradition: An Eastern Orthodox View Volume 1 Collected Works of Georges Florovsky* (Belmont, MA: Norland Publishing, 1972).

_______. *Christianity and Culture Volume 2 Collected Works of Georges Florovsky* (Belmont, MA: Norland Publishing, 1974).

_______. *Creation and Redemption Volume 3 Collected Works of Georges Florovsky* (Belmont, MA: Norland Publishing, 1976).

_______. *Aspects of Church History Volume 4 Collected Works of Georges Florovsky* (Belmont, MA: Norland Publishing, 1975).

_______. *Ways of Russian Theology, Part I Volume 5 Collected Works of Georges Florovsky* (Belmont, MA: Norland Publishing, 1975).

_______. *Ways of Russian Theology, Part II Collected Works of Georges Florovsky* (Belmont, MA: Norland Publishing, 1975).

_______. *Eastern Fathers of the Fourth Century Collected Works of Georges Florovsky* (Belmont, MA: Norland Publishing, 1976).

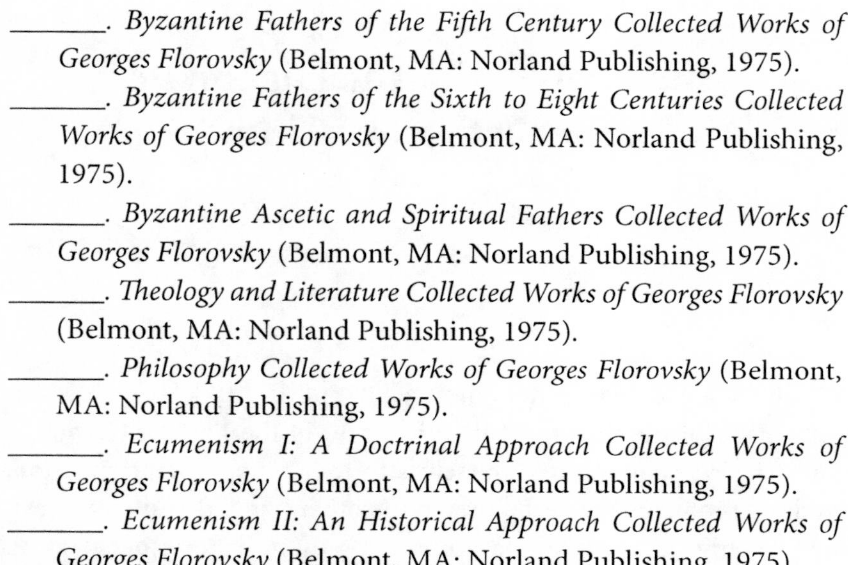

_______. *Byzantine Fathers of the Fifth Century Collected Works of Georges Florovsky* (Belmont, MA: Norland Publishing, 1975).

_______. *Byzantine Fathers of the Sixth to Eight Centuries Collected Works of Georges Florovsky* (Belmont, MA: Norland Publishing, 1975).

_______. *Byzantine Ascetic and Spiritual Fathers Collected Works of Georges Florovsky* (Belmont, MA: Norland Publishing, 1975).

_______. *Theology and Literature Collected Works of Georges Florovsky* (Belmont, MA: Norland Publishing, 1975).

_______. *Philosophy Collected Works of Georges Florovsky* (Belmont, MA: Norland Publishing, 1975).

_______. *Ecumenism I: A Doctrinal Approach Collected Works of Georges Florovsky* (Belmont, MA: Norland Publishing, 1975).

_______. *Ecumenism II: An Historical Approach Collected Works of Georges Florovsky* (Belmont, MA: Norland Publishing, 1975).

The Problem of the Diaconate in the Orthodox Church

The scope of this chapter is limited. It is not our task here to discuss in detail the history of the diaconate in the Eastern Orthodox Church. We shall address ourselves to the contemporary situation, and the problems implied in it. On the other hand, this situation can be properly understood and appraised only in historic perspective. The diaconate has obviously changed its shape and function more than once in the course of history; hence, the Orthodox theologian is guided in his inquiry by tradition, especially in controversial matters. From early times the diaconate was acknowledged as an integral part of the threefold structure of apostolic ministry, if only in the third place. Strangely enough, the actual origin of the diaconate as an institution is still an open, and rather obscure, issue. It is generally assumed that the diaconate can be traced back to the appointment of the Seven by the apostles, described in the sixth chapter of the Book of Acts, although the name "deacons" does not appear in the text. This was the usual interpretation in the West, as early as the time of St. Irenaeus.

In modern times, however, this interpretation has been challenged. The Orthodox theologian is bound at this point to take into account that venerable exegetical tradition of which St. John Chrysostom was an authoritative exponent and witness. Speaking of the election of the Seven, in his homilies on the Book of Acts, Chrysostom emphatically and formally denies that Seven were "ordained" as deacons, for the simple reason that at that time no distinct ecclesiastical orders existed: no bishops, no presbyters, and no deacons. According to Chrysostom, the Seven were appointed for an occasional and specific task, that is, for the "service of tables." It may be argued that this interpretation simply reflected the situation in Chrysostom's own time, when the diaconate had become, especially in the East, a liturgical institution. Yet, Chrysostom in no way was inclined to minimize the importance of charitable *diakonia* in the Church; indeed, the social responsibility of the Church was one of his crucial concerns. He simply insisted that the diaconate was instituted in the Church for a different task and purpose.

Whatever may be said of Chrysostom's exegesis, it was authoritatively endorsed by the Council of Trullo (692), with direct reference to Chrysostom's witness. The question was raised whether it was permissible to have more than seven deacons in a given local Church. The local Council of Neocaesarea (c. 315) ruled that the pattern of the Seven had to be adhered to, with the reference to Acts (canon 15). The Council of Trullo, after having pondered the whole matter and, with direct reference to Chrysostom's witness, reversed the ruling, since there was no valid reason for limitation in number. Indeed, there was no identity or connection between the "liturgical diaconate," *ton tois mysteriois diakonoumenon andron*, and the *diaconia* of the Seven, which was restricted solely to the "service of tables." This "service," special and occasional, must remain, however, a "pattern of philanthropy and charitable care," *typos philanthropias kai spoudes* (canon 16). This sharp distinction between the *hierourgias diakonia* and the *oikonomia ton trofon* became a commonplace of Byzantine canonical thinking. It has been maintained by many competent scholars in the Russian Church in modern times, both by exegetes and by canonists.[1]

[1] As, for instance, by the late Professor Nicholas Gloubokovsky, the renowned student of New Testament and Patristics, and by the late Professor Alexander Almazov, a distinguished canonist and liturgiologist. See their statements in *Zhournaly and Protokoly Predsobornago Prisutstvija* (Diaries and Minutes of the Pre-Council Commission) (St. Petersburg, 1907), III, 220, 223.

The order of deacons has always been regarded in Catholic tradition as a subordinate and subsidiary office in the total structure of ecclesiastical ministry: In the documents of the early Church deacons are usually described as "servants" or "attendants" of the bishop: *tou men episkopou hyperetai eisin,* in the phrase of the first Ecumenical Council (Nicaea I, AD 325, canon 18). They constituted at that time the working retinue, as it were, of the bishop, and in this capacity were assigned various tasks, primarily in the field of pastoral administration and service to the needy. The very term *diakonia* seems to have denoted at that time precisely this special kind of service. Deacons had a wide area of duties in the early Church, but a limited and subordinate competence. They acted by the bishop's authority and under his orders, and had to report all matters to him for decision. They were not supposed to do anything without his knowledge and approval, "in a clandestine way." As the bishop's agents and representatives, acting on his behalf and in his stead, they held an influential and distinguished position in the life of Christian communities. Accordingly, they were described sometimes not only as the bishop's "servants," but also as his "apostles and prophets," as his "ear and eye, mouth, heart, and soul" *(Apostolic Constitutions,* bk. II, ch. 30, 31, 32, 43).

In conjunction with that *hyperesia,* deacons had from early times their own distinctive role in the liturgical worship of the Church and were described also as "servants of Christ's mysteries" (St. Ignatius, Trallians 2). According to the *Apostolic Tradition* of Hippolytus, deacons were ordained by the imposition of hands by the bishop, not in *sacerdotio, sed in ministerio episcopi,* and for that reason presbyters, or priests, were not supposed to participate in the rite of ordination, since deacons were not their *symbouloi* and had no share of that spirit of counsel which was the common possession of "the clergy": *non est enim [diaconus] particeps consilii in clero (id.* 9). This sharp distinction between *sacerdotium* (common to bishops and priests) and *ministerium,* or *hyperesia,* is highly significant. Strictly speaking, according to the *Apostolic Tradition,* deacons did not belong to "clergy," *kleros,* at all.[2] On the other hand, their actual prominence in the practical field could but breed and encourage ambition and pride. As early as the Council of Nicaea, they had to be recalled to "their proper limits," tois *idiois metrois,* and to be reminded that their order was lower than that of the presbyters, *ton presbyteron elattous,* since they were no more than "bishop's servants" (canon 18, quoted above). The tension continued, however, and the Council of Trullo was compelled to wrestle with the same problem once more. Deacons were still, even at that time, appointed occasionally to certain administrative positions *(offikia ekklesiastika exontes),* and granted thereby "dignity" or "honor" *{axioma).* They tended therefore to assume precedence over presbyters. The Council dismissed all such claims as license and presumption (canon 7).

What is crucial and essential in this ruling is obviously the strict distinction between "order" and "office." The ruling implies that administrative appointments or commissions do not change the hierarchical status of the appointees, in spite of the *axioma* which such appointments may confer. Now, the question immediately arises: was the "service to the bishop," the *hyperesia,* just an "office"; that is, a "commission," and assigned task? And what exactly was the relation of such "commission" or task to the "order"? The early rites of ordination are rather vague at this point. They do not specify the *charisma* conferred by ordination to the diaconate, nor do they define those functions to which deacons are ordained. Yet, the subordinate and auxiliary character of the diaconate is clearly stated. The only clue here is, perhaps, the reference to St. Stephen, which occurs in the rite described in the eighth book of the *Apostolic Constitutions* "And

[2] *The Treatise on the Apostolic Tradition of St. Hippolytus of Rome*, ed., Gregory Dix (London, 1937), pp. 15–18; Jean Michel Hanssens, S.J., *La Liturgie d'Hippolyte* (Orientalia Christina Analecta, 155), (Rome, 1959), p. 122f., 166f., 401ff.: Dom Bernard Botte, O.S.B., *La Tradition Apostolique de Saint Hippolyte, Essai de Reconstruction* (Liturgiegeschichtliche Quellen and Forschungen (Munster/W.), Hf. 39, p. 23 ff. and *passim*: Jean Colson, *La fonction diaconale aux origins de l'Eglise* (1960), pp. 97–104.

replenish him with thy Holy Spirit, and with power, as thou didst replenish Stephen, thy martyr and the follower of the sufferings of thy Christ" (ch. 18). This clause is retained in the later Byzantine rite that is still in use. It is significant, however, that St. Stephen alone is mentioned here, and is mentioned as martyr and sufferer and not as "deacon." It is rather an analogy, with an emphasis on the charismatic character of service. In the course of time most of the tasks that originally constituted the *hyperesia* of deacons were transferred or reassigned to other agents. Indeed, the pastoral care, in general, and especially the care of the poor and needy, could be exercised by bishops in manifold ways and through diverse channels. Moreover, charity and mutual service was the obvious duty of all believers and of the whole community.

Of the various duties which characterized the service of deacons in the early Church, only their liturgical function, with special reference to the celebration of the holy Eucharist, has been retained as their distinctive and proper task. In a sense, it was a conspicuous change, but it would be inaccurate to describe it as an atrophy or decline of the diaconate. Indeed, it meant a reorganization of the Church's *diakonia* at large. It implied also a new interpretation of the nature of the diaconate, still in line with the old tradition, but with sharper distinction between "order" and various "offices" or commissioned tasks. In fact, the liturgical role of deacons was becoming increasingly conspicuous precisely in the fourth century, in the period of stabilization and unification of rites. It was for the role and function of "liturgical assistants" (of bishops *and* priests) that deacons were ordained. This was their basic and primary function, and it constituted their ecclesiastical and ministerial status.

In the contemporary rite of ordination to the diaconate its auxiliary character is clearly indicated. The ordination takes place at the liturgy after the *anaphora,* that is, after the consecration of the elements; and this is meant to signify that deacons do not take any acting part in the consecration, except insofar as the whole worshipping congregation also is supposed and invited to join in prayer and to share in this way in the celebration. On the contrary, ordination to priesthood takes place before the consecration, at the very beginning of the sacramental service, so that a newly ordained priest is able immediately to join the bishop and his fellow-presbyters in the priestly action of consecration. This twofold ordination is a new way to express the traditional distinction: deacons are ordained in *ministerio,* whereas priests are ordained in *sacerdotio.* After the rite of ordination has been completed, the new deacon receives from the bishop a *ripidion,* or *flabellum,* a kind of fan, with which he is supposed "to guard" the Sacrament, originally from flies and insects. Now it is no more than a symbolic gesture, but it expresses clearly the serving role of deacons in the liturgy of the Church. In modern times the *ripidia* are made in the shape of cherubs and are accordingly called *hexapteryga,* in order to suggest an analogy between angels and deacons, since angels also are but "serving spirits." According to the contemporary rule, ordination to the diaconate may also be performed at the Liturgy of the Presanctified Gifts, which is not a sacramental service in the strict sense, but simply a special variant of Vespers with the additional rite of administering Holy Communion from the presanctified, or reserved, Sacrament. In brief, deacons are not supposed or permitted to function as such, except as assistants of the officiating priest or bishop. They are no more than assistants.

The liturgical function of the deacon is conspicuous and impressive in the Eastern rite. Western liturgiologists usually regard it as a distinctive and most characteristic feature of this rite.[3] On the whole, this observation is correct; however, if the assistance or participation of deacons in the divine service is normal, regular, and desirable, it is not indispensable or obligatory, since it is an auxiliary and subsidiary function. This assistance belongs, as it were, to the *plene esse* of the liturgical rite, to its ceremonial completeness and perfection, rather than to its very *esse.* As a matter of fact, there are no deacons at all in

[3] For instance, Anton Baumstark, *Die Messe im Morgenland* (Kempten und Munich, 1906), p. 12 ff.; "Vom geschichtlichen Werden der Liturgie," in *Ecclesia Orans,* 10 (Freiburg/Br., 1923) pp. 97 ff.

the majority of Orthodox communities today. This may be a sign of crisis or decline, but it must be considered seriously and understood properly. It is significant that as early as the fourteenth century, the great Byzantine interpreter of the liturgical rites, Nicholas Cabasilas, was rather reticent about the function of deacons.

Let us turn now to the analysis of the rite itself. First of all, the deacon is a *keryx,* a kind of liturgical herald or crier. The term itself has been used by St. John Chrysostom and by Theodore of Mopsuestia.[4] The deacon announces the beginning of the service and invites the officiating priest to give the initial blessing or invocation (*kairos tou poiesai to kyrio*), while he himself receives the permission to start. The deacon exhorts the congregation to join in prayer, and at certain particular points he stirs its attention: *orfoi-proschomen* — "stand aright," "let us attend." It is his duty and privilege to call the congregation, before the *anaphora,* to recognize each other, "to love one another," and to introduce the recitation of the Creed. It is his privilege also to invite the celebrant to proceed to the consecration of gifts. It is his task to invite communicants to approach and to receive holy Communion from the hands of the officiating priest or bishop. It seems that in the ancient church deacons were permitted, or even commissioned, to administer communion themselves, if only to the lay people, and this is still occasionally done, mainly in the Greek Church, although it is now commonly regarded rather as an abuse. In all these instances the deacon appears to be the keeper of the liturgical order. The role of a herald is, by its very nature and purpose, conspicuous, but obviously it is auxiliary and subordinate. Lessons at the liturgy are normally read by deacons, although the epistle is usually read by an *anagnostes*, or even by a layman, and probably, in older times, it was the privilege of the *anagnostes* to read all lessons. Before the reading of the Gospel, the deacon asks for the blessing of the officiating priest in a rather solemn form.

[4] The relevant texts are collected and examined in the recent book by S. Salaville and G., *Le rôle du diacre dans la Liturgie Orientale* (Paris-Athens, 1962, 'Archives de l'Orient Chrétien,' 3), pp. 34–43.

The most significant function of the deacon in the divine rite is, no doubt, the recitation of the litanies, of which, in a sense, he is the regular minister. The litanies, however, maybe said only in the context of the regular public service presided over by a priest or bishop; outside of this context they cannot be said at all. The ministry of the deacon is in this case a subordinate ministry. It is hardly accurate to describe the litany as a dialogue for there are no replies, or answers. Nor is it accurate to describe the deacon as a leader of the congregation, or as a mediator between the priest and the congregation, as it is often done, especially by Western scholars.[5] As a matter of fact, the deacon does not recite prayers — that is, the litanies — on the behalf of the congregation; he only invites it to pray. "Let us pray" is simply an invitation, not yet the prayer itself. In the phrase of such a competent student of the Eastern rite as Jean Michel Hanssens, "both the celebrant and the people pray together in litanies, though in many different forms," and the clauses of the litany pronounced by the deacon "are exhortations directed to the people rather than prayers addressed to God." Indeed, "to invite" is not the same as "to lead."

Each litany must be concluded with a doxology by the priest, who is actually the true and only leader of the congregation. It is proper at this point to quote the comments of Cabasilas: "At *the beginning the priest exhorts the people to prayer, for he is appointed to this office* and is for that reason placed in front of the people. *He is also their ambassador and mediator* (*os presbeutes auton kai mesites*). . . . After he has prayed for all his intentions, *the priest calls upon the faithful* to commend themselves to God."[6] Now, the litanies are recited by the deacon, and the priest has his own prayers to be said at the same time, *submissa voce,* within the sanctuary. There is an apparent duplication, or parallelism, of prayers; yet, the litany is incomplete without the

[5] By Baumstark, as quoted above in Note 4; by Salaville and Nowack, *op. cit.*, Note 5, pp. 117–119; also by I. H. Dalamais, O.P., "Le Diacre, guide de la prière du people d'après la tradition liturgique," in *La Maison-Dieu*, 61, 1960, pp. 34–40.

[6] I. M. Hanssens, *Institutiones liturgicae de ritibus orientalibus* (Rome, 1932), III, p. 230.

doxology which can be given only by the priest. It is much more than just an audible exclamation (*ekfonesis*). In the phrase of Cabasilas, it is an explanatory verse (*akroteleutios*), which gives the reason for which prayers may be offered at all (*prostithesi ten aitian*). The reason is the glory of God. "*The priest wants to bring all the faithful to share in his hymn of praise ... and the congregation do indeed unite themselves to his prayer,* for when he has recited the doxology, all the faithful say 'Amen,' and by this acclamation *they take to themselves as their own the prayers of the priest*."[7]

It is hardly correct, therefore, to describe the deacon as an intermediary between the congregation and the officiating priest. Indeed, the priest, who has direct contact with the congregation, is himself their mediator. The prayers of the priest and of the congregation are not only coordinated, they are truly integrated into one action of praise and intercession. The role of the deacon is conspicuous, especially in the first part of the Divine Liturgy, the *enarxis,* but it would be a gross exaggeration to consider him as a minister in his own right. There is no reason to assume, as it has been sometimes suggested, that the duplication of prayers in the *enarxis* was motivated by the Semitic conception of the Holy as totally inaccessible to ordinary people.[8] Nor is it probable that this duplication had been introduced deliberately to secure the closer participation of the people in the worship, when language difficulties arose." In any case, this does not apply to the Byzantine liturgy, in which the language of the people has been always used. It is important to underline that this duplication of prayers in the *enarxis* has nothing to do with the habit of reciting the *anaphora* in secret (*mystikos*). In this case, there is actually no duplication at all: the part of the prayer which is recited now by the priest "in secret," the parts of it audibly intoned by the priest, and the responses of the people, constitute in fact one single and continuous prayer, which is offered by the celebrating priest in the name and on behalf of the whole

[7] Nicholas Cabasilas, *Sacrae liturgiae interpretatio*, c. XII and XIV, *MG CL*, c. 393, 397.

[8] *Ibid*, c. XV, c. 399,401.

Church as gathered at that time for celebration, and in which both the celebrant and the congregation participate jointly, if *diversis* modis. The *anaphora is* indeed the common *prayer* of the Church, *publica et communis* orario.[9] Characteristically, at this point the deacon has no distinctive role of his own (*precantur celebrans et populus*).

It would be out of place to engage now in further discussion of this matter, important as it undoubtedly is. The secret recitation of the *anaphora* was an unfortunate device to emphasize the august mystery of the Eucharist, but, in fact, it only obscures the common and corporate nature of the eucharistic celebration, especially in the situation when the people are not aware of the content of the prayer offered by the celebrant on their behalf. Strangely enough, it is often contended today that the congregation should not know the text of the *anaphora,* and special editions of the Euchologion are sometimes produced for the use of the worshippers, in which all secret prayers, including the *anaphora,* are simply omitted, under the pretext that they do not concern the congregation, being, as it were, a kind of private prayer of the officiating clergy. That, of course, is poor and confused theology, in flat contradiction of the open purpose and intention of the eucharistic rite itself.[10]

At present, however, we are concerned only with the liturgical function of the deacon, and are interested in the rite only insofar as it helps to clarify the nature of the diaconal assistance. There is nothing in the Divine Liturgy that might authorize us to regard the deacon as being more than a subordinate liturgical assistant of the officiating or celebrating priest. Certain parts of the rite are normally performed by deacons, always under the authority of the priest and in conjunction with his function, and they can be properly denoted as *ta diakonika;* but only the priest is the acting minister of all public rites in the Church.

We have noted, in the earlier part of this chapter, that, while the assistance of the deacon in the celebration of the divine liturgy was

[9] This was the hypothesis of Père Dalmais, *op. cit.*, Note 6, p. 37. Baumstark did not think so: *Die Messe in Morgenland*, p. 12.

[10] Baumstark, *Vom geschichtlichen Werden* , p. 97 ff.

regular, traditional, and normal, it could not, and should not, be regarded as mandatory or necessary. In other words, it does not belong to the essential structure of the eucharistic rite. Nothing essential is missing in the rite when the priest celebrates alone, and this situation is formally anticipated in the rubrics of the *Euchologion*. Indeed, in our time Divine Liturgy is more often celebrated without the participation of the deacon than with it. Of course, in this case, the priest himself has to perform certain functions of the deacon, as, for instance, the recitation of the litanies. This may create some practical inconveniences: the priest will have to say both the litanies and his own secret prayers, which are supposed to be said simultaneously. These inconveniences, however, can be easily obviated, and moreover, the rite itself will be enriched if the priest reads aloud his own prayers before the concluding doxology. It seems that the whole rite may assume more unity and cohesion if celebrated without the deacon's assistance, so that its basic purpose and ultimate aim are better focused and enhanced. On the whole, the participation of the deacon is a matter of convenience, not of substance.

A further question now arises: does the participation of the deacon, in its contemporary form and shape, really serve that ultimate purpose for which the eucharistic rite is intended and instituted, or may it, in certain cases, obscure and even impede that purpose? It is a grave and crucial question, and a delicate one, so that often it is cautiously avoided. It is significant, however, that in the Russian Church, in the early years of this century, the usefulness of the diaconate, in its contemporary form, and even its necessity, were vigorously challenged by certain prominent bishops, of the conservative wing of the Russian episcopate of that time. It has been contended that it was simply useless and to no purpose to have deacons in the parish churches; that it was, rather, a meaningless custom, or just a fashion; and the hope has been expressed that the parish diaconate might go out of fashion altogether and rather soon[14] The reasons for such radical intervention were mixed and obviously "situation conditioned." The problem was neither deeply probed, nor traced to its basic theological presuppositions. Nevertheless, this challenge, coming from competent and authoritative quarters, cannot be easily dismissed or ignored.

As a matter of fact, in the Russian Church, for various and manifold historical reasons, the diaconate has lost, in modern times, its spiritual significance and has degenerated into a kind of ceremonial or artistic office The deacon has become practically a musical officer in the Church. His participation in the rite was sought mainly because it was expected to add to the external impressiveness of the rite, to its emotional and esthetic appeal The main requirement of a deacon, accordingly, was to have a good and powerful voice and artistic skill, his function was divorced from the true purpose of the rite. Here it seems proper to mention one characteristic abuse which, unfortunately, has become almost a custom in many communities deacons are often permitted to serve without preparation, that is, without the required fasting and without the intention to receive communion at the celebration in which they are taking part. It is true that, in this case, they are not supposed or allowed to function at all in the sacramental part of the divine liturgy, and their role is limited to the *enarxis,* that is, to the recitation of litanies and the reading of lessons, although the discipline on this point is often rather lax In fact, this restriction itself only underlined the abnormality and ambiguity of the usage.[11] The deacon came to be regarded as an accidental participant in the rite, in which he was invited to perform certain functions of artistic and decorative character, without being spiritually engaged in the celebration of the mystery. Indeed, this is not only an abuse, but a characteristic abuse, reflecting the current misconception of the diaconal office. The deacon has lost his proper position in the liturgical office.

This misconception of the diaconal office is rooted to a great extent in the general overemphasis on the esthetical aspect of the divine

[11] See my article, "Corpus Mysticum: The Eucharist and Catholicity, in *Church Service Society Annual*, No. 9, May 1936–1937 (Cupar, Scotland), pp. 38–46.

rite which has been growing in modern times, especially in the Russian Church. The choir has assumed a disproportionate role in the rite, and the rite itself has become a sort of artistic performance. The esthetic aspect is indeed essential to the sacred rite, in which there is ample room for art. Art and esthetics, however, must be subordinate to the spiritual purpose of the rite, but they tend to run an independent and autonomous course. The modern history of music in the Russian Church is a conspicuous example of such distortion, butt it would be out of place to discuss this complex subject at length at this point.[12] Only against this general background is it possible to understand properly the current shift in the character of the diaconate.

The other important factor in the process was the growing custom of infrequent communion. Whatever may be said, and is being said, in the defense of the habit of non communicating attendance which still prevails and is often even enforced in Orthodox communities, in spite of the vigorous challenge and appeal of such a great and saintly master as Father John of Kronstadt and many others before and after him, one cannot underestimate the obvious spiritual danger inherent and implicit in this habit. It encourages the faithful to regard the Eucharist as a kind of sacred spectacle which may be attended without any deeper engagement in the very purpose of the divine rite. By its very structure, and also by the purpose of its divine institution, the eucharistic rite is inwardly ordained toward Communion, and culminates precisely in the solemn call "to draw near," addressed to the congregation. Only in this perspective can the participants in the service find their proper place. According to the authoritative inter-

[12] For further information: A. Goloubtsov, "O prichinakh i vremeni zameny glasnago chtenija litugijnykh molitv tapnym" (On the Causes and the Time of the Change of the Audible Recitation of Liturgical Prayers into the Secret), in *Bogoslovskij Vestnik* (September, 1905), pp. 69–75; B. Sove, "Eucharistija v drevnej Tserkvi I sovremennaja pratika" (The Eucharist in the Ancient Church and the Contemporary Practice), *Zhivoje Predanie* (Paris, n.d.), pp. 179 ff.; Panagiotis Trembelas, "L'Audition de l'Anaphora Eucharistique par le Peuple," *L'Eglise et les Eglises,* II, Editions de Chevetogne (Belgium, 1955), 207–220; see also the remarks of Archimandrite Kiprian (Kern), *Eucharistija* (Paris, 1947), p. 165 ff.

pretation of the Fathers, and of the later Byzantine commentators, the liturgy certainly is, in a sense, a "sacred panorama," a comprehensive symbolic image of the whole *oikonomia* of salvation it requires and implies vision and contemplation. But obviously this contemplation finds its fullness only in communion. In other words, attendance finds its justification precisely in participation, which is the only real focus of attendance. The current over emphasis on the artistic side distorts the perspective and actually impedes contemplation. In contemporary practice, the congregation, "the Holy People," in the phrase of Cabasilas, is reduced to silence, to the role of spectator, it loses its true part in the service which is, in principle and essence, precisely the corporate action of the whole Church, as gathered for celebration, in which it is at once the privilege and the bound duty of all believers to participate. All functions in the divine rite are coordinated precisely at this point; if they are not, the inner unity of the rite may be completely lost. This is what has actually happened with the diaconal function in the contemporary situation.

It is for this reason that the question arises whether the diaconal assistance, in its contemporary form, is really desirable, even for the *plene esse* of the rite. At this point we are facing a dilemma. On the one hand, one may dispense altogether with the assistance of the deacon in the eucharistic rite, since this assistance in its contemporary form does not seem to serve the true and ultimate purpose of the rite. This has been done already on a large scale, if only for accidental reasons, and the venture seems to have been justified by its results. The priest is able to exercise more effectively his role as a minister of unity in his local congregation," and the congregation recovers its own and proper part in the divine service. It has been not infrequently suggested that common and congregational singing be restored in order to make the participation of the people real and effective. It has been done in many communities in the Russian Church and the purpose has been achieved.

On the other hand, the existing diaconate may be reorganized and restored to its proper role of liturgical assistants of the priests in the eucharistic service. A closer liturgical relationship must be restored between the priest and his deacon on the basis of their joint participation in the eucharistic celebration, as it is actually anticipated in the traditional rite, although the mode of their participation will be different. The concept of liturgical assistance must be clarified and properly defined; then the participation of the deacon in the service may become an organic part of the divine rite. This prospective restoration of the true liturgical diaconate can be achieved, however, only in the context of a comprehensive liturgical renewal. Valid arguments may be adduced in favor of either alternative; they must be carefully scrutinized and pondered. This would require a theological reassessment of the whole problem of ministry. The nature of Christian ministry is always defined in the Orthodox tradition in close relation to the sacraments, especially to the holy Eucharist. The theological key to the problem of the diaconate lies in the doctrine of the Eucharist, and actually the whole problem of ministry is a eucharistic problem: the Eucharist is the heart and the center—and indeed the foundation—of the Church, which is herself the Body of Christ. The diaconate, as a distinct ministerial order, can be understood adequately only in this eucharistic setting.[13]

As a matter of fact, the permanent diaconate has survived in the Eastern Church, if in a very peculiar form. At all times there has been, in the Church a large body of deacons, both in the cathedrals and in the parishes. The composition of this group was mixed. In the Russian Church one can discern two main categories. First, there was a distinct group of those who were selected for this position on the basis of their musical ability, mainly in the cathedrals or in large

[13] See, for instance, the intervention of Archbishop Dimitry (Kovalnicky) of Kherson and Odessa at the Pre-Conciliar Consultation in 1906 in *Zhournaly i Protokoly*, as quoted above, Note 2, III, 223 f. Archbishop Dimitry was previously for about thirty years Professor of Ecclesiastical History in the Theological Academy of Kiev, and later its rector. Subsequently he served as Bishop of Tambov, Archbishop of Kazan, and finally of Kherson and Odessa, and was an influential member of the holy governing Synod of the Russian Church (d. 1913).

city churches. They had to remain permanently in their office simply because they were selected for special reasons, as qualified precisely for the diaconal function. Many in this group had an adequate theological training and could therefore be assigned to additional duties, including preaching and catechetical instruction, if required. Second, there was a much larger group of those who had to remain deacons because they were not qualified for promotion.

This peculiar situation can be understood only in historic perspective. The instance of the Russian Church is especially significant in this respect. For various historic reasons, which cannot be discussed at length in this paper, the clergy in the Russian Church gradually became a closed and hereditary social group, a kind of a special class, or even a caste. This situation was decreed by state law and was rigorously maintained; it could not fail to foster the development of a peculiar class-consciousness, for even the families of the clergy belonged by law to "the clergy." The unity of the clergy was a social phenomenon in the total structure of a neatly stratified society. "Clergy" was a legal status, not an ecclesiastical institution. The school system, established in the eighteenth century, was the chief factor in securing the unity of the class. It was the duty of bishops to establish schools in their dioceses, and it was the legal obligation of all the clergy to send all their boys to these schools, under severe sanctions and threats of prosecution for desertion in the case they failed to do so. These were general schools, not specifically theological, and theology was taught only in two upper forms. The course was long, the curriculum dry and heavy, and discipline oppressive. Only a tiny minority of those who were compulsorily enrolled at an early age was able to graduate. Those who left the school before graduation were in constant danger of being conscripted as soldiers, or compelled to join the ranks of peasantry, unless they were given some position in the Church. This explains the disproportionate inflation of the lower ranks of the clergy in the Russian Church, and it affected the social status of the diaconate. Most deacons, especially in the rural parishes, had a very inadequate education, and could not be promoted to any higher or responsible position Moreover, their economic situation was often alarmingly poor. This created a sharp social split within the ranks of the clergy. It is true that this system was legally abrogated about a century ago, in the era of Great Reforms in the 1860s, but its consequences were still felt quite strongly, even in the early years of this century, and inveterate habits continued. The diaconate was, in fact, a professional group in the Church rather than a vocational one. The abnormality of this situation has been sharply exposed by many bishops of the Russian Church, especially in the period of pre-conciliar discussions in 1904–07, and then at the Great Council of 1917–18.[14] These social conditions complicated the problem of the nature and function of the diaconate in the Russian Church. The existing permanent diaconate could not fulfill the purpose that would vindicate its existence. In other Orthodox Churches the situation was different, according to the historic and local conditions, but the basic problem was always the same. Many problems of the past are now obsolete and antiquated, especially in the Churches behind the Iron Curtain, but the memories of the past still weigh heavily on today's canonical and theological thinking.

The contemporary problem of the diaconate, as it is conceived and discussed rather intensively in the West, is more the problem of *diakoni* in a wider sense than that of the diaconate as a distinct hierarchical order. In the Eastern Churches the situation is different. In spite of the crisis and confusion out-lined above, the Eastern Church is primarily concerned with the liturgical diaconate. This does not mean that the Orthodox Church is indifferent to the great and grave problem of *diakonia,* of the social responsibility and service of the Church, but it may be contended, from the Orthodox point of view, and in the light of the historic tradition of the Eastern Church, that *diakonia* in this sense cannot serve as a basis for the diaconate as an order. *Diakonia* is but a function or a task, and it is the task of the whole Church. It may be further contended that this task can be ac-

[14] See the remarks of Father Kiprian, *op. cit.*, pp. 137 ff.

complished rather by the laity in the Church, under special commission from the hierarchy and under its supervision. In certain cases an ordination to minor orders may be desirable. As a matter of fact, many of the diaconal tasks, in this large sense of the word, have been for a long time successfully exercised in the Orthodox Churches by lay people in the field of missions, of education, and religious education in particular, of charity and social service. For these tasks, from the Orthodox point of view, there is no need to restore a permanent diaconate. These tasks and duties belong to the common competence and responsibility of the whole Church. In this connection one should think rather of the restoration of the old and traditional office of the deaconesses (of which there has been constant talk in the Russian Church during the last hundred years), of the expansion of sisterhoods and especially of medical sisterhoods, and of many other similar institutions. These arc indeed urgent and impending problems; but they are outside the scope of this paper.[15] Many of these tasks may be assigned to deacons, but rather on the basis of individual competence or vocation, and not as an intrinsic component of the diaconal ministry, in the proper sense.

[15] There is no up-to-date monograph on the history of the Russian clergy. Some information is given in general manuals of Church history, especially in that of Professor A. Dobroklonsky, Vol. IV, published in the last decade of the last century. One has still refernce to old books of Professor Peter Znamensky: *Prikhodskoe Dukhovenstvo v Rossii so vremeni reform Petra* (The Parish Clergy in Russia since the Time of Peter's Reforms), (Kazan, 1873), and *Dukhovnyja Shkoly v Rossii de redormy 1808 goda* (The Church Schools in Russia up to the Reform of 1808), (Kazan, 1881). See also N. Runivsky, *Tserkovnograzhdanskie zakonopolozhenija otnositelíno pravoslavnago dukhovenstva v tsarstvovanie Imp. Alexandra II* (The Church and State Legislation Concerning the Orthodox Clergy in the Reign of Alexander II), (Kazan, 1898).

CHAPTER EIGHT

Elizabeth Behr-Sigel (1907–1995)

Elizabeth Behr-Sigel is certainly one of the most interesting theologians whose writings have inspired people in both Europe and North America. Even up until her recent death in 1995, she was still actively pursuing writing projects and speaking engagements. She certainly was a remarkable woman, especially given the fact that she was a forerunner and advocate for women's issues in the Church at a time when very few people in the Eastern Church were discussing such issues.

Elizabeth was born near Strasbourg in 1907 to an interfaith family, her mother was Protestant and her father was Jewish. Her parents, however, raised Elizabeth in a Christian household. Eventually, she studied at the University of Strasbourg and was trained to be a pastoral assistant in Ville-Climont in the Reformed Church. She did not officiate at the Eucharist; however, she was very active in pastoral care as she visited the sick and homebound, and preached and taught when needed. She eventually married Andre Behr with whom she had three children. Upon his death in 1975, Elizabeth completed her doctoral studies, writing her dissertation on the Russian theologian and author, Alexander Bukharev, who is also known by his Church name, Archimandrite Theodore who lived in the mid 1800's. Bukharev was one of the first Russian Orthodox theologians and thinkers to begin seeking greater dialogue with the West, especially in terms of a creative exchange of theology, seeking to bring the Church into the modern era in order to address problems of modernity. Certainly, her work with Bukharev inspired her to question the often times deadened traditionalism with its ritualistic fervor in order to seek greater openness, freedom, and creativity in the Church. She was not afraid, for example, to question why women were not allowed to be ordained to the presbyterate, after all, there was a long history of women deacons in the Church going all the way back to the 5th century. Her devotion to this subject, arguing for greater openness in theological debate and dialogue, can be seen throughout her writings.

Elizabeth's life was quite extraordinary. She was friends with many people in the Russian Parisian community, especially with Frs. Lev Gillet and Sergius Bulgakov, Mother Maria Skobtsova, and Paul Evdokimov, whose own son Michael was Elizabeth's god-son. Elizabeth was frequently a guest speaker and active participant in a wide variety of ecumenical activities, especially the World Council of Churches. She was also an active member of ACTS (Association of Christians United Against Torture) as well as in the Orthodox Fraternity in France. Her writing endeavors also included writing and editing for the French Orthodox publication *Contacts.*

Her writings reflect a deep sense of the truth of the Gospel, a full life of Christ, without a false notion of Tradition nor a pseudo-spiritualism. In many ways, Elizabeth's own life is an example of her commitment to the Gospel, herself being a wife, mother, grandmother, author, professor, and ecumenist. She saw herself as a member of a larger Church which encompassed much more than the local Orthodox community in Paris. Her shared friendships with people from across the Christian spectrum points to her openness to people of all faiths and backgrounds.

The essay included in this volume is from an essay which was published by the WCC on women in the Church. In it, she briefly traces the historical roots of women in the Church and calls to question the role of women in the Church today, which unfortunately is quite limited. She calls for a renewed review of the role of women and their place within the community of faith.

For Further Reading

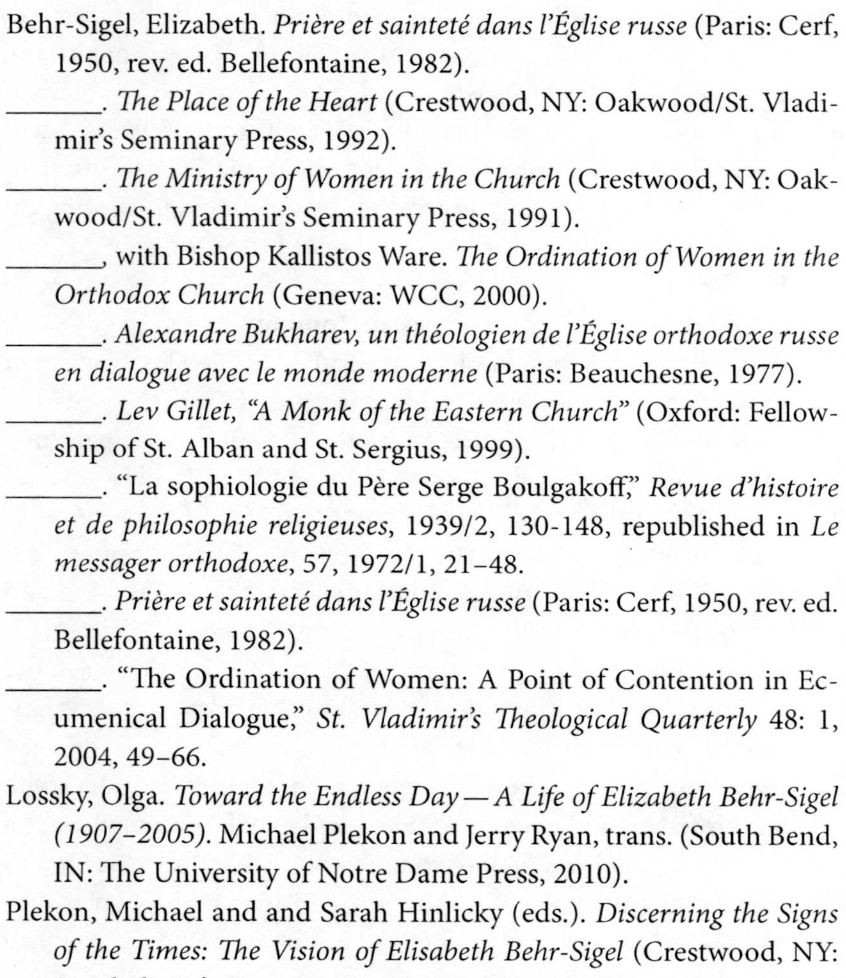

Behr-Sigel, Elizabeth. *Prière et sainteté dans l'Église russe* (Paris: Cerf, 1950, rev. ed. Bellefontaine, 1982).

_______. *The Place of the Heart* (Crestwood, NY: Oakwood/St. Vladimir's Seminary Press, 1992).

_______. *The Ministry of Women in the Church* (Crestwood, NY: Oakwood/St. Vladimir's Seminary Press, 1991).

_______, with Bishop Kallistos Ware. *The Ordination of Women in the Orthodox Church* (Geneva: WCC, 2000).

_______. *Alexandre Bukharev, un théologien de l'Église orthodoxe russe en dialogue avec le monde moderne* (Paris: Beauchesne, 1977).

_______. *Lev Gillet, "A Monk of the Eastern Church"* (Oxford: Fellowship of St. Alban and St. Sergius, 1999).

_______. "La sophiologie du Père Serge Boulgakoff," *Revue d'histoire et de philosophie religieuses*, 1939/2, 130-148, republished in *Le messager orthodoxe*, 57, 1972/1, 21–48.

_______. *Prière et sainteté dans l'Église russe* (Paris: Cerf, 1950, rev. ed. Bellefontaine, 1982).

_______. "The Ordination of Women: A Point of Contention in Ecumenical Dialogue," *St. Vladimir's Theological Quarterly* 48: 1, 2004, 49–66.

Lossky, Olga. *Toward the Endless Day—A Life of Elizabeth Behr-Sigel (1907–2005)*. Michael Plekon and Jerry Ryan, trans. (South Bend, IN: The University of Notre Dame Press, 2010).

Plekon, Michael and and Sarah Hinlicky (eds.). *Discerning the Signs of the Times: The Vision of Elisabeth Behr-Sigel* (Crestwood, NY: St. Vladimir's Seminary Press, 2001).

_______. "To Become Permeable to Christ: Elizabeth Behr-Sigel's Theological Vision," *The Ecumenical Review* Vol. 61 no. 2 (2009).

Women in the Orthodox Church

"What a strange Church the Orthodox Church is . . . a Church of contrasts: at the same time so traditional yet so free, so ritualistic . . . and so lively. A Church where the pearl of great price of the Gospel, is lovingly preserved, sometimes covered dust . . . but a Church which can sings its Easter joy as none other."

Of all these contrasts mentioned by Archimandrite Lev Gillet, a great contemporary Orthodox spiritual writer, better known by his literary pseudonym "a Monk of the Eastern Church,"[1] the position of Orthodox women provides a particularly striking illustration. We see there juxtaposed and intermingling the liberating message of the gospel and outmoded taboos, a theological doctrine of humankind both spiritual and personal, and misogynistic stereotypes inherited from patriarchal societies. A universally present icon of the Mother of God radiates a tender and deep femininity. But the altar is barred to women. The women bringing spices to the tomb on the first Easter morning, were the first to announce that Christ was risen from the dead are honored in the Orthodox Churches with the title "apostles to the apostles." But the reading of the gospel in public worship remains and is still limited to male ministers. And so we can go on. And yet fresh currents are flowing beneath the hard shell of impenetrable customs and rituals. Today as in the past, women participate actively in the life of the Orthodox Churches in various ways. When they come into contact with the acids of modernity, a new awareness emerges. One

[1] A Monk of the Eastern Church, *Orthodox Spirituality* (London, 1945), pp. 64–65.

of the signs of the times is a call that we should discern between the living Tradition and fossilized traditionalism, particularly regarding the place of women. Will it be aright? Will it be followed up?

The common calling of all the baptized, both men and women, is prophetically declared in the sacraments of Christian initiation, administered by the Orthodox Church in deeply symbolic rites to all, with no gender distinction between the sexes. Baptism by immersion symbolizes passing, being born, to New Life in fellowship with the death and rising again of Christ. As the "Monk of the Eastern Church" explains, the sealing with the Holy Spirit of various parts of the body, chrismation, or confirmation, makes each one, male or female, an anointed of the Lord, another Christ in their fellowship by the Spirit with the Anointed One, Jesus Christ. The words, "As many of you as have been baptized into Christ, have put on Christ," (Gal. 3:27) are sung by the choir when the newly baptized male or female, clad in their baptismal robe, are received into the Eucharistic community, the visible Body of Christ, of which they have become full members. However, at that very moment, where all distinctions seem to be put aside, there follows a contrasting rite: male baptized are received into the sanctuary behind the iconostasis. For women and girls, the doors remained closed. Today, a growing number of Orthodox women view this rite as discriminatory and sometimes to manage to get in changed.

What is the teaching on women of those known as the Church Fathers, who have great authority in the Orthodox Church?[2] The accusation that they are misogynists comes mainly from Western feminists, who base their argument on the Latin tradition from Augustine to Thomas Aquinas and Bonaventure. Some Orthodox voices have joined this cry, like those of the Greek-American Byzantine hymnography specialist Eva Catafygiotou-Topping[3] and the

[2] See France Quere. *La Femme et les Pères de l'Eglise*, Paris, DDB, 1997.

[3] Eva Katafygioutou-Topping. *Holy Mothers of Orthodoxy*, Minneapolis (USA), 1987.

Romanian theologian Anka Manolache.[4] On the Orthodox side a more profound study of the issue of gender in the theology of humankind of the Greek Fathers has been undertaken in the article, Male and Female in Cappadocian Theology" by Verna Nonna Harrison.[5] The true founders of the doctrine of humankind in Orthodox theology are the Cappadocian Fathers — Basil of Caesarea, Gregory of Nyssa, and Gregory of Nazianzus. They, together with Maximus the Confessor after them, strenuously affirm the ontological unity of humankind beyond the distinction between men and women, according to the order of creation. That order has been damaged by sin, which is essentially separation, but is restored in Christ according to the order of redemption. At the center of their theology of humankind lies Genesis 1:27–28 and Galatians 3:27–28. "Wives, as husbands, have the privilege of having been created in the image of God. The two natures are equally honorable, declared Basil to a woman who seemed to doubt it" (*On the Origin of Man Homily* 1, 18). Commenting on the baptismal hymn in the Letter to the Galatians, he emphasizes that the image of Christ is present in all the baptized. It overrides differences of race, social standing and sex, "As in the portrait of the emperor, the beauty of the face transfigures the material used by the artist, be it wood or gold, making it unimportant" (*Treatise on Baptism*, quoted by Harrison). Summing up the doctrine of humankind in the Cappadocian Fathers, Gregory of Nazianzus declares, "The same creator for men and for women, for both the same clay, the same image, the same death, the same resurrection" (*Discourses* 37, 6).

Behind this discourse there lies the images of the actual women who inspired it: women martyr Julitta, whose example Basil exhorted Christian men and women to follow. In his eulogy of her, he puts in her mouth an exegesis of Genesis 2:21–22 which today would be con-

---

[4] Anka Manolache, "Orthodoxy and Women," in Jeane Becher (ed.), *Women, Religion and Sexuality*, Geneva, WCC, 1991.

[5] Verna N. Harrison, "Male and Female in Cappadocian Theology" in *Journal of Theological Studies*, Oxford, 1990 vol. 8. See also, *Contacts*, no. 179, 1997 Vol. 2.

sidered feminist! Further, such women were Macrina the Elder, confessor of the faith and grandmother of Basil the Great and Gregory of Nyssa; Nonna, mother of Gregory of Nazianzus, who brought her husband to the Orthodox faith; Gorgonia, her sister, described as a woman instructed in Scripture, constant in prayer, and generous to the poor, "privately instructing the men and women in her entourage but remaining silent in Church and in public." The most significant person symbolizing the position of women in the Cappadocian community was Macrina the Younger,[6] the elder sister of Basil the Great and Gregory of Nyssa. Her brothers speak about her as their teacher. Gregory's "Dialogue on the Soul and on the Resurrection," a conversation that he had with his dying sister: a text sometimes compared to Plato's *Phaedo*, was inspired by the conversation he had with his sister on her deathbed. Women, for the Fathers, far from being just a sexual objects, were the "complementary other" with whom they conversed, their companions, and at times their teachers in spiritual struggles. Their egalitarianism is placed in the eschatological perspective of the completeness of the end of time, when genital sexuality will be transcended. Monasticism is an attempt to complete that fullness. Within the context of an alternative society it represents, the basic equality of men and women expressed in their doctrine of humankind is most easily although not exclusively achieved.

It should be added that the patristic period coincided with the development of the diaconate of women. It was a ministry in the service of women as a response to their particular needs within a patriarchal society. But, as the research of Evangelos Theodorou has demonstrated,[7] it also had a theological, catechetical, and philanthropic roles, conferred in a genuine ordination.

---

[6] On Macrina the Younger, see Ruth Albrecht, *Das Leben der Heilgen Markrina auf dem Hintergrund der Thekla-Traditionen*, Gottingen, 1986. On the martyr Julitta and her eulogy by St. Basil, see pp. 9–13, 237–241. Likewise Ruth Albrecht, pp. 201–203.

[7] Evangelos Theodoru, "Institution des Diaconesses dans l'Eglise orthodoxe" in *Contacts*, no. 146, 1989 no. 2.

The female face of Orthodox Christianity, is largely unknown and is still to be explored. Little is known of the life of Christian women during the dark centuries following the Hellenistic age up to the time of the splendor of Byzantium.

Following the missionary growth of Byzantine Christianity and especially after the fall of Byzantium, the patriarchal agrarian societies on the seabord of the Mediterranean and in Eastern Europe became the homeland of Orthodoxy, and the clear teaching of the gospel and the Fathers on humankind lived on there deep in the Church's conscience. But, like the treasure hidden in the field of the gospel parable, it lay buried beneath the dead wood of outmoded taboos, like the concept of the monthly ritual impurity of women based on a misogynistic interpretation of Leviticus, and truisms about their weakness and inferiority. The seeds of the gospel, however never cease to bear fruit. The flame of women's holiness has never been extinguished. The Church has canonized new martyrs, great monastics, and princesses like Olga of Kiev, venerated with her grandson Vladimir as "equal to the Apostles." She has also canonized ordinary laywomen like Juliana Lazarevskaia in Russia at the dawn of the modern era, whose heroic charity was extolled in her biography written by her son.[8]

Nearer to our own day we have the example of "women believers"—simple peasants and aristocrats, virtuous women and prostitutes—in the great Russian literature of the nineteenth century: the princess Maria of *War and Peace*, Sonia in *Crime and Punishment*, and the sorrowing mothers seeking consolation from the *starets* Zosima in *The Brothers Karamazov*.

What is the situation today? What is the position of women now in the Orthodox Church? During the 20th century, it ceased to be exclusively Eastern, either geographically or culturally. As a result of emigration, Orthodox communities of varying sizes have been established and settled in Western Europe, America, and even Australia. Traditionally Orthodox countries such as Greece, Romania, and Rus-

[8] Elizabeth Behr-Sigel, *Prière et sainteté dans l'Eglise russe*, Bellefontaine, pp. 109–113.

sia, are becoming Westernized. To what extent has this intermingling and marriage of different cultures changed the life and position of Orthodox women? A full examination of the subject would exceed by far the bounds of this chapter. I shall simply make some observations.

In the course of the recent, often tragic, history of the Orthodox churches, women have taken on considerable responsibilities. This was particularly the case in Russia under the Soviet government. It was a well known that it was women — often older women, the famous "babushkii" or grandmothers — were the ones who saved the parish structures of the Russian Orthodox Church from the total destruction planned by the atheistic state. The grandmothers arranged for their grandchildren to be secretly baptized. But they also showed themselves to be willing to form groups of twenty faithful, to whom under legislation instituted under Krushchev, the government could, at their request — a request that put them into a compromised position-make available a state owned place of worship. It was also often woman who would consent to take on the position and responsibility of the *starosta, i.e.* the responsible lay person of the parish, thus serving as the intermediary — the buffer — between the secular authorities and the priest, whom she sought to protect from their harassment.[9] The survival of a parish depended to a large extent on the courage, determination, and savoir-faire of a few elderly women.

It should be remembered that as the same time other Russian Christian women were to be found in the ranks of the so-called dissidents. They published *samizdats*, illegal literature, organized underground religious seminaries, and were sentenced to heavy prison time or to the gulag. What has become of them? We hear little of them nowadays.

Alongside the Christian women dissidents in the USSR, mention should also be made of an Orthodox nun who performed her ministry-truly diaconal ministry according to her biographer-among Rus-

[9] Editors note: the *starotsa* or parish warden is the lay leader of the parish council or parish vestry, the lay organization that helps govern the local parish.

sian emigration in France, initially in the inter-war period and then under the German occupation. She was Mother Maria Skobtsova, a former revolutionary socialist who returned to the Church. She was a friend of the great Russian religious intellectuals such as Fr. Sergius Bulgakov and the philosopher Nicolas Berdiaev. Like Pastor Bonhoffer, she was a key figure in the Christian resistance to Nazi barbarism. For having organized an escape network for Jews in Paris, she was deported to Ravensbruck concentration camp and died there, almost certainly gassed shortly before Easter 1945.[10] Steps are being taken for her to be canonized by the Orthodox Church.

Today, after the fall of communism, younger women, often new converts, are taking over from the grandmothers of the Soviet period. These new Christians quite often have good university education, and are working as assistants to overworked priests. They act as social workers, and also as bookkeepers, accountants, and architects, and are breathing new life into parish structures. It is women who are taking on the basic diaconal work of the Church among the victims of harsh economic change, such as old people, street children, large families and the handicapped.

Among these women, who are effectively deaconesses but without the title, there are some who desire recognition from the Church in the form of a blessing of their ministry, or indeed an actual ordination. The desire is to be found here and there among certain educated women have been theologically trained. Such a desire has ancient roots in Russian history. Although the ancient order of deaconesses fell into disuse, it was never officially abolished in the Orthodox Church. A campaign to restore it was mounted in the mid 19th century-perhaps through Protestant influence-by women of high aristocracy, they were encouraged by enlightened bishops such as the famous Metropolitan Philaret Drozdov of Moscow. The call was taken

[10] Mère Marie, *Le Sacrement du Frère*, Paris-Lausanne, 1995: Serge Hackel, Mère Marie, Paris, YMCA Press, 1992 (in Russian); Serge Hackel, *One of Great Price*, London; Elizabeth Behr-Sigel, "Mère Marie Skobtsov," in *Messenger orthodoxe*, no. 111, 1989 vol. 2.

up again at the beginning of the 20th century by the Grand Duchess Elizabeth, but in the tragic events of that period-Elizabeth Feodorvna was assassinated at the beginning of the Bolshevik revolution-it came to nothing. She has recently been canonized. But her bold proposal lies dormant in the archives of the Patriarchate of Moscow. It is not on today's agenda of the Russian Orthodox Church. As it emerges from a long ice age, it has flowing through it a fundamentalist and anti-Western current. Only a small minority of women know about the proposal and are interested in it. For various reasons, which would be interested in examine, the militant feminism which as developed in the West remains as a whole alien to Russian Christian women. They say that they have no need of it. As a legacy from monastic spirituality, the principle of obedience to one's "spiritual father" who is a priest or a monk, although their spiritual mothers, far from being disputed, finds enthusiastic supporters among new women converts. Paradoxically, in new parishes and fellowships, which are springing up in Russia, these deeply committed "submissive women" often from the most dynamic and even dominant element. The Church, like Russian society, is, according to Veronique Lossky, who knows them well, "contradictorily at once patriarchal and matriarchal."[11]

Elsewhere too, Orthodox women today are taking an active part in Church life, both in countries of Eastern Europe and the Middle East. Where Orthodoxy is the traditional form of Christianity, and in the *diaspora*, where in the West in the course of the 20th century we have witnessed the birth and establishment of Orthodox communities. As mothers and teachers, they have always had an essential role in passing on the faith within the family. But today their role goes beyond the family circle. Religious education and catechesis of children and young people is carried out by women, either alone or in equal partnership with male catechists. They sing in in church choirs, the role of which is so important in Orthodox worship. They are sometimes choir leaders. And-at least in the churches resulting from Rus-

[11] Veronique Lossky, "La femme et le sacerdoce" in *Contacts*, no. 174, 1996 vol. 2.

sian emigration-that they are members of parish and diocesan councils and diocesan assemblies, which are responsible for the election of bishops. In all these ways they participate in different aspects of the life of the community. A significant step forward was taken when, during the second half of the twentieth century, when in various local Orthodox churches, particularly in Greece and in the *diaspora* in France and the United States, women were admitted as students to theological schools and faculties. They are now beginning to teach in them. Women Orthodox theologians share in ecumenical dialogue at all levels, particularly in the heart of the ecumenical World Council of Churches. It is a new situation, throwing up paradoxes. As Orthodox woman who is competent to do so can occupy a New Testament teaching post in a prestigious theological faculty such as that of Thessalonika. She is, however, not permitted to read the gospel in the worship of the people of God. An Orthodox theological declares unanimously that, "all acts denying the dignity of the human person, all discrimination between men and women based on gender, is a sin,"[12] but access to the altar remains forbidden to women.

As responsible theologians in the Orthodox Church-both men and women-have become aware of these contradictions, the question of the admission of women to the sacramental ministry has arisen. That question no longer comes to them only from outside in the course of ecumenical dialogue, but it has also become for them an internal problem.[13] The first international conference of Orthodox women, in the monastery of Agapia in Romania (1976), and at the Orthodox Academy of Crete (1989), expressed the wish that the possibility of the admission of women to a sacramental ministry be responsibly and calmly investigated. At the international Orthodox consultation in Rhodes in (1988) on "the ordination of women and

[12] "La place des femmes dans l'Eglise orthodoxe et la question de l'ordination des femmes," in *Contacts,* no. 146, 1989 vol. 2, p. 102.

[13] See the following chapter. Also E. Behr-Sigel, "L'ordination des femmes: un problème oecuménique," in *Contacts* no. 150, 1990, vol. 2. English translation in *Sobornost* 13:1 1991, and Theology, 1994 vol. 2 (SPCK).

the place of women in the Church," convened and organized by the Ecumenical Patriarchate, a resolution to restore the diaconate for women was unanimously passed. More recently, this same wish has been vigorously taken up by Orthodox women meeting in Damascus (October 1996) and in Istanbul (May 1997) in the course of conferences dealing with the gospel them, 'Discerning the Signs of the Times" (Matthew 16:3).

For reasons of liturgical symbolism, the ordination of women to the presbyterate remains unacceptable to most Orthodox. But does that make it a real heresy, a departure from Christ's teaching? The first Orthodox theologians confronted this question, for which they were not prepared, were inclined to think so. Today, their responses are more nuanced, as can be seen in the accompanying study by Bishop Kallistos Ware, which is both rigorous and open.

Fr. John Meyendorff, of blessed memory, in a book published more than thirty-five years ago, but still relevant and recently republished wrote, "One of the basic problems confronting theologians today is to be able to distinguish between the Church's holy Tradition-a legitimate development of revelation-and the human traditions which are only an imperfect expression of it, and, very often, contradict and obscure it."[14] There is a growing number of Orthodox theologians, men and women, who wish to see an *aggiornamento* of certain "traditional" practices regarding women in our historic churches: practices marked, as stated in the conclusion of the Rhodes consultation by "human weakness and sin," which have prevented "Christian communities from putting an end to ideas and customs which in practice amount to discrimination."[15]

My desire is that the Church become what it already is in the supreme reality of the mind of God: a community of faith, hope, and love, of men and women, of mysterious human persons, unutterably equal yet different, made in the image and reflecting glory of God

[14] Jean Meyendorff, *L'Eglise orthodoxe hier et aujourd'hui*, Paris, Ed. Du Seuil, 1995, p. 9.

[15] *Contacts,* no.146, 1989 vol. 2, p. 102.

the Three in One. That is the great Orthodox vision of the Church. It remains for it to be transplanted into concrete historical terms. That is a humanly impossible task, but it one to which we feel we are called, trusting in Christ's promise to send the Spirit, the Giver of Life, the Spirit of Truth, who will guide his disciples into all truth (John 16:13).

CHAPTER NINE

Nicholas Berdiaev (1874–1948)

Of all the authors included in this book, Berdiaev is the only non-professional theologian represented. In 1901, Berdiaev became acquainted with Sergius Bulgakov, who was a Marxist and later returned to his Orthodox roots. Due to the harsh circumstances under the Soviet communist regime, Berdiaev along with other Russian intellectuals were deported from their homeland and forced to live in the West. Berdiaev left Russia in 1922 and eventually emigrated to Berlin where he established the Russian Academy of Theology and Philosophy. However, life in Berlin was difficult for Berdiaev and his family, as it was for thousands of Russian immigrants due to the lack of language skills and job openings. So Berdiaev left Berlin for Paris, where he became acquainted with other Russian intellectuals who were already living there. By this time, Bulgakov was teaching at the St. Sergius Theological Institute and was active in the Russian émigré community. Berdiaev never accepted an official teaching post at St. Sergius, but rather accepted a teaching post at the Sorbonne where he taught Philosophy. He was also active in the Russian Christian Student Movement as well as Orthodox Action.

Every Sunday, the Berdiaevs hosted a weekly gathering in their house in Clamart, a suburb of Paris. Notable persons, such as Helene Iswolsky, Mother Maria Skobtsova, and Jacques and Raissa Maritain, were frequent guests at these meetings.

Berdiaev was a dedicated scholar and philosopher, writing numerous essays, articles, and books, many of which were translated into English soon after his death. While very much a faithful Orthodox Christian, he never held an official teaching post in the Orthodox Church nor was ordained to official Church ministry. He was an active layman, focusing his attention on the nature of freedom in Christ, that humanity has been given the greatest gift and this cannot be taken away from us, not from the government, and not even by the Church. Berdiaev saw the inconsistency between Orthodox teachings and doctrine and the rampant clericalism, abuse of power and authority, and hypocrisy among its leaders, especially the hierarchy. This essay, "Discord in the Church and Freedom of Conscience," was originally published in the Russian language journal *Put'* in 1926 (*Put'* Oct./Nov. 1926, No. 5, pp. 42–54). The themes highlighted throughout the essay — freedom of conscience and freedom of God — is compared with the human authority and power of the hierarchy which is still an important topic in the contemporary theological reflection in Christianity today, especially among the Orthodox and Roman Catholics.

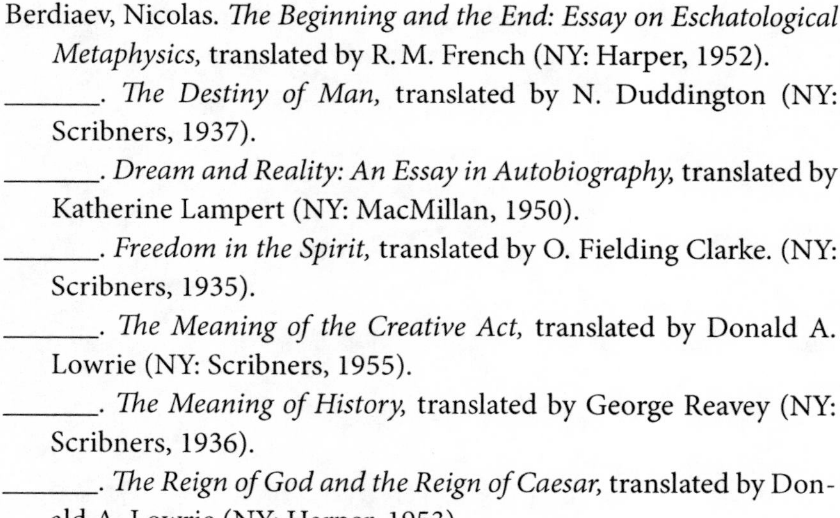

For Further Reading

Berdiaev, Nicolas. *The Beginning and the End: Essay on Eschatological Metaphysics,* translated by R. M. French (NY: Harper, 1952).

_______. *The Destiny of Man,* translated by N. Duddington (NY: Scribners, 1937).

_______. *Dream and Reality: An Essay in Autobiography,* translated by Katherine Lampert (NY: MacMillan, 1950).

_______. *Freedom in the Spirit,* translated by O. Fielding Clarke. (NY: Scribners, 1935).

_______. *The Meaning of the Creative Act,* translated by Donald A. Lowrie (NY: Scribners, 1955).

_______. *The Meaning of History,* translated by George Reavey (NY: Scribners, 1936).

_______. *The Reign of God and the Reign of Caesar,* translated by Donald A. Lowrie (NY: Harper, 1953).

______. *The Russian Idea,* translated by R.M. French. (NY: MacMillan, 1947).

______. *Spirit and Reality,* translated by George Reavey (London: G. Bles, 1946).

______. *Slavery and Freedom,* translated by R.M. French (NY: Scribners, 1939).

______. *Truth and Revelation,* translated by R.M. French (NY: Harper, 1953).

Lowrie, Donald. *Rebellious Prophet* (NY: Harper, 1960).

See also Fr. Stephen Janos' website dedicated to Berdiaev: http://www.berdyaev.com, accessed August 2007.

Discord in the Church and Freedom of Conscience

Clericalism is alien to Orthodoxy. This negative phenomenon rather was developed upon Catholic soil. But we are now witnessing the birth of Russian clericalist tendencies and clerical ideology. Our Orthodox youth, even in their better parts has been affected by this malady. Among the youth, this is a childhood disease of Russian religious renaissance: a passionate reaction to a long period of separation from the Orthodox Church. Among the elders, the pre-Revolutionary generation, this is more likely to be a geriatric sclerosis, a complete incompatibility with creativity and freedom.

The last Council of Bishops in Karlovtsy stepped on a path of a schism in the Church. It devastated the Metropolitans. It practically condemned the Student Christian Movement. It fomented a poison of malicious suspicion, desiring to infect healthy souls with its senseless mistrustfulness. Its clericalist tendencies produced a frightful shock, forcing one to think about the primary questions of the Church's self-consciousness. And this is a positive aspect of this miserable Council. Sometimes good arises out of evil. Divine Providence even makes use of evil for purposes of good. The pus-filled boil burst open. And this is good. The horrible blow was delivered to the authority and prestige of the Russian bishops in Yugoslavia and Bulgaria, which has governed all these years by spiritual fear. This ordeal must likewise be painfully experienced by all those who were susceptible to the illusions of clericalism.

A certain part of Russian youth, which was ardently and sincerely religious, but which had not completely thought through or even grasped the fundamentals of Orthodoxy, developed a tendency to consider each bishop to be infallible, and seeing him as something like the pope. The generation, which developed a reaction against the Revolution's destructive calamity, and which needs to lean against an unshakable pillar of authority, has developed a fear of the freedom of spirit, a freedom of choice. However, such tendencies must lead to tragic conflicts of conscience.

It is only within Catholicism that the concept of external, infallible, hierarchical authority has been fully developed, with its resultant conclusions. In Orthodoxy such a concept can only be incomplete and contradictory. If one can live satisfactorily with one Pope, then by trying to live with twenty-five popes who are constantly arguing and condemning each other, one can easily land in an insane asylum. Actually, Orthodoxy differs from Catholicism not because it has twenty-five popes instead of one, but because it does not have any popes. This must be thoroughly understood.

Orthodox consciousness does not know of any infallible authority of its bishops. Only the whole Church, only the Church's *sobornost'* (catholicity), enjoys infallibility within itself, and those who bear it constitute the whole people of the Church of all Christian generations beginning with the Apostles. The 1848 Encyclical of the Eastern Patriarchs states: "Infallibility is found in the oneness of the Church's ecumenicity, united by mutual love and the unchanging dogmas, along with the purity of rites. It is not entrusted to the hierarchy alone but to the whole people of the Church which constitute the Body of Christ." The bearers and guardians of Christian Truth are the whole people of the Church and not the hierarchy alone. And there are no formal and legal guarantees for expressing the internal authority of the Church. A single Orthodox individual can be more correct than the predominant majority of bishops. There was a time when St. Athanasius the Great, while still a deacon, *i.e.* in an insignificant hierarchical office, was the defender of true Orthodoxy against almost the whole of the Eastern episcopal establishment which was inclined towards Arianism. Clericalists of that time who supported the external hierarchical authority, should have been against Athanasius the Great and on the side of the Arian bishops. It is entirely conceivable, for Orthodox consciousness, that the lay author A. S. Khomiakov expressed the spirit of Orthodoxy much better than some Metropolitans who were influenced by scholastic theology, both Protestant and Catholic.

Orthodoxy was tolerant of a wide variety of freedom of religious thought. The great advantage of Orthodoxy is found in precisely its lack of external guarantees, that it does not view the Church in terms of the kingdom of this world, analogous to the State, which demands formal juridical conditions, believing as it does, in the direct activity of the Holy Spirit. A question which is presently obscure but which must be acutely posited, is the question whether Orthodoxy does or does not recognize freedom of conscience as the preeminent basis of spiritual life. [Russian poet and thinker Feodor Tyuchev once wrote with reference to Pope Pius IX: "they were overcome by the fatal word — freedom of conscience is nonsense." These words, so dear to our Slavophiles, make sense and are justified only if Orthodoxy itself firmly affirms that freedom of conscience is not nonsense but is the greatest treasure of Christianity. But we are living in a time of fear and timidity in the face of the freedom of conscience, refusing to take upon ourselves the burden of freedom, the burden of responsibility.

Today's clericalist tendencies reflect a Catholic distorted view in the understanding of the Church and Church authority. And this Catholic view is especially strong among those who consider themselves fanatically and exclusively Orthodox, who hate Catholicism and are incapable of understanding its positive qualities. Today there is a reaction not only against Russian anti-religious thinking, which is very good, but also against Russian religious thought of the XIX century, which is rather ingratitude and an uncalled-for breach of continuity. The Russian religious, Orthodox thought was exceptionally freedom-loving, it nurtured the idea of the free spirit, the freedom of conscience and was preparing a creative spiritual reform, a spiritual renaissance which was wrecked by the forces of the long growing atheistic revolution and its inseparable forces of deadening reaction which quenches the spirit. Now the creative and regenerative movements in the Church are curbed and paralyzed by the lies of the Living Church and the falseness of Church reform in Soviet Russia.

For me the problem of the freedom of conscience is fundamental in Christian consciousness and it must be articulated with the greatest clarity and radicalism. Freedom always enjoys primacy over authority. Even in the Catholicism the search for unshakable authority with its perceptible signs is, in the final analysis, a fiction based on illusions. The Pope's infallible authority assumes that it is accepted and confirmed by the free will of the believing Catholic.

Papal authority is not an external objective reality, it is not a reality of a natural and a material order, such as the reality of a stone thrown at us or a tree branch striking us from without, but it is a reality of a spiritual order. But the Papal authority becomes a spiritual reality only as a result of an act of faith, which is an act of freedom, resulting from the acceptance of a religious subject.

The particularity of the predominant Catholic perception is that it sincerely wants to quickly put a stop to the exercise of the freedom of conscience, that it does not recognize the permanence of its exercise. In principle, the Orthodox perception does not recognize this curb on the freedom of conscience, or that such exercise is the exclusive prerogative of the highest Church organs. Freedom of conscience acts without ceasing. That freedom keeps the catholicity of the Church alive. The life of the Church is the unity of love in freedom. In essence, everything, which is significant spiritually, in the Catholic world as well, presumes the freedom of conscience, the creativity of the free spirit, and not the action of an external formal authority.

Freedom of conscience in Orthodoxy does not mean Protestant individualism. Within itself, in its depth, it is united with *sobornost'* (catholicity). The Reformation was absolutely correct in its affirmation of the freedom of conscience but in the end it placed itself upon the false path of individualism. Freedom is not the isolation of the soul, opposing it to all other souls and to the whole world. In the realm of freedom, of Christian freedom, there is a mystical union of that which is uniquely individual with the universally common. But freedom can never be ended or interrupted, it cannot be delegated to another, it can only be enlightened.

I can never accept anything against my free conscience, not even God Himself, since God cannot be a violence over me. My humility before the Highest can only be an enlightenment and a transfiguration of my free conscience from within, as my mystical communion with a Higher Reality.

Even an Ecumenical Council, Orthodoxy's highest organ, does not enjoy formal authority. An Ecumenical Council does not have formal and juridical signs, consciously discernible, does not have a legalistic status. A Council should not be made into an idol or an absolute. A Council could be a Robber Council, having all signs of legitimacy. Well-known is a sharp criticism of St. Gregory of Nyssa who did not want to attend them. An authentic Ecumenical Council is one in which the Holy Spirit is truly present. The authenticity and the spirituality of an Ecumenical Council is being discerned and affirmed by the free conscience of the people of the Church. The Holy Spirit acts within the Church's people, in the Church's *sobornost'* (catholicity) and makes a distinction between truth and falsehood, between authenticity and imitation.

The order of ecclesiastical existence as a spiritual existence, is distinguished in that it has no external guarantees, it has no legal or materially discernable signs of authenticity. Everything is resolved through spiritual life, through spiritual experience. The Holy Spirit does not act like natural forces and social forces. There are no analogies here. Too much of such analogy is a temptation and is an attempt to identify the Church with this world.

The Church's hierarchical structure is historically inevitable. Canonical development is a secondary development and not of the first order. Of primary order is the spiritual life only and that which develops within it. This is what holds the Church in its holiness. The confirmation of the primacy of external hierarchical authority is always a self-deception and an illusion. Those who definitively submit themselves to the external hierarchical authority are the ones whose internal convictions are identical or comparable with the authorities. No one has ever submitted to external authority if his conscience definitely opposed it, or the submission was only in accordance with purely external discipline.

This must likewise be said about Catholics. External authority of itself has never been able to convince anyone of anything. Conviction always arises from within and always presumes a collaboration of the freedom of conscience and God's Spirit. Clericalism is convincing only for convinced clericals, for those who treasure the clerical structure of life more than anything else, those who desire and anxiously await the triumph of clericalism and its party. The defenders of authority and enemies of freedom usually recognize complete and unlimited freedom for themselves but they do not want others to have it. Such are the least humble and the most self-willed people around.

This is obvious from the example of the direction of the Rightist-clericalist trend in the emigration. The extreme and at times fanatical supporters of the Karlovtsy Synod's line against Metropolitan Evlogy represent the extreme rightist monarchist group which selects the highest Church organ and the Metropolitans not on the basis of ecclesio-canonical principles but on the basis of their particular political sympathies and Black-Hundreds reactionary aspirations. If the Synod of Bishops and the Council of Bishops would adopt a more liberal and freedom-loving direction for the Church, if they would break with the Rightist monarchist course, then their present supporters would desert it and would begin to reject its ecclesiastical authority. The Communists are just like that: they recognize complete freedom for themselves but do not let others breathe freely.

All these extreme Right monarchists in the emigration recognize complete freedom of conscience and freedom of choice for themselves and admit authority of the Church where they want and where they like, clothing with authority those metropolitans and bishops who cater to their whims and sympathize with them. In Berlin, I heard Russians say on more than one occasion that they do not recognize the authority of the Metropolitan Evlogy, to whose jurisdiction they are subject, because they don't like the direction he is taking. These people would never listen to the voice of the Church, which would condemn their aspirations and political sympathies, nor accept it as the Church's voice. They never wanted to listen to Patriarch Tikhon, *i.e.* the highest organ of the Russian Orthodox Church. Nor did the bishops who did not like the direction the Patriarch was taking, listen to him. The very formation of the Synod of Bishops was contrary to the wishes of the Patriarch and was an arbitrary act.

All these self-willed people of the Rightist camp have never recognized freedom for the Church and always supported the State's dominance over the Church, not so much of the State but of their own political direction and interests. The first Karlovtsy Council, which was condemned by the Patriarch, was conducted under the banner of the Rightist monarchist organization which exercised its dominance over the Church. Of what use is hierarchical authority here? They do not recognize it when they don't like it.

Today, within the Rightist émigré circles, Church authority is recognized where it endorses and encourages the reactionary restorative political desires, where there is an aura of the spirit of obscurantism and the spiteful paranoia over the "Judeo-Masonic" conspiracy. No one pays much attention to canons unless they are needed for a false and hypocritical cover. It is quite clear that, from the canonical point of view, legitimacy is on the side of Metropolitan Evlogy, but the Rightist-clericalist sector recognizes that the ecclesiastical authority belongs to the Synod of Bishops inasmuch as the latter expresses their spirit and their aims. The Rightist-clericalist sector in fact consists of those people who want to dominate the Church with their politics and monarchist type of government. It also recognizes the primacy of freedom over authority but only of their own freedom. It projects its freedom or its will upon the organ which it likes and which is convenient for them. This lie must be exposed and it is being exposed by life itself.

The Karlovtzy episcopate is a certain party, a certain trend and it is not the voice of the Church. The pretension of such a trend of the émigré Orthodox Church to autocephaly and as the head of the whole Russian Orthodox Church is pathetic and laughable. A significant part, not all of them, of the émigré hierarchy consists of bishops who deserted their flocks and for that reason it cannot have any significant moral authority for the whole of the Russian Orthodox world. Not a single bishop or priest in the emigration has any moral right to pass judgment upon bishops and priests who are doomed to a martyr's life in Russia. There are those who speak with disdain and judgment about Patriarch Tikhon and about Metropolitan Benjamin. This is a godless and a repulsive manifestation. No one can know how the disdainful and judgmental individual would behave himself in Soviet Russia. Would he not join the Living Church, as did a number of former Black Hundred supporters, since they are so experienced in servitude and spying? We now know that both Patriarch Tikhon and Metropolitan Benjamin, in their own ways, suffered martyrdom.

We have entered upon a lengthy epoch of Church discords. For one who knows Church history, there is nothing new in this. But we, Russians, have become used to a lengthy period of peace and stability in the Church. The Orthodox people lived in a stable milieu, in a strong cohesion of Church and State. In the 20th century, the Russian world experienced some stormy movements, which resulted in a crisis and catastrophe, but the Church remained in appearance in a state of deathly calm and immobility. Perhaps the catastrophe is the result of the Church's inertness. The monarchy protected the Church's repose but along with this it stood in the way of any creative activity, even forbidding the calling of a Council.

Many Orthodox people thought that this calm and inertia would be eternal. But for a more acute view it was evident that not everything was all right and peaceful in the Orthodox Church. Internal processes took place, internal contradictions occurred which were not exposed because the Church was enslaved by the State. The prevailing style of the imperial Church was one of deathly inertia and immobility. There were no Church discords or disputes because there was very little creative activity, or it was so insignificant that it was powerless to express itself. When disputes arose in the first century Church, there was also a stormy creative life. Church disputes could be the other side of a vital internal life, of religious tension and internal struggles of the spirit.

We are entering upon such an epoch, one very difficult and trying, full of responsibility but also joyful in seeing the beginning of a creative movement. The structure of the Orthodox soul must undergo a change. A new order is coming to Orthodoxy. One must prepare his soul for a violent era of discords. There is no turning back to the old calm and stability nor can there be. One cannot divest oneself of the burden of the freedom of choice; one cannot lean against an external unshakable pillar for support. We must find support within the depth of our own spirit.

We are witnessing that history of the Orthodox Church which is seeing the end and liquidation not only of the Petrine Synodal period but of the whole Constantinopolitan period in Christianity's history. We are now at the beginning of a new Christian era. The Church must redefine its relationship to the world and to the processes that are taking place there. The Church must be free and independent of the State, of Caesar's kingdom, of worldly moods. It must relate to the creative processes of the world in a more meaningful way, to bless the world's move towards Christ and Christianity, which are as yet unrecognized, to welcome the prodigal son's return to the Father in a way other than was done up to now.

In times of a historical crisis and change, during the destruction of the old world and the birth of the new, the Church's hierarchy does not always, or in a timely manner, become fully cognizant of the magnitude of the events taking place, nor does it assess the religious significance of what is taking place and its effect upon the Church. A part of the hierarchy remains completely in the past and longs for restoration of the old, peaceful, immobile life. It is not sensitive to the historical reality. It is blind to that which is taking place in the world. It looks upon the tragedy of mankind without love or compassion. It remains full of pharisaical self-justification and with a closed mind.

Another part of the hierarchy begins to sense that some changes are taking place but without being fully conscious of them. A third part recognizes these changes more fully. Such a variation of feeling and consciousness engenders strife within the hierarchy itself and results in discord within the Church. As always, ideal motivations will become compromised with personal and class agendas, class struggle and personal competition.

The Karlovtsy bishops, the Karlovtsy Synod and the majority of the Sobor represent the trend within the hierarchy which completely finds itself in the decaying past, the period in Orthodoxy which is withering away. They neither see nor understand what is taking place. They are spiritually blind and are embittered at the tragedy that is taking place in the world and in mankind. They are contemporary lawyers and Pharisees for whom the Sabbath is greater than man. The last Karlovtsy Council and its condemnation of everything creative in Christian movement is the final convulsion of the Church's expiring era. It is Monophysical in spirit in that it rejects man; it is Caesaro-papist in the flesh in that it deifies Caesar upon earth. This kind of a trend must hurl anathemas at everything that is taking place in mankind and in the world. It has been made captive by malicious mistrustfulness and suspicion. It sees only the advent of evil, since it is only interested in the old life and hates any new life.

It is tied not to the eternal in the Church but only to that which is corruptible and transient. It stands in the way of the emergence of young life in Orthodoxy. Such a tendency not only lacks spiritual truth but it has no canonical truth. The Rightist Synodal trends within the emigration is formally compatible with the Leftist [Living Church] synodal trends in Soviet Russia. There is no freedom for the Church in either place.

Spiritual truth and canonical truth is completely on the side of that part of the hierarchy, which guards the freedom of the Church, which places the Church above worldly elements and political passions, which discerns the magnitude of the historical revolution, which has taken place and which precludes forever any possibility of returning to the past. This portion of the hierarchy abroad is represented by Metropolitan Evlogy. The point here has nothing to do with Metropolitan Evlogy's personal views, but in that he is the instrument of the Highest Will, of Divine Providence, during this difficult and torturous transitional period being experienced by the Orthodox Church abroad. Such was Patriarch Tikhon for all Russia. It is clear that here we have help from God.

Neither the Patriarch nor the Metropolitan can be spokesmen for any kind of an extreme trend in the life of the Church, and they rarely are the initiators of anything other than a placid movement. Their mission is to maintain the Church's equanimity in the face of discord and disturbances. But in their mission they should not interfere with emerging creative initiatives, they can give them their approval and incorporate them into the basic course of the Church's life.

The equilibrium of the Church's life, her unity, cannot be supported by way of compromise with the decaying segment of the hierarchy that condemns creative life and stands in the way of letting the Church enter into a new epoch. This decaying trend is doomed to be sloughed off. The Church's development is found on the opposite side of that deadening policy, which chokes off the spirit. I believe that a split is inevitable sooner or later. The possibility of a temporal truce is of course cannot be excluded, but it won't be substantial. The Orthodox Church will not cease to exist because of it and will not lose its unity. Essential is the unity in truth and not a compromise of truth with falsehood. The fear that the reactionary-restorative trend will fall off for good and then die is not a religious-ecclesiastic, but rather political fear, since this would be the mortal blow to the entire Rightist monarchist movement. This blow must be administered since that movement stands in the way of the healing of Russia and the Russian people. It is blocking the begetting of a better life.

The extreme Rightist party in Orthodoxy adheres to the idea of an ecclesiastic nationalism. It wants to isolate Orthodoxy from the Christian world. It does not understand the ecumenical spirit. In all likelihood we will experience a new Old Believer and an Old Ritualist split, but in the worst possible meaning of those terms. The old split somehow had the people's truth in it, which will not be so in the new split. This new split is possible in Russia itself as well as in the emigration. One should prepare for it spiritually. It will demand courage and decisiveness.

Our own epoch in the Church's life presents us with a very difficult and complex spiritual problem. What does it mean, when a bishop — well-known for his ascetical life, an authentic monastic, who carries out the testaments of the Holy Fathers, who is known for his spirituality — turns out to be spiritually blind, unable to test the spirits and sees in the world around himself and in mankind nothing but evil and darkness and is doomed to disseminate about himself nothing but condemnation and gloom? This is a very alarming problem that calls forth some thoughtful concern. Apparently asceticism in and of itself does not bring about higher spiritual achievements and does not result in spiritual insight. It might even dry up and harden the heart. The devil is also an ascetic. Another element is necessary in the spiritual path without which asceticism is deprived of its transfiguring and enlightening purpose. Asceticism without love is fruitless and dead.

"If I speak in the tongues of men and of angels, but have not love, I am a noisy gong or a clanging cymbal. And if I have prophetic powers, and understand all mysteries and all knowledge, and if I have all faith, so as to remove mountains, but have not love, I am nothing. If I give away all I have, and if I deliver my body to be burned, but have not love, I gain nothing.

"Love is patient and kind; love is not jealous or boastful; it is not arrogant or rude. Love does not insist on its own way; it is not irritable or resentful; it does not rejoice at wrong, but rejoices in the right. Love bears all things, believes all things, hopes all things, endures all things" (I Cor. 13:1–7).

The hierarchs who gathered for the Council of Bishops in Karlovtsy failed to carry out the testaments of Apostle Paul. There is no love in their words and deeds, only a profound malevolence, a lack of love for man and for God's creation. They are neither "long-suffering" nor "merciful." They "put on airs," are "irritated," "conceive of evil," they "shield" nothing, they "hope" for nothing, they "bear" nothing. The monk-ascetic can observe the commandment to love God but if he does not observe the commandment to love his neighbor, does not love man or God's creation, if he sees nothing but evil in man, then his love for God is perverted and distorted. Then he is nothing but "a noisy gong, a clanging symbol."

The monastic ascetical malevolence, lack of love, suspicion of the world of man and of any activity in the world is a perversion of Christian faith. Christianity is the religion of love of God and love of man. Love for God alone without love for man is a perversion of the love for God. Love for man without love for God (humanism) is a perversion of love for man. The mystery of Christianity is the mystery of Godmanhood. The monk-ascetic in whom the heart has hardened and cooled, who loves God but treats man and the world without love is a practical, living Monophysite. He does not confess the religion of Godmanhood. He is the culpable source of the advent of Godless humanism in the world.

Orthodoxy has experienced this Monophysite tendency and now we are seeing its evil fruits. We are witnessing the last vestiges of a Monophysite, misanthropic Orthodoxy, or—more correctly—of a psudo-Orthodoxy. This spirit is bound for oblivion. It evilly acts against man and condemns any progress in life. This problem is pointedly raised in the discord within the Church. Presently there is a struggle for Christianity as the religion of Godmanhood that unites within itself the fullness of love for God and man. Asceticism without love is dead. It makes one blind, without vision. It makes of man a self-made eunuch [refers to Skoptsy, a Russian Manichean heresy]. This truth must be realized through suffering in the time of our discord. He who is exclusively concerned with the salvation of his soul while being cold and cruel to his neighbor, that person kills his soul. The bishops who carried out their resolutions at the Karlovtsy Council show no signs of Christian love. They are carrying out a deed without love, one, which is inimical to man. They are Monophysites in the spiritually-ethical meaning of that word no matter how loudly they profess the irreproachable ecclesiastical and dogmatic formulas. In this is the metaphysical meaning of current state of things.

Much is being said in out time about Churcifying life. This is the maxim of the Russian Student Christian Movement. The maxim is undoubtedly sincere but it needs clarification and an explanation of its context since one can attribute completely different meanings to it.

The Churching or Churchification of life could be understood in the spirit of a false "hierarchism" or clericalism, in the spirit of the old Byzantine theocratic idea that has been done away with in history and cannot be restored. Some understand Churchification as a submission of all facets of life to hierarchical authority, subject to their direct rule. This is more like a Catholic rather than an Orthodox understanding of Churchification, a Catholic theocratic idea, from which even many Catholics free themselves. It is not understandable where such an idea came about among a certain part of our youth, which looks upon the hierarchy as possessing some kind of infallibility and a special charisma of knowledge and teaching authority. Actually, there is no such teaching in the Orthodox Church although some individual hierarchs espoused it. Basically, it contradicts the principle of *sobornost'* [catholicity] that lies in the foundation of the Orthodox Church. The *sobornost'* of the Church, which cannot have any kind of a formal and juridical expression, is incompatible with the assertion of the infallible authority of the episcopate and its exclusive charismatic privileges in doctrine and teaching authority.

The Spirit breathes where it wills. For the Orthodox, the Church is not an unequal organization. The priesthood has, before anything else, a liturgical meaning, and in this it is inerrable and does not depend upon human qualities or talents. But the Christian truth is revealed to and is guarded by the whole people of the Church amongst whom may be people with a special kind of individual gifts of teaching.

To the priesthood belongs the leadership on the spiritual path for the salvation of souls but not on the path of creativity, which is the prerogative of mankind. For example, *starchestvo*, spiritual leadership of *startsi*, *i.e.*, elders, which is so characteristic of Orthodoxy, proves that even spiritual gifts for the guidance of souls are not directly linked to the hierarchical order. The *starets* is an individual, gifted with personal charisma, discerned by the people, a spirit-bearing individual and not of a particular hierarchical order. The *startsi*, more often than not, were persecuted by bishops. Very enlightening in this sense is the life of Father Leonid, one of the first great *startsi* of the Optina monastery.

It is without question that disciplinary power, without which Church administration would be impossible, belongs to the bishop within his diocese. But this does not constitute infallible authority or a special gift of teaching. The bishop is at the head of the hierarchal structure of the Church; he maintains the unity of the Church and preserves Orthodox Tradition. But the lordship over all creative life of the individual and of people does not belong to him. He does not lord over the people's knowledge, over their social endeavors. Not even creative initiative in spiritual life belongs to him. Even Catholics recognize that internal priesthood belongs to all Christians and in a certain sense all Christians are priests. It is only in the external plan that the Catholics affirm the hierarchical principle in an extreme form.* Orthodoxy recognizes the potential general priesthood even more. This is in conformance with the teaching of the Apostles and many teachers of the Church. Meanwhile, hierocraticism is a deviation and a distortion, is the refusal to recognize that the Holy Spirit acts in all of the Christian mankind, that Christ is present among His people. This is the temptation of the Great Inquisitor, in Dostoyevsky's *Brothers Karamazov*, the rejection of the Spirit's freedom and the throwing off of the burden of the freedom of choice, the delegation of responsibility to the few and its removal from the conscience of all Christians. It isn't fair to blame only the Catholics for this.

The "Churchification" of life can be understood in a diametrically opposite sense, to see in it precisely the placing of greater responsibility upon all the people of the Church, upon all Christians, a more powerful action by freedom of the spirit. One can and must recognize as potentially Churchly that, which does not have an official, formally juridical stamp of Churchliness.

The Churchification of life is an invisible process, it does not hit one in the eyes. God's kingdom comes invisibly, in the depths of people's hearts. The people are tired of the conventional lies of external Churchliness, which symbolically sanctifies life without any real transfiguration and improvement. The authentic Churchification of life does not include only the processes that formally belong to the Church's hierarchy and are subject to a symbolically established form of sanctification. It primarily covers those processes, which truly change and transfigure life in accordance with the spirit of Christ and in which Christ's truth becomes manifest. These processes on the surface can remain free and can appear autonomous, but within them Christ's Spirit can act. Bukharev, one of the most remarkable of Orthodox theologians, says it well when he speaks of the "descent of Christ upon the earth," about our assimilation with Christ in every act of our life.

The Churchification of life is an actual, an ontologically real Christianization of life, the introduction of Christ's light, Christ's Truth, Christ's love and freedom in all spheres of life and creativity. Such a process demands spiritual freedom. It cannot be the result of an action or of a coercion on the part of an external authority.

The Churchification of life is not merely a sacramental process, a process of the sanctification of life, but it is also a prophetic process, a creative process that transfigures life, changing it and not merely sanctifying it. For this reason it cannot flow from the exclusive, authoritative provenance of the hierarchy because Christian freedom must act in that process.

The assertion that Divine grace acts only under authority and not in freedom is mistaken and arbitrary. It has been pointed out that freedom has been responsible for many mischiefs in this world, that it has been dark and without grace. However, authority has also been responsible for no small amount of mischief and it did increase darkness and malice in the world. There is no guarantee in either authority or freedom since behind authority there can be a manifestation of malicious freedom, self-volition and arbitrary rule. But freedom can be enlightening and full of Grace. The Spirit of God acts through freedom.

Where God's Spirit is, there is freedom. Without freedom God's Will can not be executed in this world. Man's free conscience may have been darkened by original sin but it has not been destroyed. Otherwise the image and likeness of God in man would have been erased and he would have been incapable of receiving any revelation and religious life would have been impossible for him. Man's freedom was reborn and enlightened from within through Christ's redemption and a free conscience was affirmed in man as a direct result of Christ's light within him.

Fearless affirmation of the freedom of spirit, freedom of conscience has a special significance in our critical epoch, in this epoch of ecclesiastical trouble and religious storms. Freedom is harsh, and it requires the strength of spirit. But this harshness and this strength are much needed today. Exactly in our epoch, it is impossible to lean exclusively on an external authority, on a pillar that towers above us and is not within us. We have to experience this absence of any external guarantees and external unshakable support in order to realize this. Only then that immovable foundation will be discovered within us.

This does not mean in the least that God has abandoned us. The work of the Holy Spirit might even be greater than ever. The vacillation of all external authorities, the crushing of all illusions have the providential significance. This has been sent to us as a test of our Christian freedom, of our internal fortitude. Not a single Orthodox Christian is exempt from the freedom of choice, from carrying out the act of a free conscience. One cannot cowardly run from this seeking a safe shelter. The highest levels of hierarchy will need the free conscience of Christians, the freedom of their choice, during this time of trouble and confrontations. God needs man's free conscience, man's free resoluteness, man's unfettered love. The whole meaning of the Creation lies in this. The rejection of the freedom of conscience as the supreme origin and the primary principle of religious life is the rejection of the world's purpose, is a slavish opposition to God, is a temptation and a derangement. The spirit of a free conscience is not the spirit of a formal and indifferent liberalism. It is part and parcel of the very content of Christian faith.

Everything that I said here I said not about that freedom, which I demand from God, but about that freedom, which God demands from me. The discords in the Church that are now taking place inside Russia and in the emigration, demand firmness, fortitude and strength, they demand the power of freedom in us. Without the spirit of freedom one cannot conquer the temptation of Communism and can offer nothing in its stead.

It has not been given to us to cast off the burden and difficulty of freedom nor the striving towards freedom. As paradoxical as it sounds we, in a certain sense have been forced towards freedom by the very tragic events taking place in the world. Our consciousness must stand on the highest levels of the historical events. The sorrowful events that took place at the Council of Bishops, have their positive side — they liberate us from illusions and enticements, in their negative ways they remind Christians about their birthright, about their higher calling. The suspicious attitude towards the Russian Student Christian Movement, the most valuable thing in today's emigration, teaches the youth that Christian rebirth is impossible outside of the freedom of spirit. It is clearer now than ever before, that the Orthodox Church holds fast not to external authority, not to an external organizational unity, but to the internal freedom of the Spirit, Christ's freedom, the freedom and grace in man, through the action of the Holy Spirit.

CHAPTER TEN

Anton Kartashev (1875–1960)

The Russian Church historian Anton Vladimirovich Kartashev was born into a mining family from Kistim in the Ural mountains of Russia. He eventually attended the St. Petersburg Ecclesiastical Academy and graduated in 1899. He stayed there and taught Church history. For several years, Kartashev also was an assistant librarian at the Imperial Public Library in St. Petersburg.

Kartashev was invited to be Russia's first and only Minister of Religions in the Provisional Government of A. Kerensky (1917) and was instrumental in organizing the All-Russian Church Council of 1917–18. This was a very important post, because it was the first time in over two hundred years that the entire Russian Orthodox Church — bishops, priests, deacons, and clergy — met face to face as a council or *sobor*, in order to discuss very important theological and pastoral matters. After being arrested by the Bolsheviks, he escaped to the West. From 1925–60, Professor Kartashev taught Church History, Old Testament and Hebrew at St. Sergius Orthodox Theological Institute in Paris where he was a colleague of both Bulgakov and Afanasiev, and mentor the young Alexander Schmemann. Kartashev devoted his teaching and writing not only to Church History but to ecumenism and a greater understanding of what divides and what unites Christians in Christ. He and authored many books and articles, many of them on the nature of freedom in the Church and on ecumenism.

This essay, "Individual and Communal Salvation in Christ," was published in *Put'* in 1934 which highlights several important themes. Kartashev emphasizes that the basic structure of Christianity is the community. While we are all individuals who come to baptism alone, we are incorporated into a much larger and wider community, which the Apostle Paul alludes to as the body of Christ, at other times he uses the image of a building or temple. The New Testament gospels use similar communal images, such as the flock of sheep and the vine which are found in the Gospel of John. As a community, Christians have a great responsibility for one another, and for the world around them. In his essay, Kartashev promotes social action among Christians, that we are supposed to bring what we experience and learn in Church to the world around us, what he calls "Churchifying life." He does not call for a Christian government, a secular promotion of a monolithic "Church-State" but he does emphasize the need for greater influence of the Church in the daily life and routines of Christians. Of all the essays included, this one by Kartashev shows us that the entire Church — both clergy and laity — have an important role in the world around us. He certainly does not advocate a fleeing from the world, a type of sacred and profane dichotomy, but rather that Christians embrace the world around them. Unfortunately, too many contemporary Christian bodies seek to live apart or separate from the world which creates a false division between the sacred and the secular, a theme that also runs throughout the writings of Kartashev's student, Alexander Schmemann. As more and more Christians fall into sectarianism and fundamentalism, this essay by Kartashev is a breath of fresh air, especially in the contemporary Church which tends to see the world in negative terms.

For Further Reading

Kartashev, Anton. *On the Biblical Criticism of the Old Testament* (Paris: YMCA Press, 1947).

_______. *Way to Ecumenical Council* (Paris: YMCA Press, 1932).

_______. *The Restoration of Holy Russia* (Paris: YMCA Press, 1956).

_______. *History of the Russian Church 2 Volumes* (Paris: YMCA Press, 1959).

_______. *The Ecumenical Councils* (Paris: YMCA Press, 1963).

Individual and Communal Salvation in Christ

Each time the question arises about communal, political, cultural, and not merely individually-spiritual significance of the Gospel and the Church, one must first know: at which level is the inquiry made? Practical thinkers are generally satisfied with the premise that Christianity "in some manner," the manner of which is not delved into too deeply, did have an influence not only upon the souls of individual believers, but upon whole nations, their institutions, their lives and their accomplishments as a whole. Thus they could expect to see the Church's full participation in every one of today's painful and burning issues. These problems have become world-wide and all-encompassing. One cannot run and hide from them in some desert. Practical thinkers oblige the Church to participate actively in these problems on the basis that the Church is one of the ideological forces along with other such forces that govern nations and mankind and, therefore, it must make use of the same methods as those of other forces, *i.e.*, propaganda, the organization of masses and the rule of a majority. With the obvious exclusion of coercion and armed revolutionary struggle.

Metaphysical and mystical minds cannot look at all this so simply. Although the historical fact of Christianity's influence on world culture, even for them, is beyond dispute, the manner and methods of such influence are not seen by them to be so uncomplicated nor in some cases, acceptable. They see the individual human *persona*, its heart, its soul, as the only object of Christianity's direct influence.

Following the Christian transfiguration of the "inner man" the whole milieu in which the spiritually renewed person lives and acts must, of itself, be transfigured from within, imperceptibly and gradually: community, state, and culture. These latter entities live and develop in accordance with their own natural laws, alien to Christianity, but they can be subjected to its influence and to some degree, be transfigured. They cannot be fully permeated by Christianity inasmuch as they are unrelated by their nature. These are categories of a cosmic, and not a spiritual order. The Lord placed Himself in opposition to "this world," and the Apostle of Love commanded us "not to love this world." The category of "community" is from "this world," thus the Christian heart must not adhere to it. Social life is a kind of a mechanical linkage of personalities and is fatally subject to a certain mechanical conformity with a law, which is alien to the realm of spiritual freedom which is the Christian religion, the Church. It is only in this spiritual "society", the communion of saints in the Church, where the human personality is embraced in its royal fullness, and not as a mechanical molecule or particle. Only that single "community" is genuinely a Christian one. By being an actual and living member of that mystical community, the individual Christian, and through him, the whole Church, "spontaneously spiritually" and thus internally, unnoticeably, enlightens, elevates and transfigures the external and fallen society. All other methods, except this one that comes out from the depths of the personal, transfigured spirit, are methods that are not Christian. In certain fortuitous cases they may even be acceptable for a Christian conscience. In others, they are perceived by it as something alien and even antithetic to Christianity.

Thus, the multitude of Christian Churches and denominations, with small, uncharacteristic and numerically insignificant exceptions, relate to the social sphere with a cool ascetical indifference, dispassionately, with estrangement, and even with hostility. It is especially characteristic and significant that the Eastern Church — the most ancient and closest group to the cradle of Christianity and to the voices of the first Evangelical preaching — is in principle permeated with that ascetical, eschatological indifference towards cultural and historical achievements. This does not call for any special proofs. This is evident in every line of the Eastern liturgy, which more than adequately reflects the spirit of Eastern piety, as well as every line of the didactic literature of the Fathers and the *startsi*, the leaders of Eastern holiness.

Instinctively in line with, and true to that spirit, the Orthodox conservative milieu, both clerical and lay, looks upon all appeals for social action as appeals of the flesh, pagan, non-Christian, and distracting from the Church and even away from Christianity. We must admit this in good conscience in order not to obscure the difficulties of attempting to attract the Church towards social action.

Meanwhile, Orthodox dogmatics and Orthodox ethics, as well as all Christian ethics demands without exception, from every Christian and from the Church, in addition to individual ascetic efforts, ascetic efforts in social service; in addition to personal, individual salvation, the salvation of society as well. Social and communal, not only in the sense of the mystical communion of saints in the Church, but in the sense of a more efficient drawing of human society, alien to the Church, onto the path of Christian salvation. In a broad perspective, this is a maximum Christianization of human society, saturating it with the principles of Love, so that the society be like a Church. We usually speak of the "Churching" of society. This does not mean turning it into a church, but precisely the transfiguration of its aims, forms, and methods, in the image of the Church and in the spirit of the Gospel.

For us, all these are self-evident conclusions from the dogma of God-manhood. The Christ is not only the High Priest and Prophet, but he is also a King. As the King, He is not just the Ruler of the mystical, invisible, intimate kingdom of souls. But, that kingdom of souls must unavoidably become incarnate into a visible, external and even material life of the inwardly Christianized community of mankind. The mystical theocracy must become manifest and prove its reality in an external theocracy or more to the point, an external Christocracy.

When Roman Catholic Christians sing "*Christus vincit, Christus regnat, Christus imperat*," one is justified in asking them, in the words of Apostle James: "Show me your faith apart from your works" (James 2:18). Christians, in good conscience, carried out various examples of Christocracy throughout their history: in the creation of Christian governments, Christian culture, philosophy, scholarship, art, literature, philanthropy. Throughout all of the Middle Ages Christian nations believed without any doubt that all human creativity must be carried out "in the name of Christ"; that Christ reigns over all undertakings of mankind, especially those common to all people and society as well as activities of the State. They believed that the kings and rulers of nations were merely servants of Christ and the Church in all their earthly and human dealings. In principle, Christians could not nor did they have the right to think otherwise. But, alas! in later times Christians fell away from their enduring, child-like faith. They doubted its rightness. They pusillanimously forfeited their commanding and leading position in culture to the secular-dominated enlightenment that was not merely emancipated from religion, but was hostile to it. The conductor's baton guiding mankind in its worldwide cultural structuring has long ago fallen into the hands of secular forces. The Church has been pushed aside and often forcibly banished from any influence in the sphere of social life with the declared aim that it would not dare to Christianize life and build the visible Kingdom of Christ.

Thus the Church's rival and enemy — worldwide secularism — tells the Church where its strength lies and where is its vocation in the social sphere. It wants to be the soul, the center and the head of all life — the position once held by the Church. Being universal, secularism wants to usurp the place of religion, to abolish it and to replace it. It has already paganized all spheres of life. The Church must once again conquer those lost positions, to baptize and Christianize anew all governments, laws and communities, science, culture, economics and technology. This inescapable struggle for a new Christianization of the world removes all ascetic doubts from us: is it lawful, is it Orthodox, to summon the Church to serve society? It is too late to have doubts when a defensive war is going on with the principal enemy of Christ's Kingdom. For the enemy, the Church's ascetical retreat into the area of merely the personal, individual salvation of faithful souls is, pure and simple, a surrender and capitulation of the Church. This is just what the enemy wants. To annihilate the Christocratic realism of the Church—this is the aim of "the prince of this world." The Church that does not participate in the activities of this world is no longer Christ's Kingdom. It is a kind of an impotent Buddhism. This is a desertion from the field of battle in the age of the Gospel's decisive struggle with the world's anti-Christian onslaught.

On the contrary, today we must sound the alarm and mobilize all those who believe in Christ and all the forces of the Church, in order to work for the resolution of all universal problems common to all mankind from a Christian perspective, from the Church's point of view. We can grant the Order of ascetics and hermits the privilege of following their own contemplative life-style, as to any such specialized Order within the Church. But the obligatory type of the Church's ministry and of Christian activism (especially in this war time for the Church) must precisely be social service in the broad meaning of that term. It is self-evident—and this is basic for a Christian—that this "Christian social service" must take place only upon the firm foundation of the internal belonging to the Church, in accordance with her mystical and authoritative direction, being nourished and transformed by the power of the Church's grace. By no means can this be on a self-standing, simply humanitarian basis. Only then it will not be diverted from the path of the Gospel and will have the means to channel the general trend of even secular culture towards the goals of Christ's Kingdom.

The Church must be able to provide her answers for all questions of social life. Not the technical questions of course, but those of principle nature. The Church's sphere is axiological, she must be able to evaluate everything in conformity with the Kingdom of God. A free market or a planned economy, capitalism or socialism, democracy or Caesarism, pacifism or militarism, nationalism, fascism, communism, *etc.*, absolutely all forms and expressions of mankind's collectivism must be evaluated by the Church. The Church must give its members direction and guidance for each of the existing systems of common life and how each one must conduct himself within these systems, both in principle and in practice. One may need to struggle against some, defend another, reform the third one, recreate the fourth in accordance with one's own new plan.

The question — where or in what spheres of the Church can one look for such guidance for social service, leads to the problem of the forms of Church authority. Not having an infallible center in Rome, we do have sufficient, efficient and viable forms of "*Sobornost*"" in all its degrees, from the lowest to the highest "ecumenical," that allow us to function with assurance, knowing that we can always find control, judgement, direction and help — without recourse to the Old Testamental "*Urim and Thumim*" — within that "Sobornost.""

Would the Church's participation in the world's social structure imply that the hierarchy or the priesthood would be diverted from their altars or from their specifically Apostolic "service of the Word"? Would this lead to the secularization of pastors and their preoccupation with the vanities of the world? By no means. The Church, as any organized establishment, follows the principle of the division of labor. If the priesthood is for service of the Word and the altar, then there is a substantial reservoir of talent among the multitude of laity for every kind of social service in the name of Christ. In the Church, the layman vocation is primarily an obligation for public and cultural service. For the maximum effectiveness of such service the laity, in common with their pastors, but primarily and specifically the laity, should be organized into a number of special brotherhoods or leagues and to make up, on the whole, as a technically perfected army of Church servants with every type of spiritual weaponry. This army must be interspersed into the system of common life and common relationships and from there, shape the activities in the spirit of the Gospel and thus try to achieve the transfiguration of the world in the image of the Church, thus "Churchifying" life.

There are two methods for the Church to influence culture and society. Let's, conditionally, call one method "clerical." This is when the Church, through the hands of her hierarchy, takes over the power of the State, when she forms her own ecclesiastical parties in politics, when she forms her own schools, her own social and economic factions. We will call the other method "molecular," when the Church, through her members and through its brotherhoods and organizations, participates in the numerous government and cultural establishments, corporations and organizations, in the various already existing political parties, in educational institutions, universities, in the public press, in secular life in general, for the purpose of disseminating her Christian influence. Such a method is more feasible and adaptable. Its feasibility is prompted by the fact that today there are no longer any patriarchal conditions where all governments, the whole nation, all institutions, were solidly Christian. Then all theocratic designs were carried out directly, through clericalism and government enforcement. There is nothing like this today in the nature of things. Today, real and not just nominal, Christians constitute a minority even in officially Christian States. Being a minority they have neither the right nor the opportunity to impose their Christocratic plans upon the heterodox and unbelieving majority. All they can do is work for Evangelical foundations by way of the "molecular" influence within the common forms of life. This predominant method does not exclude, in necessary situations, the implementation of specific methods, which we conditionally defined as "clericalism."

It is the "minority" status of Christians in our times within the secular forms of government and society that precludes the practical influence of purely ecclesiastical and canonical entities made up of parishes and dioceses. While these sacred institutions are absolutely essential for the intimate and mystical life within the Church, these canonical organizations are frequently completely overlooked within the structures of the extra-ecclesial secular society. Parishes as entities, are meaningful only within the boundaries of their specific denomination and cannot as such, have a meaningful vote power in political, economic and cultural matters. Individual Christians who make up these parishes must, either personally or as organizations or brotherhoods, participate in the institutions of secular society and thus introduce that, which is necessary for the Church, into the common way of life.

The canonical system of Church organization is thus inadequate for the Church's service within society among the heterodox and unbelieving majority. Here, the organization of brotherhoods and leagues consisting of Christian members sharing a common profession or specialty could be the most effective way for working in the interests of the Church. Without the development and strengthening of such a system one cannot expect the Church to be successful in efforts for the Christianization of life on a broad field.

This Christocratic process of the transfiguration of the cosmic, pagan and anti-Christian way of life into a life compatible with the spirit of the Gospel, is difficult and far-fetched. However, no individual Christian nor the Church as a whole can live without the hope that they somehow are creating on this earth, in this sinful and imperfect milieu, a kind of a *City of God*. They save not only their own souls but are saving their sinful society, their common life and all of their common historical creation, carrying out not only their own salvation, but at the same time, the salvation of society in Christ, creating a new Theocracy–Christocracy.

LaVergne, TN USA
13 June 2010
185872LV00001BA/114/P